WITHDRAWN

Changing Family Patterns in the Arab East

CHANGING FAMILY PATTERNS IN THE ARAB EAST

Edwin Terry Prothro *and* Lutfy Najib Diab

American University of Beirut

AMERICAN UNIVERSITY OF BEIRUT

1974

Changing Family Patterns in the Arab East
Published by the American University of Beirut
Copyright 1974. All rights reserved
Library of Congress Catalog Card Number: 73-85671

301.42
P967c
1974

Printed in Beirut, Lebanon, by the Heidelberg Press

CONTENTS

PREFACE

A STUDY OF FAMILY PATTERNS carried out by two social psychologists may seem a little unusual, and a preferatory remark on how this came about may be in order. My own interest in racial attitudes had led me to cross-cultural studies in the development of attitudes, values, and other "cognitions." While completing a monograph on child rearing in Lebanon, I became increasingly aware of the significance of family patterns in the development of personality, including those attitudes and values which had been of major interest to me. In reading on the subject of the family, I was surprised to find that there had been "far more systematic field research among the Bantoid peoples of Africa" than among the peoples of Arabic Islam, one of the world's major cultures. I was also struck with the extent to which the classical, stereotyped picture of the Islamic family did not agree with my own observations in the Middle East over a period of nearly two decades.

At the same time, my colleague Lutfy Diab was completing a series of studies on attitude change—especially change in response to group pressures. During my discussions with him on the "actual" versus the "ideal" family in Islam, he too became interested in the influence of the family group on attitudes. As a native of Lebanon, he was acutely aware of both consistency and change in traditional Arab family patterns, and shared my interest in accumulating data on this subject.

In early 1966 I was awarded a three-year grant (later extended to four years) for a study of "Changing Patterns of Family Life in the Arab Levant." It was this grant, MH 11574, from the National Institute of Mental Health, which made the study possible. I am grateful to the Institute for this as well as other assistance, formal and informal, institutional and individual, and hope that they, and our relationship, will continue to flourish.

The path of scholarship is never smooth, but this investigation, begun with such enthusiasm, seemed quickly to attract the Evil Eye. First we became deeply involved in university administration during a turbulent period for universities everywhere. My own appointment occurred about the same time that the decision was made to award the grant. Then, no less a journal than the *Reader's Digest* singled out this study for special attention in an article entitled "The Great Research Boondoggle."[1] To our happy surprise, this attack had no effect on the project. No one of the National Institute of Mental Health ever mentioned the article to us. An editorial in *Science* gave a masterful reply,[2] and the incident was apparently closed. We concluded that magazine articles too may have their boondoggle aspect.

Next came the 1967 war in the Middle East. Most of our work in the village of Artas, near Bethlehem, was carried out in 1966. The interviewer had completed all the village interviews by early 1967, and on June 5 she went to the Amman airport with the records in her suitcase, planning to fly to Beirut for one of our regular consultations. After her suitcases had been loaded on the plane, and while she was waiting for her flight number to be called, an announcement over the loudspeaker ordered everyone to the nearest air raid shelter. The plane, with the luggage, departed for an unknown destination, and shortly thereafter Israeli planes began bombing the runways. Some three weeks later the interviewer, the Artas records, and the investigators were reunited in Beirut. There have been sporadic closing of borders and airports in the years since the 1967 war but these have not seriously impeded the gathering of the data, with one exception. We had planned to include a Syrian village in the study, but it proved to be impossible either to obtain formal permission to conduct such a study or to conduct it with the informal agreement of the local notables.

There were of course many fortunate aspects of the project. Chief among these was the dedicated work of our many assistants. Among those to whom we owe thanks are the interviewers who gathered data: Miss Huda F. Akil, Miss Leila Biksmati, Miss Bushra Budayr, Dr. Leila S. Khoury, Miss Hayat Salam, Mr. Abdel Mawla Solh and Dr. Nahid Ussayran. We similarly appreciate the diligent help of our research assistants: Mr. Assadour Choungourian, Mr. Andrawus Khuri, Miss May

---

[1] Schulz, W. "The great research boondoggle" *Reader's Digest*, March 1967, 91-96.
[2] Abelson, P.H. "A partisan attack on research" *Science*, 9 June 1967, 1315.

Majdalani, Miss Salwa Makdah, Mr. Muhammad Shuraydi and Mrs. Roxann A. Van Dusen.

The text of this report reveals the extent to which we have been inspired by the publications of William J. Goode and John Gulick.

Finally we wish to express our warm and continuing appreciation to Najla and Salwa, who taught us so much about Middle Eastern family life.

EDWIN TERRY PROTHRO
Beirut, 1973

CHAPTER ONE

The Contemporary Revolution in Family Life

F AMILIES are found in all societies, and in an impressive variety of forms. These two basic facts have long stimulated students of human behavior, and were the starting point of this study.

In the latter half of the nineteenth century, when Darwinism was at its peak in social thought, a number of scholars attempted to find an evolutionary continuum along which they might arrange the various forms of family life. Efforts were made at describing, or imagining, family life of apes, prehistoric men, and contemporary primitive men, and arranging the described patterns into a putative time sequence. These theories had considerable impact outside the field of social science. Political radicals (e.g. Engels) announced the need for further development, beyond the existing family, characterized as it was by exploitation of women and children. Psycholanalysts looked to prehistoric family crises for explanations of impulses imbedded deep in the unconscious. Unfortunately, the evidence on which these evolutionary theories was based was flimsy, and there was no firm basis for choosing among rival theories (Bell & Vogel, 1968, p. 4). In spite of their attractiveness to others, the theories could not hold the support of sociologists.

Although evolutionary family theory was generally abandoned by the early twentieth century, studies of the family continued to proliferate. Many of these were concerned with the contemporary Western family as a "primary group," and with its many problems of poverty, divorce, etc. Such studies were less concerned with history or with cross-cultural comparisons than with differences within cultures (Farber, 1964, pp. 16-21).

At the same time, studies of families in other societies increased in number and in adequacy. These stressed the uniqueness of cultures, which were

1

no longer viewed as mere stages in evolutionary development toward Western cultures. The interrelations and interdependencies of institutions within cultures were emphasized.[1] A "functionalist" theory emerged, which focused on the functions which the family served for the whole society, for other social institutions in the society, and for individuals. This theory, or approach, lent itself readily to the study of changes within a society (e.g., studies of the changing functions of the American family) as well as to comparisons among societies.

The Trend toward the Nuclear Family

Before the middle of the century, enough information was available on families all around the world to permit new efforts at describing how families change over time. These explanations were less grandiose and less simplistic than the earlier evolutionary theory. Indeed, students of the family began to avoid the term "evolution" and spoke instead of change, development, or modernization of the family.[2]

The major change noted, in Western and non-Western societies alike, was a shift from the extended family, with its large network of kinship ties, to the nuclear family of husband, wife and children. The rise of the nuclear family was found to be associated with urbanization, industrialization and general modernization. The extended family predominated in less modern societies, and in those where agriculture was more important than business and industry (Davis, 1948; Ogburn & Nimkoff, 1950).

The thesis of a world-wide trend toward the nuclear family, associated with urbanization and industrialization, has been subjected to a number of criticisms in recent years. These criticisms point toward a refinement of the thesis, not to its rejection. In the first place, the thesis as stated ignores the fact that in societies with low levels of complexity, where subsistence is based on hunting and gathering, families are usually nuclear. If these societies become more complex, and especially if they begin to practice settled agriculture, we might expect in them a shift from nuclear families

---

[1] This approach may have been encouraged by the prevailing *Zeitgeist* of the Age of Relativity.

[2] White (1959, p. 135) argued that it is a mistake to speak of the evolution of the human family, for the family is an integral part of society. In his view, the study of the evolution of societies as wholes is the proper approach. Toulmin, in his survey of 'would-be disciplines,' notes that most students of whole societies turned away from evolutionary approaches around the beginning of the century, but are now turning back (1972, p. 385).

to extended families (Winch, 1970). The thesis does not apply, then, to societies with very simple levels of subsistence.

A number of writers have also pointed out that a nuclear family is only *relatively* independent of the extended kinship network. Even in highly industrialized modern cities, there are visiting, exchange of telephone calls and letters, as well as many bonds of affection, between members of a nuclear family and their relatives. There is no sharp dichotomy between nuclear and extended families. Consequently, when one refers to a shift away from the extended family, he is referring to a lessening of kinship ties rather than to a break with them or an abandoning of them.

Finally it must be noted that although industrialization and urbanization are "associated with" the trend away from the extended family, they are neither necessary nor sufficient conditions for the emergence of the nuclear family. The nuclear family was found in the United States *before* its industrial revolution (Furstenberg, 1966). Japan is a modern, industrial, urban society in which there is today relatively great emphasis on extended family ties. On the West Indian island of Barbados there is "the same small nuclear family, articulated with the larger society in precisely the same way as we find in industrialized Western society, but without urbanization and industrialization" (Greenfield, 1961, p. 319). Evidently, there is no simple cause and effect relationship between industrialization and urbanization on the one hand and the emergence of the nuclear family on the other.

Worldwide Convergence in Family Patterns

As the volume of firm data on families of many cultures grew, and broader generalizations about changing families became possible, scholars presumed again to explain the past and predict the future of the human family. In our opinion, the most solidly-grounded of these attempts was that of William J. Goode. In 1963 he published a report which drew together data from the West (the Americas, Europe, Australia and New Zealand), Arabic Islam, Sub-Sahara (black) Africa, India, China, and Japan, to demonstrate a worldwide trend toward the conjugal family. He presented evidence that, in spite of wide differences in starting points and in rates of change, all cultures are converging toward similar patterns of family life. Moreover, he predicted that they would continue to do so over the next twenty years or more. He entitled his work *World Revolution and Family Patterns*, but this "revolution" is one in which there is consid-

3

erable stability, with changes in family patterns occurring selectively and at different rates in different societies.

The conjugal family as seen by Goode is a nuclear family (parents and children) with some emotional ties to close relatives. Thus, the father may have warm ties with his siblings, the children with their grandparents, etc. These ties may express themselves in visiting, exchange of gifts on special occasions, exchanges of telephone calls and letters, voluntary consultations in times of crisis, and the like. The parents and children will ideally have their own residence, but one or more relatives may live with them on occasion. This family type can be distinguished from the extended family, where there is a network of kin who have many interlocking rights and expectations and obligations, and where those with authority (e.g. elders and males) exert considerable moral control over their relatives. As can be seen from these descriptions, conjugal and extended families differ in *degree* to which certain variables are present. Both types involve obligations, expectations, rights, authority, and control among kin.

Because the conjugal family is widespread in the modern Western world, the revolution in family life is sometimes described as "Westernization" of the family. Such a term, says Goode, may obscure our analysis "by leading us to believe the countries are changing only under the impact of Western influence, whereas often the most important pressure is *nationalist and indigenous*" (pp. 18-19, emphasis ours). Moreover, the Western world is itself still undergoing the revolution, as he amply documents. We would agree that the term "modernization" is more neutral, and more accurate in describing the changes now occurring in the direction of the conjugal family.

The independent variable to which he gives most attention is industrialization, but this term is used in a rather special sense to include not only growth of manufacturing industries, but also to development of any business or trade where there is "freedom to use one's talents and skills in improving one's job" (p. 169, original in italics).

Industrialization reduces the cohesion of the extended family by reducing the control which elders hold over new opportunities. Because lower classes exercise least control of job opportunity, the impact of industrialization is strongest among them, and lower class patterns are the first to change (p. 13). *Urbanization* is frequently mentioned in conjunction with industrialization, and it is asserted that, at least in the modern world, it is not possible to distinguish clearly between their separate effects (p. 169 and p. 374). Indeed, he states flatly that "the modern system

4

of industry *never* occurs without both urbanization and bureaucratization" (p. 11, emphasis ours).

In addition to the interwoven factors of industrialization and urbanization, the factor of *ideology* is also important in bringing about the revolution in family life. The ideals of the conjugal family are radical, for they assert rights of the individual, and emphasize his own desires and abilities. They place an emphasis on romantic love. They stress liberty for personal decision, equality of the sexes, and fraternity on a voluntary basis. As Goode says, such personal freedom has special appeal to youth, to the educated, to women, and to all who are at a disadvantage by birth in the present scheme of things. Ideological variables are reasonably independent of industrialization and modernization, but they cannot operate without some support in that sector. Ideology can hardly survive where there is no opportunity for its expression in the society and the economy. Urbanization and industrialization offer opportunities for individualism, and alternative supports to the individual who no longer has the full support of the extended family.

Communications and mass media also play important roles in disseminating ideology, demonstrating alternative patterns of living, and providing an impulse to improvement of one's lot in life. Goode mentions mass communications in passing as one aspect of industrialization, but a number of other students of social change have given communications (including schooling as well as mass media) a central role (Lerner, 1958; Rogers, 1969; Kahl, 1968). The difference in point of view is one of emphasis, for all students of modernization recognize that a multiplicity of factors are involved. Nevertheless, the difference in emphasis is important—both for theorists and for social planners.

Communications is an instrument of change in ideology, and if we use the term broadly to include education, it is the major instrument for bringing about such changes. As we have indicated, Goode stresses the appeal of an egalitarian ideology to the disadvantaged, and looks to industrialization to provide opportunity for such persons to practice that ideology in matters relating to the family. We should recognize, however, that an egalitarian ideology can affect the advantaged also, and thus in at least some cases produce changed practices without the support provided by industrialization. For example, a young lady may assert her right to discard the veil because she is financially independent, thanks to a job she holds strictly from merit and achievement. In this case industrialization has provided support for the disadvantaged. But it is also possible, and far more effective, for the young lady's husband or older brother to acquire from education or mass media a changed ideology, and to encourage her to discard the "outmoded" veil. We would say in the latter instance that communications had served as the instrument of ideology, implementing change even in the absence of the supports of industrialization.

To summarize, there is worldwide change occurring in family life. The extended family, and all that it implies in terms of control of youth, status of women, arranged marriages, and the like, has been challenged by an ideology of individualism and egalitarianism. This ideology is propagated by mass communications and supported by industrialization, especially when accompanied by urbanization, for the conjugal family fits better the needs of an industrial urban society than does the extended family. Around the globe, as Goode has made plain, the trend is toward the conjugal family.

Changes in the Islamic Family

The traditional Middle Eastern family has been described as extended, patrilineal, patriolocal, patriarchal, endogamous and occasionally polygynous (Patai, 1969, pp. 84–92). In these families, the status of women was depicted as low. Their chastity was jealously guarded—often by seclusion and veiling. Divorce was easy for men to achieve, and common. Marriages were arranged by parents, and took place at an early age. Fecundity was prized, and sons particularly desired.

The pattern of family life in the Levant was usually described as that of the traditional Middle Eastern family until the end of World War I. Bliss' descriptions of women, marriage and family in Lebanon, Syria and Palestine, published in 1917, are similar to some of those by Lane, describing Egyptian life a century earlier. Both of these descriptions are reasonably close to that of Stern (1939), who discusses marriage in the early centuries of Islam. Evidently, changes in family life in this part of the world occurred slowly until a few decades ago.

During the latter half of the nineteenth century, several Egyptian writers, spurred by their contacts with France and other European nations, began to examine the weaknesses of Egypt's social structure and to propose among other things wider education as a remedy. One of these, Qasim Amin, published at the end of the century a book entitled *Liberation of Women (Tahrir al Mar°a)*, in which he argued that the strengthening of Islam should begin in the family. Consequently, the position of women

6

had to be improved. Not only did he advocate education for women, but he even argued, albeit cautiously, against seclusion and veiling (Hourani, 1962, pp. 164 ff.). In the early twentieth century a number of other writers joined "the Modernists" and took up the call for the (partial, gradual) emancipation of women (Baer, 1964, pp. 44 ff.). Their ideas were spread by the "mass" media of the day, in books, pamphlets and articles. They stressed their belief that emancipation of women was compatible with the Quran. The movement soon spread to the Levant, where the belief of the Young Turks in emancipation was also having an impact. In 1928 a Lebanese woman, Nazira Zein-ed-Din, published a book on unveiling and liberation. The immediate impact of this intellectual movement toward "modernism" as it related to women and the family was not great. For years there was more exhortation than action, but the groundwork for change was nevertheless being laid. One tangible result was the formation of a number of women's welfare associations, and many of these continue to thrive today.

Most students of Islamic society specify the 1920's as the decade when change began to be noticeable (Patai, 1969, p. 133; Chatila, 1934, p. 5; Woodsmall, 1936, p. 22; Daghestani, 1932). This was the period when the Ottoman Empire was replaced by a French mandate in Lebanon and Syria and an English mandate in Palestine. In the mandate period, there were increasing relations with the West. The upper classes were of course in closer contact with Westerners than were others. They read more European authors; they traveled more. It is hardly surprising, then, that changes in the role of women began in the upper classes.

By the thirties, students of families in the Levant spoke not only of the traditional family, but also of change, particularly in the cities and among the upper class. It was at this time for example that upper class urban women of the Levant began to give up the custom of veiling in considerable numbers. As Gulick points out (1968, p. 152), these changes cannot be attributed to a mysterious "urban influence." Rather, we would argue, they result at least in part from the city dwellers' greater exposure to communications from and with persons who practice different customs and follow different rules—with impunity. Exposure may take place while one is traveling abroad, or may occur at home via mass media, or may result from direct contact in local schools, offices or other meeting places. When those with different behavior and different beliefs are seen to be powerful and successful rather than objects of ridicule or scorn, there is a psychological impact on the observer which some have called "the demonstration effect." Demonstration sometimes leads to emulation.

7

Mass communications and egalitarian ideology have, we believe, played important roles in bringing about changes in patterns of living. The role of industrialization has to date been less significant. For one thing, there is in the Levant little modern industry, for "much manufacturing still takes place in small workshops in which few people outside of the owners' family are employed " (Berger, 1964, p. 210). In addition, business and industry in the Levant are usually based upon and developed within the extended family (Benedict, 1968; Khalaf & Shwayri, 1966; Tannous, 1941). In villages and cities alike the extended family often serves as a vehicle of change and agent of economic development (Farsoun, 1970, p. 267; Williams & Williams, 1965). Industrialization does not yet challenge the authority and control exercised by the senior members of the extended family.

In discussing the changing Muslim family, we must not overlook the fact that the "Middle East is a fascinating land of great contrasts " (Beck, 1957, p. 340). There are age differences, urban-rural differences, class differences and regional differences in attitudes, values, and practices. Perhaps we can best catch the vividness of the contrasts by quoting a newspaper reporter who flew from Beirut and Cairo to several states of the Arabian peninsula (Anon., 1970, p. 8):

> As the Saudi Arabian Airlines jet descends into Jedda, the pretty, dark-haired stewardesses dressed in green miniskirts disappear behind a curtain.
>
> They emerge a few minutes later shrouded in full-length, black veiled robes, properly garbed to set foot on the homeland of the Prophet Mohammed.
>
> "When you put on the *abaya*," says the English-speaking Saudi stewardess, "you lose your shape, your age, and your identity. You become a non-person."
>
> The transformation was repeated in reverse in Kuwait. There two wives of government officials boarded an airliner for Beirut, wearing the long black veiled *abayas*.
>
> As soon as the plane was airborne, however, the women doffed their robes, revealing chic, colorful dresses, settled back and ordered a couple of whisky-sodas.
>
> Thus does jet travel, crossing the cultural gap of centuries, dramatize the vast contrast in the feminine condition of the Arab World—from the Western freedom of Beirut and Cairo city life to the oriental seclusion of the Arabian desert.

8

A Study of Change

In this study we have attempted to determine change in a number of aspects of Sunni Muslim family life in several cities and villages of the Levant. We have, whenever possible, compared our data of the late sixties with those of earlier studies. We have also pursued the question of change by comparing in our study women married earlier in the century with women married more recently.

Information on differences in rate of change have been sought through comparisons of different localities (including both cities and villages) and different social classes.

Following the lead of Goode, we have noted the interrelations between changing family patterns and other aspects of a modernizing society—industrialization, urbanization, communications and the spread of an egalitarian ideology.

Our basic aim was to shed some light on the conditions under which change occurs, and thus to facilitate prediction of the future development of the Muslim family in the Levant.

CHAPTER TWO

Approach to the Study of Sunni Families
of the Arab Levant

T HE TERM "Arab Levant" is used here to refer to three states of the
Eastern Mediterranean: Lebanon, Syria and Jordan. These
states are all members of the Arab League, and their inhabitants
have been Arabic-speaking for many centuries. The great majority of
the people in the area are Sunni Muslims,[1] but in Lebanon the Muslim
half of the population is about equally divided between Shiites and Sunnis.
The Levant is more or less in the middle of a Muslim "culture continent"
extending from Morocco to Afghanistan. In this "continent" of more than
seven million square miles, with a population of more than 160,000,000,
the Muslim family is everywhere a major element of the culture (Patai,
1969, pp. 13 ff.).

This part of the Fertile Crescent "for several millennia has been ecolo-
gically characterized by agricultural villages and commercial towns and
cities" (Gulick, 1968, p. 112). Although urbanization is proceeding at a
rapid rate (Abu-Lughod, 1973, p. 107), the present population pattern is
still similar to that of the preindustrial West, in which a "great capital
city towers above the rest" (Issawi, 1969, p. 116). We initially planned
to interview women in the towering capital city and in one Sunni village
of each of the three countries. We were able to complete the study in the
three cities of Amman, Beirut, and Damascus, and in the Jordanian village
of Artas[2] and the Lebanese village of Buarij, but events following the June

---

[1] The proportion of Muslims in the population is about 94 per cent in Jordan, 92 per
cent in Syria and perhaps 50 per cent in Lebanon.

[2] At the time of this writing the village of Artas is in Israeli-occupied territory, but at
the time of our interviews it was, functionally as well as legally, part of Jordan. At the
time of the studies of Granqvist just after World War I, it was a Palestinian village.

11

War of 1967 made it impossible to carry out our plan to study a Syrian village. On the other hand, we were able to add Tripoli, Lebanon's second city and largest Sunni city, to the group. The principal data, then, came from four cities and two villages.[1]

Most of the data were derived from interviews with wives. The basic questionnaire was designed to cover a number of important features of family life, and particularly those features thought to have undergone change over the past half-century (see Appendix). This questionnaire was the basis for individual structured interviews of about a half-hour's duration. We completed 1717 interviews with married women and 88 with divorced women. A supplementary interview, based in part on a schedule developed by Stephens (1963), was conducted with 131 of the wives and eight of the divorcees.

In addition to the interviews, we studied the records of the Sunni religious courts in Tripoli and Sidon, the two largest predominately Muslim cities of Lebanon. We also drew upon census reports, statistical abstracts, monographs and other published material where available.

We had hoped to find as interviewer in each locality a Sunni woman of that nationality with some education in the social sciences who was known and accepted there. We were partially successful. In Beirut, Tripoli, and Damascus our interviewers met all the criteria of education, religion, sex, and nationality. In Artas and Amman the interviewer was a Jordanian woman with a Ph.D. degree, but she was Christian.

In Buarij, the interviewer was a Lebanese Muslim, but he was a male. Although he had the advantage of knowing the people of the village, it was definitely a disadvantage that he was male, for this fact brought the modesty code to bear on the interviews (see Chapter VI). He was able to interview about half the women in comparative privacy, but the other half of the interviews were joint rather than individual, with the husband doing most of the responding. Indeed, in nine cases the husband was interviewed without the wife being present.[2] Obviously the data from

---

[1] Well over 90 per cent of the inhabitants of Amman, Damascus, Artas and Buarij are Sunnis. Tripoli is about three-fourths Sunni. Beirut was a Sunni Muslim city up until the end of World War I. Today the Sunnis are the largest minority in the city, and they (as other sects) tend to live in districts where they are in the majority (cf. Prothro, 1961, pp. 13-14).

[2] In these nine interviews, factual data on age of wife at marriage, number of children, and the like were obtained, but for obvious reasons the more subjective questions were not posed. For the sake of convenience, we refer, throughout the monograph, to all interviewees as wives.

Buarij are not strictly comparable with those of other localities, and caution is in order in interpreting differences found between Buarij and other places.

Classification, by locality and social class, of persons who responded in the basic interview is found in Table II-1. Of the 1717 interviewees, 279 were from the two villages and 1438 from the four cities. In the cities, 236 of the interviewees were judged by the interviewer to be upper class, 826 to be middle class, and 376 to be lower class. Judgments of social class were based on education of husband and wife, occupation of husband and the condition of the home (size, general condition and appearance, furnishings, conveniences, and servants were all noted).

The judgments in each city were made by the interviewer in that city— occasionally in consultation with the junior author. Such judgments were probably fairly reliable with regard to intra-city comparisons, and probably conformed fairly well to general opinion within the city. Nevertheless, an upper class family in Amman, say, might not meet some of the criteria for being upper class in Beirut. Housing, servants and income which would qualify one for upper class in Amman might be judged middle class in Beirut. It should also be noted that social class was estimated at the time of the interview and was not an estimate of social class at the time of marriage. We have not dealt with the question of social mobility of interviewees.

In the villages every married woman (or her husband) was interviewed. In the cities the interviewers began by interviewing Sunni women of their acquaintance and then proceeding to persons known to the interviewees. This "snowball" technique was pursued with some attention given to seeking wives of all three social classes. Nevertheless, the lower class was under-represented in every city. It is evident that such a technique for selecting interviewees cannot yield a true sample of city women, and that our use of "sample" in referring to those who were interviewed is an extremely loose usage. Nevertheless, we do have data on nearly two thousand women of all ages from six localities and we believe these data can provide some insight into the changing society of the Arab Levant.

The supplementary questionnaire was given principally to village respondents: 30 from Buarij and 71 from Artas. A few were given in the cities, but they were found to be generally inappropriate for city women.

The number of wives and husbands in the basic sample who had completed at least primary school can be determined from Tables II-2 and II-3. Primary schooling consists of about five years of study, but no close

13

check on replies was possible, so these data might best be thought of as showing "some" schooling and a basic literacy. It is evident from these tables that husbands were more often literate than were wives, and that in the villages literacy is on the increase, for younger persons (those married recently) were more often literate than were their elders. In view of our use of education as one criterion of social class, it is not surprising to note that lower class persons are more often illiterate than are those of other classes, though the size of the class difference is noteworthy.

Four Changing Cities

The Levant can be characterized as an area of high urbanization, of rapid increase in mass communications, and of slight industrialization.

The traditional high degree of urbanization in the Middle East has shown a notable increase since 1920 (Lapidus, 1969, pp. 99–100). Indeed, Issawi (1969, p. 113) describes the area today as "overurbanized." He cites data to show that the area is more urban than most other under-developed areas of the world. The Levant today is also modernizing at a rapid rate, if we use new building, increase in communications, improved education or growth in tourism as criteria of modernization (Churchill, 1967). At the same time, *industrialization* is developing slowly and the area is still in the pre-industrial era. The Arab Levant therefore presents an excellent opportunity for the study of modernization with little indus-trialization.

The population of Beirut in 1922 was only 140,000 and the suburbs were small villages of a few thousand more (Hudson, 1968, p. 59). By 1967 it had a population of over 400,000 (Churchill, 1967, p. 29) and the entire metropolitan area had more than twice that number (Khalaf & Krongstad, 1973, p. 117). The city of Tripoli increased in size about as rapidly in the same period. In 1922 its population, including the major suburb Mina, was a little less than 40,000. By 1961 it was estimated to have 210,000 inhabitants (Gulick, 1967, p. 31).

The 1960 census of Damascus gave a population estimate of 530,000 and the 1970 census indicated an increase of 58 per cent in one decade, to 835,000. The rate of increase has evidently accelerated of late, for the eleventh edition of the Encyclopedia Britannica (1910) estimated the population to be between 155,000 and 225,000.

The most spectacular recent growth of any of these cities took place in Amman. In the early years of this century it was only a village. In 1921 it became the headquarters of the Amir (later King) Abdullah, and in 1928 was declared capital of Transjordan. Nevertheless, as late as 1939 its population was no more than 20,000. The creation of the state of Israel gave greater importance to Amman, and produced a flood of refugees from former Palestine into Jordan. By 1958 the city was estimated to have 170,000 inhabitants (Hacker, 1960, pp. 24-35 and p. 65). The official census of 1961 counted 246,475 persons in the city and 413,332 in the Amman district.

Industrialization in the area has not kept pace with the urbanization. In Jordan and Syria, about four per cent of the labor force is in industry. In Lebanon, the figure is approximately 12 per cent. As Churchill observed in his survey of Arab cities: "Industry, with few exceptions, is confined to light manufacturing. . . ." (1967, p. 21). Moreover, the industrial sector's share of the gross national product of Lebanon, about 13 per cent, seems to have increased not at all in the past decade or two (Hudson, 1968, pp. 66-67; Khalaf, 1971, p. 158). In Syria the increase from 1953 to 1966 was from 12 to 15 per cent, and in Jordan, from 7 to 12 per cent. Issawi (1971, p. 316) notes that the Arab Levant is less industrialized than Latin America or the part of Asia outside the Middle East, where more than 15 per cent of the gross national product is attributable to manufacturing. Observers seem agreed that the Levant is a pre-industrial, or perhaps it would be more accurate to say, lightly-industrialized, region. Berger has discussed the many barriers to industrialization of the area (1964, pp. 402-409). The implication of his analysis seems to be that there must be a certain degree of modernization before industrialization can begin.

As we saw in Chapter One, increased communications is often seen as a spur to modernization. There is considerable evidence that a "communications explosion" has occurred in the Levant. For the young, schools are a major vehicle of communication. It is in schools that one may learn of the "modern" world, and come to think in modern terms. The proportion of the population in primary school doubled between 1948 and 1968, and the proportion of primary students who were female also increased (see Table II-4). Of the four cities, Beirut ranks first in literacy and in proportion of children in school. It is followed by Tripoli, Damascus and Amman in that order (Churchill, 1967, p. 33).

Contacts with foreigners may also serve to communicate and demonstrate novel behavior patterns. Amman, Damascus and Tripoli have only a few thousand foreign residents each, but nearly seven per cent of the population of Beirut is made up of residents who are from Europe

15

or North America. Tourists are numerous in all three countries. According to the United Nations *Statistical Yearbook 1970,* the number of tourists (including those from Arab states) was in 1969 three quarters of a million for Lebanon[1] and nearly half a million for Syria. Jordan, which had almost as many tourists as Lebanon before the loss of Jerusalem in 1967, was third in 1969, with only 340 thousand. Contact with foreigners through travel abroad is probably common among middle and upper class males of the Levant, less common among females of those classes and uncommon among lower classes. The Jordanian census of September 1961 found that nearly four per cent of the population was then outside the country. Such data are not available for Syria and Lebanon. However, one study (Sayigh, 1962) of 190 Lebanese business men found that more than 70 per cent of them had traveled outside the country *before* entering their present career. Evidently the inhabitants of cities in the Middle East have had considerable opportunity to observe the ways and mores of foreigners.

Exposure to modernity through other media has increased enormously in recent years. This growth is best documented in Lebanon. Hudson cites evidence that the number of radio sets increased by a factor of 10 from 1948 to 1963, and "the population has been theoretically blanketed" since 1963 (1968, p. 72). There are 37 daily newspapers in Lebanon. In Beirut, 85 per cent of adults read newspapers regularly. There is good evidence that frequency of cinema attendance per capita is one of the highest in the world. In the late 1960's attendance per habitant was about twice that in the United States, according to data reported in the United Nations *Statistical Yearbook 1970.* There are two television companies with six channels which transmit in Arabic, French and English, and 79 per cent of all Beirut Lebanese homes had television in 1970 (Anon., 1971, p. v). Obviously, the communications revolution has occurred in Beirut.

Observers have noticed the abundance of radios, newspapers, and cinemas in Tripoli, Damascus, and Amman as well as in Beirut, though precise data are not available. It would probably be fair to estimate that Damascus and Tripoli rank behind Beirut in "exposure to modernity through mass media," and that Amman ranks behind them (Churchill,

[1] In speaking of consumption habits and appetites for new products, one economist has pointed out that the demonstration effect and emulation of foreigners are "quite strong in a small touristic country like Lebanon " (Khalaf, 1971, p. 203). One qualification seems called for, however. It is in the capital city that the impact is strong. In Tripoli the tourist industry is "disproportionately small considering the city's size " (Gulick, 1967, p. 94).

16

1968; Hudson, 1968, p. 80; Patai, 1969, pp. 493 ff.). In all four cities, however, exposure is increasing at a rapid rate.

In these four cities, then, there has been in this century, and especially in the past 20 years, rapid population growth and a sharp increase in communications, but little increase in degree of industrialization.

Two Changing Villages

When one compares the observations of anthropologists who studied Buarij and Artas before World War II with those of our interviewers, it is evident that modernization in the Levant has not been limited to the cities. Even without extensive data for comparisons, one must be impressed by the differences in reports of life today and of 30 or 40 years ago. Indeed, the villagers themselves are acutely aware that many changes have occurred.

The Buarij of Fuller's time was "a world apart" inhabited by peasants bound together by ties of land, kin and religion. They were loyal to each other and to their village. The rhythm, the texture, and the scope of their lives seemed largely determined by needs and requirements of farming, family, and religion.

The Buarij of 1967 is still largely a peasant village, and matters of land, kin and religion continue to be important. But it is no longer a world apart. It has grown larger, more accessible to the outside world, more prosperous and—to the regret of many—less unified and less cohesive. The population has grown from around 235 to perhaps 550, the number of stores from one to seven, the number of large buildings from two (mosque and coffeeshop) to more than a dozen. To the five main families has been added a new one which immigrated from the town of Baalbeck (some 50 kilometers away).

Relatives still build near one another, but the houses are now of reinforced concrete or concrete blocks. Only seven of the mud-brick houses remain. The practice of keeping animals on the ground floor of a two-storey dwelling has been abandoned by more than 90 per cent of the families. The thorn hedges which kept animals in have also been abandoned.

Communications have improved dramatically. The road joining the the Beirut-Damascus highway is paved, and vehicles drive back and forth to the nearby towns of Chtoura and Zahle. In summer about 50 families (as opposed to about a dozen in 1936) escape the heat of Beirut and suburbs by renting rooms or floors of houses in Buarij. The importance

17

of this resort trade is recognized by the villagers. Daily newspapers and weekly magazines are widely read. Virtually every house has electricity and a radio, and many have telephones and television. About 100 boys and 20 girls are in the village primary school, and 12 boys go to elementary school in a village 3 kilometers away. Illiteracy, at least for males, is rapidly disappearing (Tables II-2 and II-3).

Today it is only the oldest villagers who measure time in reference to personal events. Virtually every adult male and many adult females use watches. Clocks are everywhere found in homes. The Western calendar has replaced the Muslim calendar for everything except religious holidays. The age of a child is now determined by his calendar date of birth rather than by comparison with the age of some neighbor's child. Records of precise dates are kept.

Everyone seems to feel that religious practices are on the decline. Nevertheless, they still observe fasting during the month of Ramadan, as in Fuller's day, and six have made the pilgrimage to Mecca, which was only "longed for" in 1936. The Spring Festival and its preceding "Thursday holiday," which Fuller thought might have roots going back to the ancient Canaanites, have simply disappeared. In describing these festivals to Fuller, the villagers said "it has always been so." To our interviewer, 30 years later, many could not relate on what date the festival had fallen.[1] Nevertheless, the "folk religion" of shrines, the evil eye, and the like still flourishes.

The ties of land, kin and religion seem to have weakened somewhat in thirty years, but it is in the unity, cohesion and group loyalty that the greatest change has occurred. From Fuller's description it appears that Buarij had escaped the village split and subsequent feuding which Patai has described as typical of Middle Eastern society (1969, Chapter VII). Today it is evident that Buarij too has a "dual organization." Two of the largest clans in the village are bitter rivals. Members of opposing groups avoid greeting each other. They never pay visits and of course do not intermarry (we found no instance of a Romeo and Juliet match). In February, 1964, at the time of municipal elections, feeling was so high that a young man of one group was shot, and a member of the opposing group sentenced to death (later commuted to 15 years) for the murder.

---

[1] Our colleague Peter C. Dodd noticed that these villagers now look forward to the Easter festivities in the nearby Christian town of Zahle, and suggests that Easter may now be the villagers' Spring Festival. It is possible that the change followed improved transportation.

18

In 1967 the older villagers spoke with nostalgia of the old days when villagers had the feeling of unity and cohesion described by Fuller.

Although Granqvist did not give a detailed description of Artas in the 1920's, it is evident from her incidental remarks, and from her photographs, that the village of her day was quite different from that of 1967. Transportation was on foot or on the back of a donkey, mule or horse; today one can go from Bethlehem to Artas by taxi in a few minutes. Communication was by word of mouth, and announcements were made by shouting which could be heard throughout the village in early evening (1950, p. 150). In 1967 there were newspapers for the increasing number who could read, and transistor radios for the many who could afford them. There was no cinema in Artas, but young people attended those of Bethlehem, if we may judge from the complaints of interviewees. In the twenties, some twenty boys went irregularly to school in the years there was a teacher, but the girls went not at all (1947, p. 151). In 1967 there were two elementary schools of six grades each, with 120 boys in one and 90 girls in the other. In addition 8 boys and 7 girls attended high school in Bethlehem.

The village has grown from 495 persons in 1927 to about 1475 in 1967.[1] In Artas too there is dual organization, with two rival clans. There are two village mayors (*mukhtars*). Many of the people reported that this rivalry had prevented the bringing of electricity to the village, the founding of an Artas-Bethlehem bus line, and even the utilization of the new mosque for Friday prayers. Artas is modernizing, but slowly, and clan rivalry may be one reason changes are not occurring more rapidly.

[1] The Jordanian census of 1961 recorded a population of 1,016.

TABLE II-1

Number of Persons Responding to Basic Interview—
Classified by Year of Marriage, Social Class and Place of Residence

Year of Marriage	1960's				1950's				1940's				1930's				Before 1930				Totals
Social Class+	U	M	L	(T)	U	M	L	(T)	U	M	L	(T)	U	M	L	(T)	U	M	L	(T)	
Artas				(42)				(65)				(44)				(25)				(32)	208
Buarij				(16)				(21)				(15)				(10)				(9)	71
Amman	17	61	51	(129)	9	55	30	(94)	8	21	22	(51)	6	12	7	(25)	2	7	7	(16)	315
Damascus	3	56	7	(66)	5	61	4	(70)	8	33	8	(49)	1	23	3	(27)	1	17	4	(22)	234
Tripoli	24	101	64	(189)	20	90	85	(195)	5	40	37	(82)	3	16	10	(29)	1	10	7	(18)	513
Beirut	36	60	18	(114)	34	90	7	(131)	26	47	5	(78)	19	16	00	(35)	8	10	00	(18)	376
Totals	80	278	140	(556)	68	296	126	(576)	47	141	72	(319)	29	67	20	(151)	12	44	18	(115)	1717

+ Socioeconomic class designations are "U" for Upper, "M" for Middle, and "L" for Lower socioeconomic classes. "T" stands for the total number in the subsample.

Note: Unless otherwise indicated, numbers in subsequent tables are percentages which are based on the number of cases shown above. The number of cases in many of the cells is quite small, so any conclusion based on differences between one pair of percentages alone would be unjustified. Only differences and trends which show up fairly consistently could be considered significant.

TABLE II-2

PER CENT OF WIVES WHO HAD COMPLETED AT LEAST PRIMARY SCHOOLING

(percentages are based on the numbers shown in Table II-1)

Year of Marriage	1960's				1950's				1940's				1930's				Before 1930			
Social Class	U	M	L	(T)	U	M	L	(T)	U	M	L	(T)	U	M	L	(T)	U	M	L	(T)
Artas				(33)				(18)				(9)				(8)				(3)
Buarij				(37)				(14)				(00)				(00)				(00)
Amman+																				
Damascus	++	98	57	(94)	100	85	++	(81)	25	79	13	(59)	++	52	++	(48)	++	24	++	(23)
Tripoli	92	56	8	(44)	95	28	2	(24)	80	10	00	(10)	++	00	00	(10)	++	00	00	(00)
Beirut	100	100	11	(86)	100	99	14	(95)	100	100	00	(94)	5	94	—	(46)	100	70	—	(83)

+Not ascertained.

++Percentages not shown for cells with fewer than 5 cases.

TABLE II-3

PER CENT OF HUSBANDS WHO HAD COMPLETED AT LEAST PRIMARY SCHOOLING

(percentages are based on the numbers shown in Table II-1)

Year of Marriage	1960's				1950's				1940's				1930's				Before 1930			
Social Class	U	M	L	(T)	U	M	L	(T)	U	M	L	(T)	U	M	L	(T)	U	M	L	(T)
Artas				(74)				(46)				(40)				(16)				(19)
Buarij				(75)				(76)				(80)				(40)				(11)
Amman+																				
Damascus	++	98	71	(95)	100	97	++	(96)	100	94	12	(82)	++	91	++	(85)	++	71	++	(59)
Tripoli	100	59	2	(45)	70	37	5	(26)	60	20	00	(13)	++	19	10	(24)	++	40	00	(22)
Beirut	100	100	6	(85)	100	99	43	(96)	96	100	80	(97)	100	94	—	(97)	100	100	—	(100)

+ Not ascertained.
++ Percentages not shown for cells with fewer than 5 cases.

TABLE II–4

INCREASE IN PROPORTION OF POPULATION IN PRIMARY SCHOOL
OVER TWO DECADES

Country	Year	No. Students in Primary School	Population Estimate (thousands)	% Population in Primary School	% Primary Students Female
Jordan	1948	25,092	600	4.2	26.1
	1968	229,691	2,100	10.9	42.8
Lebanon	1947	137,455	1,200	11.5	37.5
	1968	425,840	2,620	16.3	45.5
Syria	1948	205,765	3,068	6.7	28.5
	1968	813,225	5,700	14.3	34.0

Source: *United Nations Statistical Yearbook*, 1949-50 through 1970

CHAPTER THREE

Courtship, Engagement and Marriage

If you fear that you cannot treat orphan girls with fairness, then you may marry other women who seem good to you: two, three or four of them. But if you fear that you cannot maintain equality among them, marry one only. ...Give women their dowry as a free gift.

SURA 4

ONE OF THE OLDEST STORIES of a search for a spouse in Middle Eastern literature is the account in Genesis of how Isaac, son of Abraham, came to marry Rebekah, daughter of Bethuel the Syrian. Although written some centuries ago, it could easily describe the search for a bride of a Palestinian of the early twentieth century.

When Abraham the Mesopotamian, dwelling in Palestine, decided that the time had come for Isaac, only son of his favorite wife, to be married, he sent his favorite servant back to their home town to find a bride. The servant took along gifts of jewelry for the prospective bride and her family. He made his way to the home of Bethuel, son of Abraham's brother, and there met Rebekah. The father readily accepted the appropriatness of a marriage between Rebekah and Isaac. The servant then gave presents to Rebekah, her brother and her mother. When the servant felt the time had come to return to Palestine with the bride, the mother and brother agreed to her departure only after hearing from Rebekah's own lips that she was willing to go. When the party arrived back, Rebekah veiled herself as they approached Isaac. Upon learning that this girl was the cousin his father had sent for, Issac took her to his tent and she became his wife.

The Arabs consider themselves to be descended from Abraham,[1] and their traditional marriage customs show many similarities with those of that ancient patriarch. In describing a "Palestinian" village of 1960,

---

[1] Through Ishmael, not through Isaac.

25

Lutfiyya (1966, pp. 129 ff.) mentioned the father's responsibility in the search for a bride, the use of intermediaries in the search, the necessity for giving a dowry to the bride and her family, the preference given to patrilateral cousins as suitable mates, the necessity that the bride's family give their consent, the acceptance by the son of father's choice, and the veiling of the bride as she is carried to the groom.

Many scholars have noted that marriage customs of the Arabs have changed little over the years. Granqvist discovered numerous parallels between the customs of her Artas villagers and those of the inhabitants of ancient Palestine. Goode (p.91) mentions that a report of the search for a bride in Syria of the nineteen-thirties was little different from that in Egypt a hundred years earlier.

In spite of the remarkable stability of Arab marriage customs over time, some changes have occurred in the twentieth century. Our interviews point up changes in several significant areas. To date, however, the changes have been accommodated within the customary patterns for engagement and marriage.

Finding a Spouse

In the Arab Levant, as in most agrarian pre-industrial societies, marriage traditionally has been in the hands of the elders (cf. Berelson & Steiner, 1964, p. 397). In Artas Granqvist (1931, p. 33) found that possible marriage combinations were discussed even before a child was born, and that a number of children were promised in marriage shortly after birth. It was taken for granted that marriage was a family affair, and that all normal persons married, so the only question facing the elders was the choice of an appropriate mate. A young man might try to persuade his parents to chose a certain girl, but in the long run he (and the girl chosen, if her parents agreed) had no alternative to submitting to the parental decision. Elopements were severely frowned upon, and led inevitably to exile from the village.

In Buarij of the thirties, the elders were described as a little more liberal. Girls had some feeling of helping determine decisions on a future mate, for they discussed among themselves the "merits and demerits of village youth" and their inclinations carried at least some weight with their parents (Fuller, 1961, pp. 53 and 66). Moreover, elopements sometimes occurred because the man could not afford the cost of marrying properly, and such marriages were usually accepted after a time. Marriages were usually arranged by the parents, but these arrangements seem to have involved consulting the young people.

The arranging of marriages in cities was traditionally a bit more complex than in the villages. Although there were more young people of marriageable age in the city, there were not necessarily more *eligible* young people—relatives, or from one's native village, or from one's quarter of the city, etc. In addition, city girls were more secluded than village girls, so their existence might not be known. It was therefore the custom for the father of a young man of marriageable age, usually at the request of the son, to ask the women of the family to visit around among appropriate families, sometimes under the guidance of a professional matchmaker, to find an appropriate bride (Lane, 1963, p. 162; Daghestani, 1932, p. 127). The decision on appropriateness involved questions of religion (of course), family (cousins were preferred), wealth, land and personal qualities.

Several studies in Arab cities have shown an increasing tendency to consult the girl before making the final choice of a husband. In Amman in 1955, questioning of a small group of married women showed that only one fifth of the older women (age 40 and over) had participated in the choosing of their husband either by making the selection or by giving consent, whereas three-fifths of the younger women (age 15 through 35) had done so (Hirabayashi & Ishaq, 1958, p. 38). At about the same time, a survey of students in several cities of the Middle East revealed that "In more liberal Lebanon... the girl is not only gaining more and more freedom in the selection of her mate, but is also being steadily relieved of many of the other restrictions on her premarital freedom of association " (Muhyi, 1959, p. 47). Another survey of seven Arab cities, including Beirut, Tripoli and Amman led to the following observations (Churchill, 1967, p. 36):

> "Premarital interaction between the sexes is extremely conservative. Gossip is a dread fear of girls.... In the upper and middle classes the girl can choose eligible men of good reputation and assured income. Arranged marriages still are quite common in lower class Moslem families, and in all classes Arab mothers are inveterate marriage brokers, although the details...will formally be worked out by the men."

The custom of finding a spouse through one's relatives is indeed very much alive in the Levant, as can be seen from Table III-2. In Beirut as in Artas, the most common way of meeting the future husband was through relatives. In all four cities, however, this custom seems to have declined somewhat in recent years.

27

The fact that the wife met her husband through her relatives or his does not necessarily imply that the marriage was arranged without her consent. The majority of city mothers said that they had been consulted and had agreed to the arrangements or that they had suggested the arrangement and obtained parental consent. In Buarij about three fourths of the mothers said they had been consulted. Only in Artas did the majority say that the marriage was all arranged without consulting the prospective wife. Even in Artas, though, a majority of the mothers of unmarried girls said they intended to consult their daughters about any future arrangement of a marriage.

The degree to which the elders determine who marries whom is reflected by the substantial minority of wives who say they never saw their husbands before the day of the engagement (Table III-3). In the cities, about half the older wives (i.e. those married before 1940) say they saw their husbands for the first time on the day of the engagement. There has been some change with time, but even among those city wives married during the sixties about one fourth say they did not even see their husband before the engagement. Again we must note that although these data show control of marriage by elders they do not mean that consent of the bride was not obtained or that these marriages were made against the wishes of the brides. Korson (1969, p. 160) found that 30 per cent of his sample of Muslim college students in Pakistan looked upon meeting the future spouse before marriage as unnecessary.

In Buarij the girls (in 1936) could go out of the house daily to the fountain to fill the household pitcher and on feast days they went out, properly escorted, in their best clothing. Almost any young person in the village would have at least some opportunity to see another in whom she had any interest. Moreover, we found that boys and girls were (in 1966) permitted to attend chaperoned parties and picnics, and that young people of both sexes attended evening gatherings. It is not surprising then to find that most of the Buarij mothers—old and young alike—had seen the prospective groom before the engagement.

In view of the compact nature of Artas, and the preference for village endogamy there, one might expect that in Artas too the familiarity of village life would outweigh the avoidance patterns, so that prospective brides would have some acquaintance with their prospective husbands before the engagement. Table III-3 shows that such is not the case. Artas is quite different from Buarij. Our interviewers found that marriage there is still a joining of two families, of two clans. The decision rests with

28

the father, though he may consult the girl. Even in the 1960's, we found that betrothal of children sometimes occurred. Some of the incidental effects of the beginnings of village modernization work *against* acquaintance of the couple prior to marriage. Many of the young men of the village now work in Kuwait or other Gulf states, and return to the village to claim a bride they have never seen. Also, there is less feeling now against marriage with someone from a neighboring village, and such engagements are rarely preceded by opportunity for personal acquaintance. We had the feeling that our interviewees in Artas would not approve of an engagement based on strong personal feeling between two young people, because such feeling would testify to a violation of the modesty code.

Among younger mothers, there is a class difference on this matter. Almost all of the upper class mothers had met their husbands before the engagement. Here again we find modernization beginning with the upper class.

With respect to choice of a mate, we can conclude that the ancient practice of the father choosing a bride for his son, usually through the women of his family, and of the bride's family deciding for her whether to accept, leaving to her only the formal words of consent, is slowly undergoing modernization. As young people have more freedom, they have more opportunity to meet a prospective spouse before the engagement, and thus to participate more actively in the family decision on marriage. Even among the most modern classes of Beirut, however, the final decision is not a private one, and is almost always arranged through senior members of the families concerned.

Age at Marriage

Behavioral scientists have found that early marriage of girls is common in agrarian societies which have parental arrangement of marriages, bride-prices, high concern with premarital chastity, and joint households (Berelson & Steiner, 1964, p. 305). All of these characterize the society of the Arab Levant, so we are not surprised to learn that in traditional families the girls married early. At the same time, all of these characteristics are undergoing change as the society modernizes, so we could expect the age at marriage to be increasing.

No firm data are available on age at marriage in the early twentieth century. Ottoman Law required that a girl be at least 9 years of age, and Arab tradition generally, but not invariably, demanded that a girl

29

have attained puberty (Goode, 1963, pp. 104-105). Lane believed that many Egyptian girls of the early nineteenth century married at 12 or 13, and most before 17 (p. 161). Granqvist found child marriage in Artas to be "very general," (1931, p. 34). She also cites a number of other observers who seemed to think that 12 or 13 was a normal age for the marriage of Arab girls in the Eastern Mediterranean (1931, p. 38).

If these low estimates of age at marriage were correct, then the situation had changed by the 1930's. Patai cites data which indicate that 19 or 20 was the average age at marriage of Muslim Palestinians of that decade (1958, p. 146). Churchill's 1952-53 survey in Beirut found that the *mothers* of those interviewed had had an average age at marriage of between 17 and 18 (1954, p. 33). Of all Sunni women signing marriage contracts in Beirut in 1936, the median age was approximately 19 and the mean about 20 (Abu Khadra, 1959, p. 38). Fuller asserted that the girls of Buarij married in their late teens (1961, p. 53). Apparently the age at marriage of girls had increased substantially from the early twentieth century to the 1930's.

Data on age at marriage of males in the early part of the century are even more varied than data on females. In Artas men were considered of marriageable age "shortly after puberty" and Granqvist found "very few unmarried males of marriageable age" (1931, p. 38). Fuller thought that boys married "in their early twenties" (1961, p. 53). In 1931 the average age of marriage of males in five Palestinian villages was around 26. Estimates for Syrian city males in the 1930's ranged from 17 to 20 for the working class and from 25 to 30 for the educated bourgoisie (Chatila, 1934, p. 27). The Beirut survey of 1952-53 found that of the few *fathers* of interviewees on whom the data were available, median age at marriage had been just under 25. In marriage contracts signed in Beirut in 1936, the median age of husbands was about 29 and the mean was 31. In spite of the sparsity and variability of these findings, we can at least conclude that in the Arab Levant around the thirties males did not usually marry early. If they had done so at the turn of the century, the custom had begun to disappear in the period between the World Wars.

Age at marriage of our interviewees is shown in Table III-4. There is evidence everywhere of a steady increase over time. Before 1930 the average age of brides ranged from 14 in Artas and Damascus to 18 in Beirut. By the 1960's the averages range from 17 in Artas to nearly 22 in Beirut and Amman. The days of child brides seem definitely in the past, and the overall trend toward later age at marriage is unmistakable. There are some class differences, with upper class women generally marrying later than the others.

Age at marriage of the husbands of these women is shown in Table III-5. The contrast between age at marriage of men and age at marriage of women is strong. Our Muslim women married "early" by Western standards, but not the Muslim men. Before 1930 the average ranged from 21 in Buarij to 30 in Beirut. In the 1960's the range was from 24 in Artas to 30 in Beirut. Only in Buarij and Amman was there increase over time in average age at marriage. Elsewhere there was either little change or a slight decrease. There is a hint in the data of greater age at marriage of upper class males as opposed to males of other classes, but differences are small and there are several exceptions. On the whole, the data reveal rather advanced age at marriage of males, especially in comparison with other preindustrial societies,[1] and little change over time.

If the age at marriage of women is increasing, and the age at marriage of men is not, then it follows that differences in age are decreasing. A comparison of Tables III-4 and III-5 shows that this is generally the case with our couples, though it does not hold in Buarij. Even among couples married in the 1960's, however, there are still average differences of 6 to 9 years in the six localities studied—fairly large by Western standards (Goode, 1963, p. 47). It is interesting to note by way of comparison, however, that Korson (1965, p. 595) found an average of difference of 6.8 years in a study of Muslim marriages in Karachi. Gulick (1955, p. 60) reports a tradition in a Lebanese Christian village that seven years is the ideal age difference between husband and wife.

The findings that Muslim women of the Levant are today older at marriage than formerly, and that the age difference between husband and wife at marriage is decreasing, are in accordance with the expectations and with the surmise of Goode (pp. 110-111). Less expected was the rather advanced age at marriage of the men, and the fact that—at least for the past four decades—there has been no consistent or significant increase in their average age at marriage. Goode believes that the average age at marriage of Muslim men is increasing. As evidence he cites Churchill's data on Beirut (1954, pp. 32-33), which found that male age at marriage was lower in the former generation than in the "current" (1952-53) generation, but the "former generation" sample consisted of only

---

[1] Petersen (1968, p. 537) has made a similar observation on age at marriage of Egyptian males.

24 fathers of heads of household who resided with their sons. The number of Muslims in this group of 24 is not known. Moreover, there was a selective factor operating in favor of fathers who married young, for those who were older at marriage would be less likely to survive until their sons had become heads of households.

It can be argued that our selection of a few hundred women from each city did not necessarily provide a representative sample. Asking a woman how long she has been married and age at marriage is tantamount to asking how old she is, and thus unlikely to give an accurate estimate. Moreover, there were factors in the interviewing situation which predisposed the interviewers toward selection of those married early. Intentionally or not, they rarely chose wives who were in a second marriage, although such marriages are common and, obviously, occur at a later age than do first marriages. Finally, women married early in the century were more likely to get into our "sample" if they had been young at the time of marriage, for they would be more likely in 1967 to be alive, unwidowed, and able to respond accurately to a long list of questions. It is probable, then, that our city "samples" underestimated average age at marriage, especially of wives married before 1930.

We therefore obtained data on the ages listed in the marriage contracts of the Sunni religious courts of Sidon and Tripoli from 1965 back as far as the records were available. There is no civil marriage in Lebanon, so these records should give fairly complete information on marriages in those two districts. The data are summarized in Table III-6. The evidence from these sixteen thousand contracts is unmistakable. The average age of brides has increased steadily since the decade of 1930's, and the proportion of brides married at age 15 or younger has decreased since then. The average age of grooms has been lower since 1950 than it was before then, so of course the age difference between bride and groom has been less in recent years than it was in the first half of the century. These data from the religious courts bear out reasonably well the conclusions drawn from the interviews: average age of brides is increasing while average age of grooms is not.

The increase in age at marriage of women is a sign of growing independence of women and is probably a result of the changing role of women in Islamic society. As the modesty code has become less strict, women are more often expected to remain in school beyond puberty and some are even encouraged to work outside the home until marriage. In short, the role of the adolescent girl is no longer restricted to that of a young bride.

The fact that men are marrying a bit earlier than formerly is also a sign of increasing independence of youth. The economic barriers to marriage, which keep decisions on these matters in the hands of elders, are decreasing. As we shall see later, there is today less emphasis than formerly on the *advanced* bride price. Moreover, some women work after marriage. Nevertheless, the economic burdens of getting married are still considerable, and men still marry at a later age than do those of most Western countries.

The opinions of the wives about appropriate age at marriage can be deduced from the data in Table III-7. Of those who reported having married at age 15 or earlier, a majority (everywhere except in Artas) thought it had been too early. Of those married at 16, 17 or 18, about a third considered it to have been too early. Of those married at 19 or later, very few said it was too early. There was little difference between younger and older wives on this issue. In general, a majority of all wives except those of Artas felt that marriage should not be earlier than age 17.

Courtship and Engagement

In a society in which marriage arrangements are controlled by the elders and segregation of the sexes is practiced, courtship naturally plays a minor role in determining marriages. Even in the most traditional parts of the Muslim Levant, however, the concept of romantic love does exist—at least in poetry and song. Boys and girls do catch glimpses of one another, even in highly conservative communities. With the disappearance of the veil, and the appearance of coeducation, the opportunities for the development of some feeling of friendship and mutual attraction between the sexes have greatly multiplied. Today families with adolescent daughters do much visiting and attending of family gatherings, especially where there are eligible young men likely to be present. Interested young men may visit a girl's brothers. We can guess that in some cases at least a young man, and even a young girl, might influence traditional parents to arrange a marriage with someone found to be attractive (cf. Muhyi, 1959, p. 47). There is also evidence that some young people, presumably from less traditional settings, make their own decisions about marriage and then persuade the parents to go along (Hirabayashi & Ishaq, 1958, p. 38). Nevertheless, "courtship" in this part of the world is limited by the modesty code, and it is usually in the period between the engagement and the writing of the contract that the couple begins to get acquainted.

As can be seen from Table III-8, very few of the women interviewed had before engagement gone out alone with the man they later married. Many of the women, as we have already noted, had never even seen the prospective groom before the engagement. The majority had seen him and even talked with him, but in a family or other group situation. The younger wives of Beirut were an exception. A majority of them had gone out alone before the engagement with the man they later married.

A number of observers have described the several steps involved in the arranging and cementing of Muslim marriages.[1] Although there is some variation from village to village, from season to season, and from person to person, there is a fairly consistent underlying pattern. First there is a search, or inquiry or inspection. This is initiated by the father of a young man, usually at the son's instigation. If the prospective bride is not already known to the groom's family, some of his female relatives will pay a social call on her family, observe the girl and report back their findings. If there is no specific girl under consideration, the female relatives may inquire around and then make a series of inspection visits. Their reports are weighed by the groom and the groom's father. The father may consult his male relatives. According to tradition, it is the groom's father who is in charge of this stage, as was Abraham the father of Isaac, but in practice the son usually plays the major role, and the mother and adult sisters also participate actively (cf. Table VI-31).

Preliminary soundings and visits may continue for some days, especially if one of the parties is not known in the community, until a tacit agreement has been reached by the families on the suitability of the marriage. Sometimes contact is through a third party, to avoid a possible rebuff and consequent hard feelings. Finally, the young man and his father and perhaps a brother or two approach the girl's father and male relatives. The girl's father will say that she is too young, that he cannot bear for her to leave him, etc. If he should deem the marriage unsuitable (and here he usually consults his wife, who usually consults the girl), he stands firm. If he deems it suitable, he allows himself to be persuaded to discuss the dowry or bride price (*mahr*). This is followed by a visit of the groom's family to the bride's family, to confirm the proposal. A few days later, the bride's family or her representative returns the visit and confirms the acceptance.

If agreement is reached on the proposal, including the *mahr*, there is

---

[1] Of these, the one which fits most closely with our own observations is Antoun's discussion of the "mode of marriage" in a Jordanian village (1972, pp. 116-125).

34

then an engagement reception. It is called *i'lan al-khitbah*, which means "publicizing the proposal." This is held in the bride's home, but all expenses are borne by the groom's family. Both (extended) families are present, and a few friends who may not be relatives. Rings are exchanged, to be worn on the right hand until the marriage ceremony. The opening chapter of the Quran (the *Fatiha*) is recited. The bride price is usually announced, and paid publicly. Among the more modern, the bride price may not be announced, but a gift of jewelry (e.g., a diamond solitaire) made. At this point the family of the groom, and usually of the bride, offer gifts or promises of gifts to the bride.

The more modern families permit engaged couples to go out together unchaperoned, so this period is sometimes thought of by them as the "courtship" period. Such permissiveness is still rare, however, as can be seen in Table III-9. The upper class women, particularly those of Beirut, have been in the lead, but even among them, such liberty is recent. Among the women of Artas, and the city women married before 1930, it was the custom to avoid the prospective husband altogether during the engagement period (see Table III-10). For the majority of the other women, it was the custom for the young man to call on his fiancée in her home, under the more or less watchful eye of her relatives. The relaxing of the modesty code will be discussed in Chapter VI, but the data on behavior after the engagement ceremony give us clear evidence of the direction of the change and the groups which are leading the way.

The next step toward marriage is the writing of the marriage contract. This is called *kateb el kitab* (writing the writ) or, more formally, *'aqd al nikah* (contract for intercourse). Western writers sometimes refer to this step as the engagement, but it is a much more binding ceremony than even the most formal engagement in the West. It is a contract signed by the groom, the bride's representative (e.g., her father), and witnesses in the presence of an official of the Muslim court. It is entered in the court records, and can be broken only by a divorce. Among other things, it specifies the *mahr*.

The writing of the contract usually takes place in the home of the bride, and in private,[1] but sometimes in the court. It is not in itself an occasion for a reception or a feast, but it may take place on the same day as the engagement announcement *(i'lan al-khitbah)*, as sometimes is the case, or

---

[1] Patai (1958, pp. 147-8) states that in Jordan there is a large gathering of guests, but Granqvist (1935, p. 24) noted, as we did, a strong preference for privacy on this occasion.

on the same day as the marriage ceremony, as is often the case (Table III-11), and these are occasions for festivities.

A majority of the marriages in Artas, Buarij and Amman took place on the same day as the writing of the contract. In Damascus, Tripoli and Beirut, most of the marriages were one to six months afterward. In these latter cities, a majority of the younger wives reported that they had several times gone out with their future husbands, alone and unchaperoned, after the signing of the contract. This trend toward greater freedom was led by the upper class wives (see Table III-12).

The wedding ceremony, or the "giving away of the bride," is the occasion of much celebration. However, the rite itself is a simple and straight-forward covenant, whether in city or village. It takes place in the home of the bride. The groom and the bride (either in person or through her guardian) express their consent[1] before an authorized *sheikh* and at least two witnesses while clasping right hands. The *Fatiha* is recited, and perhaps other selections from the Quran. There may be a brief sermon. Usually, in the cities, the bride then takes formal leave of her father's house, accompanied by the groom and a large group of her relatives and his. We observed that in modern and traditional families alike, this moment was an occasion for weeping on the part of the bride, her mother and sisters. The procession in the villages was usually *after* the festivities, at which time it would proceed to the home of the groom, which was often his family home. In middle and upper class urban families, the procession was often by horn-blowing taxis decorated with flowers and ribbons, to a hotel or other place of public reception. Village celebrations often involved feasting, singing and dancing which went on for several evenings. City celebrations frequently resembled those following a Western wedding, with a towering wedding cake and champagne. These latter celebrations were, as in the West, of only a few hours duration, and were usually followed by a honeymoon trip. In village and in city wedding expenses, including the bridal gown, are borne by the groom and his family.

In both villages we found some evidence of a trend toward shorter celebrations (cf. Williams, 1968, p. 95 and des Villettes, 1964, p. 112). In Table III-1 we have defined extended celebrations as those lasting three days or longer (some lasted up to one week). Although the number of cases is small, the younger wives in each place more often reported short celebrations than did the older wives. Apparently the villagers are beginning to follow the lead of the cities.

[1] For the bride, it is sometimes the case that "silence gives consent."

36

TABLE III–1

DURATION OF WEDDING CELEBRATIONS IN TWO VILLAGES

| | Buarij | | Artas | |
Date of Marriage	1940-1967	Before 1940	1940-1967	Before 1940
Duration	(N=16)	(N=14)	(N=54)	(N=17)
Extended	37.5%	57%	59%	76%
Shorter	12.5	29	41	24
None	31	7	0	0
No Answer	19	7	0	0

The Dowry (Mahr)

The custom of giving a bride price or dowry to the bride or to her family was until this century widespread in non-Islamic as well as Islamic parts of Africa and Asia. In Arabia before Islam, it was apparently the custom, and the bride price went to the bride's father or guardian. A number of writers have suggested that this practice points back to a time when women were treated as chattels. Chatila (1934, pp. 123 ff.) argues rather that the Arab dowry was a kind of potlatch, proving the generosity and power of the groom, and serving to bind families by exchanges of gifts. The Quran gives considerable emphasis to the protection of women's rights, and states clearly that the dowry should go to the bride rather than to her male relatives.

In contemporary Islamic law, there are two kinds of bride price or dowry (*mahr*). One (*mahr almathl*) is not specified in the marriage contract, but determined by what is normal and suitable for one of the bride's standing. Under this interpretation, the bride has an inalienable right to appropriate gifts (including, for example, clothing and furniture) upon her marriage. The most common type of dowry, and the one usually thought of by Arabs who mention *mahr*, is that specified in the marriage contract. The specified dowry is usually in money, even though the money is normally spent on the trousseau, gold, jewelry, furniture, or land. Under Muslim law, a marriage without *mahr* is not legal, so some amount is always specified in the contracts.

The specified dowry is of two kinds: immediate and deferred. The immediate may be paid at the time of the signing of the contract (*kateb el kitab*), or between then and the marriage ceremony. In many cases, the delay between the contract and the marriage is to permit the groom to accumulate the "immediate" payment. This payment should go to the bride and not to her father, though stories of greedy fathers are widespread,[1] and she ordinarily uses it to purchase personal possessions appropriate to her new role and status. The deferred payment is a protection for the bride. It is paid only if the husband divorces her or predeceases her. Islamic law makes no provision for alimony, so the deferred payment is an important protection for married women[2] (cf. Korson, 1967, p. 527).

The importance of the bride price in the life of the typical Arab villager has been described by Antoun (1967, pp. 294-308). The young man in his twenties who has neither wealth nor family will be unable to marry, and thus unable to achieve full manhood in the eyes of the community. Williams (1968, p. 95) describes a case in which a man labored for a Biblical period of seven years to accumulate the necessary funds for the bride price and the wedding expenses. Each community seems to have some conception of a "normal" bride price, but even in a single community this will vary with the status of the families involved, the nearness of the relationship between bride and groom, and the personal qualities of the bride. It is a matter of pride for the bride's family not to let her go "cheaply" unless she is marrying a close relative, or unless there is a "reciprocal marriage" in which one family gives *and* receives a bride to and from another family.

As Granqvist pointed out in 1931 (p. 126), the "complicated system of gifts and counter-gifts allows of great variations, so that it is extremely difficult for an outsider to know how great are the expenses which a bridegroom really has for his bride when everything is taken into account." She speaks of bride prices of 50 to 100 dinars (roughly 140 to 280 dollars) as common in the twenties, and Lutfiyya speaks of 100 to 500 or even a thousand dinars in the sixties (1966, p. 131). Antoun (1972, pp. 120 and 169) found the standard early *mahr* in one Jordanian village to be 200 dinars in 1960 and 250 dinars in 1966. When we consider that the annual per

---

[1] Of 162 marriages in Antoun's Jordanian village, 25 per cent were "exchange" marriages, so the bride received no early *mahr*. In another 5 per cent of the marriages, all of the *mahr* was taken by the father. In only 8 per cent of these marriages did all of the *mahr* go to the girl, as prescribed in Islamic law. Some of the villagers said that only the well-to-do could afford to give all the *mahr* to their daughters (Antoun, 1972, pp. 118-121).

[2] Just as some Western husbands attempt to avoid alimony payments, so do some Middle Eastern husbands try to avoid the late *mahr* (Lichtenstadter, 1948, p. 170).

capita income in the area is even today no more than 30 dinars or so, it is obvious that the bride price is a very considerable sum. In Beirut the median prompt payment specified in all marriage contracts signed in 1956 was about five hundred dollars and the median deferred payment about twice that amount (Abu Khadra, 1959, p. 56). The median of total annual income *per household* in Beirut was about one thousand dollars in 1954 (Churchill, 1954, p. 58), so here too the bride price is a significant sum.

In a few cases the bride price, and especially the early payment, is purely symbolic. Chatila (1934, p. 191) mentions that a *mahr* no greater than the legal minimum was sometimes stipulated in Syrian cities, but that such cases were regrettably rare. Korson (1967, p. 531) found in Karachi that about eight per cent of all grooms, in the upper and lower classes alike, had paid a symbolic *mahr*. Our data (Table III-13) show that the custom of requiring a symbolic[1] advanced payment is very strong in Beirut upper class families and fairly widespread among upper and middle classes in Amman and Damascus. In Tripoli and in the two villages, the bride price is not merely symbolic.

It must be understood that the absence of a stipulated advanced payment does not mean that the groom is freed of his obligations. He pays for engagement and wedding receptions, he gives his bride jewelry and other gifts which become her property, he buys her wedding outfit, he furnishes their home, etc. The fact that little *mahr* is stipulated usually means that the bride's family can take for granted that the groom will behave nobly and generously, that they accept *mahr almathl*.

A number of wives also reported that the deferred bride price was merely symbolic (Table III-14). There is no clear trend over time, but what trend there is (in Artas, Amman and Beirut) seems to be toward the disappearance of such inconsequential deferred payments. Class differences on this score are highly inconsistent. In Amman it is the lower class that accepts symbolic late payments; in Beirut it is the upper class that accepts them.

If the late payment serves to protect the wife in case of divorce, then an improvement in the status of women could be expected to be accompanied by an increase in the amount of the late payment, and an increase in the late payment in comparison with the early payment. Traditionally

[1] We have called payments of ten Lebanese pounds (about three dollars) or less "symbolic" payments.

the early payment was twice as large as the late payment. Among the older women interviewed, most of them, except in Beirut and Tripoli, reported that they had followed this tradition (Table III-15). Among the younger women, married in the sixties, only those of Artas still followed tradition. In the other places, the late payment stipulated in the sixties was either the same amount as, or larger than, the early payment.

The Sunni court records from Tripoli and Sidon (Table III-16) also show that there has been a shift away from the larger early payment. In Sidon during the twenties the early payment was the larger in 80 per cent of the marriages. By the sixties, it was the larger in only 13 per cent. In Tripoli during the twenties, the early payment was the larger in about 70 per cent of the marriages.[1] In the sixties it was the larger in only 10 per cent. From these records it is evident that the tradition of the early payment being larger than the late payment no longer holds.

The amount of the early and late *mahr* recorded by the Sunni courts of Sidon and Tripoli for all marriages occurring from 1946 through 1965 is presented in Table III-17. In the late forties, the early payment exceeded 1,000 Lebanese pounds in about 50 per cent of the Sidon marriages and in about 33 per cent of the Tripoli marriages. In both cities, the early payment rarely exceeded 3,000 Lebanese pounds. By the early sixties, the early payment was greater than 1,000 Lebanese pounds in 65 to 70 per cent, and greater than 3,000 pounds in nearly 20 per cent, of the marriages in both cities. The early payment evidently increased over two decades.

The increase in late payment was even greater. In the late forties, about a third of the stipulated late payments were above 1,000 Lebanese pounds and fewer than 10 per cent above 3,000. By the sixties, more than two-thirds of the stipulated late payments were greater than 1,000 Lebanese pounds and about 25 per cent were greater than 3,000. The late payment, then, increased more than did the early.

The information reported by the interviewed wives was in general agreement with the trends shown by the court records. For all localities except Artas and Beirut, this agreement is shown in Table III-18. In Artas the standard advanced payment was 100 dinars (roughly 280 dollars), and this held for all marriage decades. The stipulated late payment was usually

---

[1] A comparison of Tables III-15 and III-16 shows that, among the older women of Tripoli, those we interviewed were atypical. Most of our older interviewees declared that the early and late *mahr* had been the same.

only nominal before 1940; since 1960 it usually has been about the same as the advanced payment. In Beirut the older wives (married before 1940) reported in a majority of cases that the *mahr*, early and late, as specified in the contract, was only symbolic. A majority of the younger wives (married in the sixties) reported the early payment was only symbolic, but a majority said the late payment was not merely symbolic. These non-symbolic late payments in Beirut were above 5,000 Lebanese pounds in nearly half the cases. Here again we find the greatest increase was in late payment.

The data bear out our expectation that the improved status of women be manifested in an increased emphasis on the payment to be made to the wife in case of divorce, or death of the husband.

Trends and Prospects

For many centuries marriage in the Middle East has been under the control of the elders, and the role of the prospective bride (and, to a lesser extent, of the groom) has been limited to suggesting, influencing, coaxing and (usually) assenting. Marriage was a family affair, too important to be left to the caprice of the young. It required commitments, emotional as well as financial, between families. Elopements did occur, but if these were not accepted by the two families, they might end in forcible separation, exile, or even death. Romantic feelings certainly existed, as Arabic poetry amply testifies, but any overt expression of such feelings was considered, in the Levant at least, as a grave reflection on the modesty and chastity of the female. The wise family avoided any threat to honor by arranging an early marriage of daughters.[1]

This traditional arrangement is today under attack. Many media of communications emphasize independence, freedom, egalitarianism, youth culture, and romantic love. From our data it is evident that the Arab family is changing, and is accommodating greater individual freedom into the traditional pattern.

In the choosing of a husband, the trend everywhere is toward consulting the girl before agreeing to a marriage contract. In the early part of this

---

[1] The Arabs did not employ the Puritanical approach of attempting to internalize feelings of guilt regarding sex relations. Sex was and is looked upon as a blessing, and sex relations for both husband and wife are an obligation and a right. Control of young girls is the responsibility of the males in her family (see Chapter VI). The psychoanalyst would undoubtedly look upon this culture as a "shame culture" rather than a "guilt culture."

century, the girl was rarely consulted and often met her future husband for the first time on the day of the engagement. Today the prospective bride usually has met the prospective groom (in meetings arranged by relatives, to be sure) and has been consulted on whether she finds him acceptable. In Artas this consultation is still rare, but even there the mothers of young girls say they intend to consult their daughters when the time comes. In the cities it was the upper class which led this trend toward giving the girls an increased freedom of choice.

The age of girls at marriage is increasing and child brides are becoming a rarity. The average age of males is not increasing, so the average difference in age of husband and wife has decreased over the past forty years or so. Most of the wives, young and old alike, now feel that girls should not marry before about 17 years of age. These facts too point toward less control by the elders and greater opportunity for girls to exercise some influence in the choice of a mate.

The freedom of girls continues to be limited. In recent years it has become customary for the young man to be permitted to call upon his fiancée in her home, but it is still rare for an engaged couple to be allowed to go out together unchaperoned. Only among the upper classes, especially in Beirut, is such liberty widespread.

The financial obligations of marriage are borne largely by the groom and his family, and they are considerable. This fact, if nothing else, keeps the young under the control of their elders. Here too there is evidence of change. Wedding celebrations in the villages are becoming less extended than formerly. Among upper classes in several cities, the initial bride price (dowry, *mahr*) is more often symbolic (e.g., one pound) than real and substantial, as heretofore. At the same time, there is an increasing emphasis on the late *mahr*, which falls due in case of divorce, so that the wife enjoys greater protection than formerly.

In all of these data we find evidence of some increase in the freedom of youth and of the status of women over the past twenty to forty years. The trends are stronger in the urban upper class, who provide us with clues to the family patterns of the future.

TABLE III-2

Per Cent Meeting Husband Through In-Laws or Relatives

(percentages are based on the numbers shown in Table II-1)

Year of Marriage	1960's				1950's				1940's				1930's				Before 1930			
Social Class	U	M	L	(T)	U	M	L	(T)	U	M	L	(T)	U	M	L	(T)	U	M	L	(T)
Artas				(83)				(88)				(95)				(100)				(87)
Buarij				(69)				(38)				(53)				(40)				(44)
Amman	30	46	59	(49)	33	36	60	(43)	25	67	55	(55)	16	33	57	(36)	++	71	71	(75)
Damascus	++	62	71	(64)	40	72	++	(69)	37	73	62	(65)	++	100	++	(96)	++	82	++	(86)
Tripoli	58	56	55	(56)	80	68	69	(69)	60	79	78	(77)	++	81	100	(90)	++	80	72	(78)
Beirut	39	57	83	(55)	21	76	71	(61)	69	89	100	(83)	72	100	–	(85)	87	100	–	(94)

++ Percentages not shown for cells with fewer than 5 cases.

TABLE III-3

PER CENT WHO NEVER SAW HUSBAND BEFORE ENGAGEMENT

(Percentages are based on the numbers shown in Table II-1)

Year of Marriage	1960's				1950's				1940's				1930's				Before 1930			
Social Class	U	M	L	(T)	U	M	L	(T)	U	M	L	(T)	U	M	L	(T)	U	M	L	(T)
Artas				(37)				(30)				(41)				(44)				(52)
Buarij				(19)				(24)				(20)				(10)				(11)
Amman	6	36	33	(31)	22	36	30	(33)	37	33	41	(37)	67	50	43	(52)	++	57	29	(37)
Damascus	++	30	43	(30)	00	38	++	(37)	25	61	50	(53)	++	70	++	(67)	++	71	++	(68)
Tripoli	4	26	37	(26)	25	41	49	(43)	40	46	46	(46)	++	81	37	(67)	++	40	43	(44)
Beirut	3	18	39	(17)	9	27	29	(22)	12	51	60	(38)	26	31	–	(29)	37	80	–	(61)

TABLE III–4

MEAN AGE OF WIVES AT TIME OF MARRIAGE

(number in each group is shown in Table II–1)

Year of Marriage / Social Class	1960's				1950's				1940's				1930's				Before 1930			
	U	M	L	(T)	U	M	L	(T)	U	M	L	(T)	U	M	L	(T)	U	M	L	(T)
Artas				(16.9)				(16.4)				(14.7)				(14.8)				(14.2)
Buarij				(19.1)				(18.6)				(19.4)				(18.6)				(17.7)
Amman	23.8	22.6	19.6	(21.6)	20.0	19.7	18.8	(19.5)	19.2	18.0	17.1	(17.8)	16.8	16.2	16.6	(16.5)	++	16.1	15.3	(15.6)
Damascus	++	21.8	18.6	(21.4)	22.0	20.4	++	(20.6)	19.1	18.5	18.0	(18.6)	++	16.9	++	(16.8)	++	14.7	++	(14.1)
Tripoli	21.0	19.2	18.6	(19.2)	18.9	17.6	17.0	(17.5)	19.6	16.0	15.5	(16.0)	++	15.6	15.0	(15.9)	++	15.0	15.4	(15.3)
Beirut	21.1	22.0	22.1	(21.7)	20.9	19.6	20.0	(19.9)	20.1	19.0	17.6	(19.3)	19.4	19.1	–	(19.2)	19.6	17.3	–	(18.3)

TABLE III-5

MEAN AGE OF HUSBANDS AT TIME OF MARRIAGE

(number in each group is shown in Table II-1)

Year of Marriage Social Class	1960's				1950's				1940's				1930's				Before 1930			
	U	M	L	(T)	U	M	L	(T)	U	M	L	(T)	U	M	L	(T)	U	M	L	(T)
Artas				(24.4)				(26.9)				(24.6)				(26.8)				(25.1)
Buarij				(27.8)				(25.5)				(23.1)				(23.5)				(21.1)
Amman	30.8	27.0	26.1	(28.0)	27.6	26.6	24.7	(26.1)	25.6	24.7	26.0	(25.4)	27.3	22.9	22.6	(23.9)	++	25.6	20.8	(22.9)
Damascus	++	29.4	26.7	(29.1)	32.6	29.5	++	(29.8)	30.8	27.9	28.1	(28.4)	++	29.0	++	(28.7)	++	28.4	++	(27.2)
Tripoli	29.8	25.6	26.2	(26.3)	30.9	26.3	25.6	(26.4)	27.4	27.3	28.3	(27.8)	++	28.2	27.9	(28.1)	++	25.7	23.6	(25.2)
Beirut	29.8	30.3	29.5	(30.0)	31.3	28.6	29.3	(29.3)	30.4	28.8	24.6	(29.3)	29.7	29.1	–	(29.5)	29.6	30.2	–	(29.9)

TABLE III–6

AGES OF HUSBANDS AND WIVES AT TIME OF MARRIAGE
(from Sunni Court Records in Sidon and Tripoli)

Years	Number of Marriages	Mean Age of Husbands	Mean Age of Wives	Mean Age Difference	Per Cent of Wives Below Age 16 at Marriage
		Sidon (4,753 marriages)			
1920–1929	463	31.64	17.34	14.30	42.6
1930–1939	809	31.68	19.80	11.88	28.4
1940–1949	942	31.54	20.44	11.10	15.5
1950–1959	1480	28.75	20.88	7.87	9.9
1960–1965	1059	29.36	20.98	8.38	14.0
		Tripoli (11,428 marriages)*			
1920–1929	1298	29.36	19.44	9.92	29.9
1930–1939	1575	–	18.99	–	34.1
1940–1949	2480	–	19.60	–	22.2
1950–1959	3475	28.38	20.89	7.49	14.5
1960–1965	2600	28.74	20.90	7.84	16.6

*Data on age of husband for the years 1924-1949 are not available in the Tripoli court records.

TABLE III-7

Per Cent of Wives who Felt they had Married too Early

Age at Marriage		22 and above		19-20-21		16-17-18		15 and below	
Year of Marriage		'50 or after	'49 or before	'50 or after	'49 or before	'50 or after	'49 or before	'50 or after	'49 or before
Artas	%	0	0	0	0	2	0	33	44
	N*	(6)	(1)	(12)	(4)	(46)	(25)	(40)	(63)
Buarij	%	13	14	67	11	50	33	91	67
	N	(8)	(7)	(6)	(9)	(12)	(12)	(11)	(6)
Amman	%	1	0	11	9	45	32	79	79
	N	(80)	(7)	(71)	(11)	(58)	(50)	(14)	(24)
Damascus	%	2	0	14	0	54	44	93	78
	N	(56)	(17)	(29)	(14)	(35)	(27)	(15)	(40)
Tripoli	%	0	0	9	8	26	19	57	67
	N	(74)	(10)	(66)	(12)	(149)	(37)	(95)	(70)
Beirut	%	0	0	7	0	51	53	100	100
	N	(102)	(29)	(70)	(36)	(55)	(49)	(17)	(17)
All Localities	%	1	1	11	3	33	33	62	66
	N	(326)	(71)	(254)	(86)	(355)	(200)	(192)	(220)

*N indicates number of cases on which each percentage is based

TABLE III-8

PER CENT OF WIVES WHO NEVER WENT OUT ALONE WITH FUTURE HUSBAND BEFORE ENGAGEMENT

Year of Marriage	1960's				1950's				1940's				1930's				Before 1930			
Social Class	U	M	L	(T)	U	M	L	(T)	U	M	L	(T)	U	M	L	(T)	U	M	L	(T)
Artas			94	(96)				(97)				(91)				(92)				(100)
Buarij				(75)				(76)				(87)				(100)				(100)
Amman	41	88	94	(84)	89	89	93	(90)	99	95	100	(98)	100	100	86	(96)	++	100	100	(100)
Damascus	++	69	90	(69)	40	74	+	(71)	87	91	100	(92)	+	96	+	(97)	+	95	+	(95)
Tripoli	96	91	94	(92)	90	97	99	(97)	100	95	100	(98)	+	100	100	(100)	+	100	100	(100)
Beirut	11	28	39	(25)	24	46	29	(39)	39	70	60	(59)	47	37	–	(43)	74	80	–	(78)

TABLE III-9

Per Cent of Wives who Went out with Future Husband Alone During Engagement

Year of Marriage	1960's				1950's				1940's				1930's				Before 1930			
Social Class	U	M	L	(T)	U	M	L	(T)	U	M	L	(T)	U	M	L	(T)	U	M	L	(T)
Artas				(00)				(00)				(00)				(00)				(00)
Buarij				(14)				(6)				(7)				(00)				(00)
Amman	41	10	2	(11)	00	9	3	(6)	00	00	00	(00)	00	00	00	(00)	++	00	00	(00)
Damascus	++	38	00	(36)	40	14	++	(16)	00	12	00	(8)	++	00	++	(00)	++	00	++	(00)
Tripoli	42	15	19	(20)	15	12	1	(8)	00	8	3	(5)	++	00	00	(00)	++	00	00	(00)
Beirut	72	57	6	(54)	41	29	00	(31)	15	21	00	(18)	00	6	–	(3)	00	00	–	(00)

TABLE III-10

PER CENT OF WIVES WHO NEVER SAW FUTURE HUSBAND DURING ENGAGEMENT

Year of Marriage	1960's				1950's				1940's				1930's				Before 1930			
Social Class	U	M	L	(T)	U	M	L	(T)	U	M	L	(T)	U	M	L	(T)	U	M	L	(T)
Artas				(51)				(49)				(55)				(64)				(84)
Buarij				(00)				(00)				(00)				(00)				(00)
Amman	00	2	8	(4)	11	9	37	(18)	12	14	36	(24)	83	33	43	(48)	++	43	43	(50)
Damascus	++	4	17	(5)	00	17	++	(18)	29	33	50	(35)	++	57	++	(56)	++	82	++	(77)
Tripoli	00	10	15	(10)	20	21	29	(24)	00	36	41	(36)	++	69	37	(59)	++	80	71	(78)
Beirut	00	2	22	(4)	00	2	00	(2)	00	13	40	(10)	11	6	–	(9)	25	40	–	(33)

TABLE III–11

Per Cent of Wives for whom Writing of Contract and Marriage Ceremony were on the Same Day

Year of Marriage	1960's				1950's				1940's				1930's				Before 1930			
Social Class	U	M	L	(T)	U	M	L	(T)	U	M	L	(T)	U	M	L	(T)	U	M	L	(T)
Artas				(76)				(68)				(68)				(74)				(73)
Buarij				(69)				(52)				(60)				(30)				(44)
Amman	59	51	63	(57)	67	55	77	(63)	62	38	73	(57)	67	33	57	(48)	++	14	14	(19)
Damascus	++	27	57	(29)	40	23	++	(29)	12	30	12	(24)	++	26	++	(33)	++	12	++	(18)
Tripoli	00	12	21	(13)	5	8	16	(11)	00	17	11	(13)	++	6	10	(7)	++	10	29	(22)
Beirut	17	7	00	(9)	12	6	14	(8)	12	2	00	(5)	5	6	–	(6)	12	00	–	(6)

TABLE III-12

PER CENT OF WIVES WHO WENT OUT ALONE WITH HUSBAND AFTER THE WRITING OF THE MARRIAGE CONTRACT BUT BEFORE THE CEREMONY

Year of Marriage / Social Class		1960's				1950's				1940's				1930's				Before 1930			
Locality		U	M	L	(T)	U	M	L	(T)	U	M	L	(T)	U	M	L	(T)	U	M	L	(T)
Damascus	%	100	81	50	(80)	60	49	25	(48)	29	16	0	(15)	0	0	0	(0)	0	0	0	(0)
	N*	2	48	4	(54)	5	53	4	(62)	7	31	8	(46)	1	19	3	(23)	1	17	4	(22)
Tripoli	%	83	78	40	(66)	84	49	30	(45)	20	24	3	(14)	0	0	0	(0)	–	0	0	(0)
	N	24	90	53	(167)	19	84	70	(173)	5	34	33	(72)	3	15	9	(27)	0	9	5	(14)
Beirut	%	100	90	44	(86)	85	70	0	(71)	69	45	0	(50)	37	12	–	(26)	12	0	–	(6)
	N	36	60	18	(114)	34	90	6	(130)	26	47	5	(78)	19	16	0	(35)	8	10	0	(18)

*N is number responding to the question. Those wives for whom signing of contract and marriage ceremony occurred on the same day are not included.

TABLE III-13

Per Cent of Marriages with Symbolic Advanced Payment*

Year of Marriage	1960's				1950's				1940's				1930's				Before 1930			
Social Class	U	M	L	(T)	U	M	L	(T)	U	M	L	(T)	U	M	L	(T)	U	M	L	(T)
Artas				(00)				(00)				(5)				(00)				(00)
Buarij				(00)				(00)				(00)				(00)				(00)
Amman	47	46	29	(40)	55	40	27	(38)	62	24	10	(24)	17	17	14	(16)	++	00	29	(12)
Damascus	++	34	14	(35)	+–	40	++	(41)	62	31	00	(31)	++	5	++	(8)	++	6	++	(14)
Tripoli	9	4	2	(4)	20	7	1	(6)	00	3	00	(1)	++	12	00	(7)	++	00	00	(00)
Beirut	94	60	00	(61)	88	51	00	(58)	88	36	00	(51)	84	44	–	(66)	100	56	–	(76)

*An amount of 10 Lebanese Pounds (about 3 U.S. Dollars) or less was considered a symbolic payment.

TABLE III-14

Per Cent of Marriages with Symbolic Late Payment*

Year of Marriage	1960's				1950's				1940's				1930's				Before 1930			
Social Class	U	M	L	(T)	U	M	L	(T)	U	M	L	(T)	U	M	L	(T)	U	M	L	(T)
Artas				(7)				(22)				(33)				(46)				(35)
Buarij				(00)				(00)				(00)				(00)				(00)
Amman	36	24	58	(40)	22	56	90	(64)	37	76	96	(78)	83	83	86	(84)	++	100	71	(87)
Damascus	++	9	14	(10)	+−	23	++	(25)	62	22	00	(25)	++	00	++	(00)	++	6	++	(10)
Tripoli	5	00	00	(1)	5	00	00	(1)	00	00	00	(00)	++	00	00	(00)	++	00	00	(00)
Beirut	81	27	00	(39)	76	18	00	(32)	68	28	00	(39)	79	12	−	(49)	100	44	−	(71)

*An amount of 10 Lebanese Pounds (about 3 U.S. Dollars) or less was considered a symbolic payment.

TABLE III–15

COMPARISON OF SIZE OF EARLY AND LATE DOWRY (MAHR) PAYMENTS
(numbers in body of table are percentages, except for numbers in
parentheses, which show number of women replying)

Location	Larger Payment*	Decade of Marriage				
		1960's	*1950's*	*1940's*	*1930's*	*before 1930*
Artas	Early	98	95	95	100	100
	Late	0	3	3	0	0
	Neither	2	2	3	0	0
	N	(42)	(62)	(38)	(22)	(23)
Buarij	Early	25	62	79	80	89
	Late	50	33	14	10	11
	Neither	25	5	7	10	0
	N	(16)	(20)	(14)	(10)	(9)
Amman	Early	34	59	78	84	88
	Late	63	41	22	16	13
	Neither	3	0	0	0	0
	N	(112)	(82)	(49)	(25)	(16)
Damascus	Early	29	49	44	75	68
	Late	36	41	31	8	5
	Neither	35	10	25	17	26
	N	(55)	(51)	(36)	(24)	(19)
Tripoli	Early	1	12	6	11	0
	Late	45	37	31	33	6
	Neither	54	51	63	56	94
	N	(175)	(194)	(80)	(27)	(18)
Beirut	Early	8	7	3	0	0
	Late	69	70	77	60	50
	Neither	23	23	21	40	50
	N	(64)	(43)	(39)	(10)	(4)

*"Early" means that the early or immediate payment was larger; "Neither," that the two payments were equal; "Late," that the late or deferred payment was larger.

TABLE III–16

COMPARISON OF EARLY AND LATE DOWRY (MAHR) PAYMENTS REGISTERED
IN RELIGIOUS COURTS OF SIDON AND TRIPOLI, 1920 THROUGH 1965
(numbers in table are percentages, except for those in parentheses,
which show size of subsample)

Years	(N)	Sidon Larger Payment			(N)	Tripoli Larger Payment		
		Early	Late	Neither		Early	Late	Neither
1920–24	(124)	84	04	12	(643)	73	12	15
1925–29	(347)	77	10	13	(347)	65	15	20
1930–34	(371)	66	16	18	(614)	59	17	24
1935–39	(480)	53	21	26	(961)	52	22	26
1940–44	(431)	57	18	25	(1169)	40	31	29
1945–49	(532)	50	24	26	(1311)	34	29	37
1950–54	(679)	34	24	42	(1478)	23	36	41
1955–59	(829)	18	30	52	(1997)	16	39	45
1960–64	(894)	13	33	54	(2113)	10	46	44
1965	(168)	13	33	54	(487)	09	50	41

TABLE III–17

PER CENT OF DOWRY (MAHR) PAYMENTS EXCEEDING 1000 AND 3000 LEBANESE POUNDS
IN SIDON AND TRIPOLI FROM 1946 THROUGH 1965
(numbers in table, except those in parentheses, are percentages)

Years	N	Sidon				N	Tripoli			
		Early		Late			Early		Late	
		>1000	>3000	>1000	>3000		>1000	>3000	>1000	>3000
1946–47	(238)	59	10	37	8	(516)	34	4	35	4
1948–49	(180)	47	7	33	9	(516)	33	4	32	3
1950–51	(270)	47	6	34	5	(517)	35	5	32	5
1952–53	(248)	54	12	46	11	(619)	38	6	42	6
1954–55	(315)	55	9	53	12	(752)	39	7	47	9
1956–57	(328)	51	10	57	11	(767)	43	8	51	10
1958–59	(347)	62	13	69	16	(820)	50	11	61	16
1960–61	(393)	64	12	69	17	(902)	54	13	65	21
1962–63	(335)	70	14	76	23	(831)	65	17	77	28
1964–65	(334)	70	16	79	25	(867)	66	21	81	30

TABLE III–18

PER CENT OF WIVES REPORTING DOWRY (MAHR) PAYMENTS GREATER THAN 1000 AND 3000 LEBANESE POUNDS
(numbers in table, except for those in parentheses, are percentages)

Year of Marriage		1960's		1950's		1940's		1930's		Before 1930	
		>1000	>3000	>1000	>3000	>1000	>3000	>1000	>3000	>1000	>3000
Artas	Early	0	0	0	0	0	0	0	0	0	0
	Late	0	0	0	0	0	0	0	0	0	0
	N	(42)		(62)		(38)		(22)		(23)	
Buarij	Early	88	0	76	5	43	0	10	0	0	0
	Late	100	0	62	5	29	0	0	0	11	0
	N	(16)		(21)		(14)		(10)		(9)	
Amman	Early	58	0	60	0	59	0	48	0	19	0
	Late	68	27	46	12	24	2	12	4	0	0
	N	(121)		(91)		(51)		(25)		(16)	
Damascus	Early	61	33	49	22	50	27	65	46	74	58
	Late	75	43	60	37	54	31	38	27	42	37
	N	(61)		(67)		(48)		(26)		(19)	
Tripoli	Early	70	26	55	16	48	16	69	23	67	22
	Late	83	38	67	19	53	17	81	35	67	22
	N	(187)		(195)		(80)		(26)		(18)	
Beirut	Early	20	15	32	24	33	23	24	9	19	12
	Late	44	35	59	48	48	45	48	33	25	25
	N	(105)		(117)		(69)		(33)		(16)	

CHAPTER FOUR

Extended Family Ties

You are forbidden to take in marriage your mothers, your daughters, your sisters,
your paternal and maternal aunts, the daughters of your brothers and sisters, (and
certain specified others). Such is the decree of Allah. All women other than
these are lawful to you....
Show kindness to your parents and your kindred, to the orphans and to the needy,
to your near and distant neighbors, to your fellow-travellers, to the wayfarers,
and to the slaves whom you own.

Sura 4

THE TRADITIONAL ARAB FAMILY was described in Chapter One as patrilineal, extended and endogamous. That is, descent is reckoned through males rather than females, married men (and their wives) live with their father in one large household, and marriage with relatives is preferred. This picture of the traditional Arab family is still presented as the norm by some contemporary scholars:

"As in the West, descent is reckoned through the males, and the father is the head of the family; the Arab father, however, exercises greater authority. When an Arab couple are married they generally go to live in the establishment of the husband's father, a custom which used to prevail but is now rare in Western society. The Arab family is thus still an "extended" one—that is, a household generally consists of a man, his wife, his unmarried sons and daughters, and his married sons and their wives and children. Among the urban educated classes, however, the married couple usually set up their own household, forming the "conjugal" or "nuclear" family...." (Berger, 1964, p. 112).

"The traditional Middle Eastern family is *extended,* that is, it is headed by an elderly man and consists of his wife (or wives), his unmarried daughters, his unmarried as well as married sons, and the wives and children of the latter. Daughters, when they marry, depart from their own extended families and become incorporated into the extended families of their husbands, although their own consanguineal families still remain responsible for their moral conduct. The family, although it may comprise a dozen or more members, usually lives either in one

61

house or in a number of adjoining houses or, in the case of the nomadic tribes, in a number of tents pitched next to one another. All property is held in common by the extended family and is controlled by its head" (Patai, 1969, pp. 84-85).

While it is true that this traditional extended family is widespread as an *ideal* in the Arab world (Gulick, 1968, pp. 149 ff.), it is not in fact common. Indeed, it is unlikely that it has been the norm at any time in the twentieth century (Goode, 1963, pp. 123 ff.; Petersen, 1968). The *ideal* is of psychological importance, however, for it reveals wishes and values widely held, and it helps to inculcate notions of family loyalty and solidarity in each new generation.

Students of family structure have come to realize that family "types" are simply positions on a continuum. Though we speak of "extended" and "nuclear" families as qualitatively different, there are many individual and nuclear elements in "extended families," and many group and extended characteristics to be found in "nuclear families." The rivalries and tensions of "extended" families have always provoked some separation and emigration. And even in urban America, the nuclear family expresses in numerous ways its ties to relatives (e.g., Adams, 1968; Sussman, 1959). Instead of speaking of family *types*, it would be more accurate to speak of the degree to which there are extended ties, with whom the ties exist, and in what aspects of family life (cf. Castillo, *et al*, 1968). Consequently, the study of the Arab family is not merely one of determining whether they are "extended" or "nuclear." Rather, it must attempt to assess the extent, degree, strength of kinship ties—and whether these ties are loosening with time.

In this chapter we will examine some of the ties which bind members of Middle Eastern families, and the extent to which they have changed in recent years.

Marriage Ties

Almost all students of family life in Islam mention the Arab preference for marrying relatives. The ideal wife for a young man is the daughter of one of his father's brothers (*bint ʿamm*). Next in order of preference would be other first cousins. If none are available and suitable, then the young man would be expected to choose from more distant relatives. The ideal of father's brother's daughter marriage is so well established in the Middle East that a favorite expression used by a husband in addressing his wife is *"bint ʿammi"*—even if they are not in fact first cousins of the male line.

Levy says (p. 102) that the custom of cousin marriage prevailed among Arabian tribes in pre-Islamic times. The Quran does not require marriage of relatives, or recommend the marriage of cousins. On the other hand, it does not proscribe cousin marriage, as it does certain other marriages. The custom therefore survived in the Islamic era. One study of geneologies in early Islam showed that in Muhammed's own clan about one eighth (12.7 per cent) of all marriages were to a *bint ʿamm* (Stern, 1939, p. 65).

In the early nineteenth century, Lane (1963, p. 161) noticed a preference for cousin marriage in Egypt and other Arab lands, but gave no statistics. In Artas in the 1920's Granqvist (1931, pp. 80 ff.) found that a man had a *right* to marry his father's brother's daughter. Nevertheless, the demographic facts were such that these preferred marriages constituted only 13 per cent of all marriages. If one includes other cousins, the figure then reaches 26 per cent. In Buarij (Fuller. 1961, p. 65) of the thirties marriage of "first paternal cousins" was described as ideal, but less frequent than other marriages. Examinations of all Sunni marriage contracts signed in Beirut in 1936 revealed that seven per cent were between cousins (Abu Khadra, 1959, p. 37).

Is the preference for the marriage of relatives weakening in the modern Levant? Most students of this question would probably answer that *bint ʿamm* marriage as the *right* of a male has largely disappeared, but that Arabs still feel such marriages to have advantages and to be a good thing if all else is equal. Marriage of one's *bint ʿamm* or other cousin is still "vaguely preferred," even if no longer considered obligatory (Baer, 1964, p. 66; Patai, 1969, p. 176; Antoun, 1972, p. 125).

Studies of Arabs in societies where they are a minority show an interesting reversal of the expected trend away from cousin marriage. In Turkey (Aswad, 1967, p. 141) and Brazil (Williams & Williams, 1965, p. 61), the number of cousin marriages is greater than it was in the early days of Islam, and in Israel (Rosenfeld, 1970a and 1970b) endogamy among Arabs of some villages is increasing. This phenomenon is an interesting one, and merits further study, precisely because it is opposite to the presumed trend in "the Arab world." Evidently, pressures toward endogamy are greater where a community lives a more or less "encapsulated" existence. Indeed Kassees (1972) found that the members of one extended Arab family who had migrated to the United States and who continued to live in one of the centers where that family had concentrated were more "familistic" in general than were those members who stayed in Jordan.

Data to demonstrate the decline of cousin marriage in the Levant are not abundant. In a Shiite Muslim village of South Lebanon, Peters noted recently that first parallel cousin marriages were found in 15 per cent of one group and 18 per cent of another (Peters, 1963, pp. 177-179). A comparison of 1936 and 1956 Sunni marriage contracts in Beirut showed a slight *increase* in proportion of cousin marriages, from seven to 11 per cent (Abu Khadra, 1959, p. 37). Khuri's study (1970) of more than three thousand (largely Shiite) Muslim families in two Beirut suburbs from 1967 to 1969 revealed that 11 per cent of husbands born there and 11 per cent of those who had migrated there were married to father's brother's daughters. His interviewees were of all ages, so any very recent trend was obscured. Nevertheless, a comparison of his figures with those of earlier studies would certainly cast considerable doubt on the belief that cousin marriage is disappearing.

Class differences in preference for cousin marriage have been mentioned by some observers. Chatila, writing of Syria in the thirties, said that cousin marriage was less common among the middle class than the upper class, the urban lower class or the rural peasants (1934, pp. 92-93). Patai's general survey of cousin marriage throughout the Middle East (1955) led him to conclude that such marriages were declining in the middle class only. In Khuri's recent study, however, it was the high income groups which had the lowest incidence of father's brother's daughter marriage (1970, p. 602). Evidently there is need for further data on the relation between class and marriage preferences.

Our data on marriage of cousins and other relatives are found in Tables IV-1, IV-2 and IV-3. The marriages shown in Table IV-1 are father's brother's daughter marriages. Table IV-2 adds' marriages with other first cousins to those of the preceding table. Table IV-3 includes all marriages with relatives, on either the paternal or maternal side.

When we examine the village data, we find no evidence for the disappearance of the traditional pattern of endogamy. In Artas the incidence of cousin marriage among women married after 1940 is greater than that among those married before 1940, and greater than that reported by Granqvist for those married before 1925. A substantial majority of all Artas marriages, today as formerly, are among relatives. The preferred arrangement, with father's brother's daughter also shows no hint of declining in frequency.

The data from Buarij are less consistent. There were a number of elopements in the early fifties, in which the usual engagement and marriage festivities were omitted, and all of those were between non-relatives. Of the 21 couples married in that decade, only four were relatives (three of the four were cousins). In the sixties, however, there were no elopements, and there were as many marriages among cousins and relatives as in any previous decade. In Buarij too the traditional pattern of endogamy has survived. It should be recalled that dowry (*mahr*) in such marriages is expected to be lower than the village norm, and that this is no small consideration for villagers (e.g., Antoun, 1972, p. 69).

In the cities the older women, married before 1930, show the usual pattern of endogamy. A minority (14 to 25 per cent) married father's brother's sons, a few more married other first cousins, and about half (41 to 63 per cent) married some relative. Among this older group, as high a proportion of city women as village women married first cousins and other relatives. The younger city women, however, are beginning to break with the traditional patterns. Cousin marriages still occur, and marriages among relatives still account for a sizeable minority of all marriages, but the proportions are smaller than in earlier decades. The trend away from endogamy is strongest in Beirut and Tripoli. In these Lebanese cities there were 629 persons interviewed who reported they had married after the beginning of the fifties, and only 27 (4.3 per cent) of these had married first cousins. In every city, the trend seems to be away from marriage of first cousins or other relatives.[1]

As we have mentioned, some scholars believe that cousin marriage is disappearing most rapidly in the middle class, possibly because endogamy is "actuated mainly by the desire to retain family property intact" (Baer, 1964, p. 66). Our data lend no support to such a thesis. If we consider all marriages with relatives (Table IV-3), we find no strong or consistent class differences. Among all classes in the cities there is a trend away from marriage of relatives. If we consider father's brother's daughter marriage only (Table IV-1), there is some justification for agreeing with Khuri (1970) that this form of endogamy occurs least frequently in the upper classes. The number of marriages in each class in each decade is too small

---

[1] The same trend has been observed among Muslims of Pakistan. In 1965, 765 graduate students in Lahore and Karachi reported that 14 per cent of their married brothers and 10 per cent of their married sisters were married to cousins, whereas 25 per cent of their parents were cousins (Korson, 1971, p. 148).

to permit any speculation about time trends so we cannot say whether this class difference has only recently emerged or whether it has been that way for generations. All we can say is that the custom of father's brother's daughter marriage is in our samples least strong in the upper class.

What can we conclude from these data on marriage among Sunnis of the Levant? First, that the preference for relatives, and especially for first cousins, is still very much in evidence. The pattern was as strong in the two villages in the sixties as it had been forty years earlier. In the cities, endogamy was still noticeable, but on the decline. Class differences were minor, but to the extent that there were such differences, it was the upper class (as usual) which was least traditional.

Residential Patterns

Although the large extended Arab family in a single dwelling is more ideal than real, there are definite preferences among Arabs for living near relatives. Almost all early village studies in the Levant found a pattern similar to that of Buarij:

> "The spatial distribution of house falls roughly into clan quarters, joint family groups within a class tending to live next door to each other or to share a composite house, each family possessing its own separate entry door and room, or rooms. This general distribution of houses according to blood bonds reveals the close tie between clan members, including its lesser segmentations, linked to one another by bonds of reciprocal obligations and mutual interdependence."
>
> (Fuller, 1961, p. 8).

In recent years villages in the Levant have grown, and individual houses of one or two rooms are now more common than walled compounds and "composite" houses. Yet the residence patterns have remained. In Haouch el-Harimi, a village near Buarij, the survival of the pattern was seen in successive visits fifteen years apart:

> "During our first field trip in 1950, the building there and in other peripheral areas seemed to forebode a breakup of the extended family patrilocal residence patterns. But fifteen years later, with expansion having gone at an accelerated pace, it was clear that kin had followed kin into the village outskirts, and the traditional clustering of houses of brothers and their children had been preserved in the new quarters, with some lineages maintaining two or more residential foci."
>
> (Williams, 1968, p. 15.)

This "territorial dimension of the kinship structure" is of course found among Arabs outside the Levant. Berque (1970, pp. 195-200) noted it in Egyptian villages. Indeed he points out that the "same order, and almost the same pattern that cuts up the city into familial quarters, can be seen in the cemetery!"

Information is scarce on the relation between kinship and residence in cities of the Levant. Gulick refers to this scarcity as "a serious ethnographic gap" (1968, p. 160). In other Arab cities, however, there are some data to suggest that relatives live in greater proximity than they do in American cities. Petersen found that Cairo couples were much more likely than Detroit or Chicago couples to have "kin related to either husband or wife in the couple's area of residence" (1969, p. 274). In Karachi too, there is some evidence that relatives often live in a single compound or near one another. It has been noted that this residential proximity may be one of the factors which promotes marriage of kin (Korson, 1968).

Goode (p. 124) sees two residential patterns among urban Arabs. In the traditional pattern sons live with their parents for a while before breaking away. In the secular pattern, which he believes is becoming more common, the son and his wife establish their own home from the time of marriage.

In Tables IV-4, IV-5 and IV-6 we can see that a large number of our interviewees had indeed gone to live with their husband's parents, for some years at least, after marriage. In Artas about half the wives had done so, and this was as true of those married recently as of those married before 1930. In Buarij the number was considerably less than half, but there too it was reported as often by younger wives as older ones. In both villages, then, the traditional pattern of living with the husband's parents remains strong.

In his study of a Jordanian village in 1960, Antoun (1972, pp. 52 ff.) too found evidence for a "developmental cycle" in which couples would live for a time with the husband's parents and then establish separate residence. He noted a number of reasons for household "fission": population pressure, space shortage, disagreements and tensions among the women, and differences in "life styles" (often related to economic differentiation). At the time of his survey, about one fifth of all households included husband and wife (or wives) with at least one married son and spouse. Cohen (1965, pp. 50-51) noted a similar cycle in an Arab village in Israel, where in 1959 about one household in eight was composed of parents and married children.

In the cities too a substantial number of interviewees reported having lived with the husband's parents after marriage. Indeed, a majority of the older city wives had done so. The traditional pattern is still much in evidence, in cities as well as in villages. At the same time, however, it must be noted that the secular or non-traditional pattern is growing in the cities. It seems to have started earlier in Beirut, but is now found in all four cities. Of the 498 city wives who were married in the sixties, a majority had *never* lived with the husband's parents. There is also the usual class difference, with the traditional pattern strongest in the lower class and weakest in the upper class.

The tendency to live with the husband's parents for a while is not *solely* one of convenience, or inability to establish a separate home. If it were only a question of having a roof over one's head for a time, other relatives might be expected to help out.[1] Yet, as can be seen in Table IV-7, the couple rarely lived with the wife's parents. Only in Tripoli did this occur with any frequency. Similarly, it was exceedingly rare for the couple to live any period of time with brothers or sisters of the husband or wife (Table IV-8 and IV-9).

From our data we would conclude that the traditional residential pattern, in which the newly married couple lives for a time with the husband's parents, is still strong among villagers and in the lower class of the cities. It has begun to weaken, however, and the "secular" trend is evident among the upper and middle class families of the cities. Thus, although the tradition remains to a greater degree than Goode seems to have believed, the time trend is in the direction of his prediction.

Although many of the wives interviewed reported that the couple had lived with the husband's parents for some years, a majority (Table IV-6) sooner or later established a separate residence.[2] Almost all of the village wives said they were now living near the husband's parents, and nearly half that they were near their own parents as well (Tables IV-10 and IV-12). A good number of the wives, particularly in Buarij, said their own parents were from another village (Table IV-13). Evidently, in both villages, the custom was and is to establish a separate residence near

[1] Perhaps it should be recalled at this point that the expenses of the wedding from bride price to wedding gown, are borne by the groom and his parents (cf. Chapter III). A temporary home, while preparing the new abode, might be considered by Arabs as a part of the marriage obligations of the groom and his family.

[2] In a few cases the couple had moved back into the house of the husband's parents because of death or infirmity of one or both parents.

that of the husband's parents. The men occasionally bring wives from another village, but very rarely leave their own parents' village (Table IV-11). The traditional residence pattern, then, is again seen to be strong in the villages.

The residential pattern in the cities is much less traditional, and there are some differences among the cities. In Beirut and Tripoli almost all of the wives report that their parents and their husbands' parents live in the same city. A majority, however, live in another neighborhood or quarter than the one in which the parents live. This applies to husband's parents as well as wife's parents. In Damascus too the preponderant tendency was to establish a residence in the same city as, but a different neighborhood from, that of the wife's parents or husband's parents. A sizable minority, however, lived in a different city than either set of parents. In Amman, where immigration has been greatest in the past three decades, at least a third of the wives reported that their parents and their husband's parents did not live in Amman. Of those wives whose parents lived in Amman, nearly half lived in the same neighborhood as their parents. Of those whose husband's parents lived in Amman, about half lived in the same neighborhood as the husband's parents.

The large number of urban couples who do not live in the same neighborhood as that of the husband's parents is evidence for the breakdown of the traditional residential pattern. The fact that city couples are about as likely to settle in the same neighborhood as the wife's parents as they are to settle in the same neighborhood as the husband's parents also suggests a weakening of traditional patrilocality.[1]

Because the parents and parents-in-law of many of the older wives had died, it was not possible to compare the residential patterns of older and younger wives in Tables IV-10, IV-12 and IV-13. It is possible however to use another approach to the question of residential proximity in the extended family by studying the number of wives and their husbands who had *brothers* or *sisters* living nearby (Tables IV-14 and IV-15).[2]

---

[1] Traditional patterns have weakened, but they have not approached those of the West, where "the new family more often lives with or near the wife's parents, than with or near the husband's " (Lowe, 1972, p. 199. See also Berelson and Steiner, 1964, p. 320).

[2] It will be noted that the number of wives whose replies are reported in Tables IV-10 through IV-16 is smaller than the number in most of the other tables. Certain classes of replies were excluded: relative referred to had died, relative was unmarried and had no home to visit, wife was living in the same house as the relative, and relative had emigrated.

A large majority of the village wives reported that a married brother or sister of the husband lived near them. Many of these wives also had at least one of their own married siblings living in the same neighborhood. There were no consistent differences between the younger and older village wives, so we have no evidence for any time trend in residential patterns. In the villages, the residential grouping of kin is firmly maintained, by older and younger couples alike.

In the cities only a minority of the wives reported that a married brother or sister, of theirs or their husbands, lived in the same neighborhood. There were no consistent differences between reports of younger and older wives. There were no consistent class differences. On this variable, the lower class urban wives were no more similar to village wives than were those of the middle or upper class.

From these data we would conclude that the "territorial dimension of the kinship structure" is still much in evidence in the villages, and showing no sign of disappearing. In the cities, however, only a minority live near kin. This holds for all classes alike. Moreover, those who do live near close relatives seem about as likely to be near relatives of the wife as relatives of the husband. The traditional residence pattern is not predominant in the cities. On the other hand, however, it should be mentioned that these city couples live near parents and siblings more often than do couples of American cities (Adams, 1968, p. 35), and that younger Arab couples do so about as often as older Arab couples. Moreover, about one fifth of younger city wives still live with the husband's parents. Perhaps it would be fair to conclude that urban Arabs too continue to have preference for living near kin, and actually do so in a number of cases, in spite of the many factors affecting residence.

The Social and Psychological Extended Family

In his description of a Christian village in Mount Lebanon, Williams (1958, p. 15) found that there was a "social and psychological reality of extended families" even though "morphological extended families" were only temporary. It is our impression that his observations would apply equally to Muslim villages and to Muslim city dwellers. Even though the extended family is not living in one household, it is nevertheless a strong social psychological reality.

In crisis events, the extended family comes together and receives callers more or less as a unit, and callers include not only friends but all cousins, aunts, uncles and other traceable relatives. Included in such events which bring the extended family together are not only births, marriages, serious illnesses and deaths, but also such misfortunes as arrests by the police or such triumphs as election to office. The size of the gathering on such occasions is consciously noted as a measure of strength and solidarity of the group. Failure to attend is noted and remembered as a sign of estrangement, and is viewed as an offense (e.g., Antoun, 1972, pp. 63 and 73). As can be imagined, then, any year is marked by a number of occasions on which the extended family comes together.

Even when the family does not gather physically, it remains an important psyshological reality (cf. Tomeh, 1970). One turns to a member of the family for assistance in almost any area, whether it be a question of health, financial need, quest for a wife, employment, admission to school, starting a business, forming a corporation, or even emigration. It is small wonder that anthropologists have found that in the Middle East the family is an important agent of social change, of modernization (Williams & Williams, 1965).

Family groupings are not exclusively informal. There are a number of formal family associations in the Levant restricted to descendants of the same lineage carrying the same family name (Khalaf, 1968). In Lebanon alone there are about 500 such associations, Christian and Moslem, recorded in the Ministry of the Interior and the Ministry of Social Affairs. They outnumber all other non-governmental welfare agencies combined. The stated objectives of these organizations, in order of frequency of listing, are: family solidarity, benevolence, and education of family members. Unstated objectives are usually social control, political influence, and enhancement of the "family name." The organizations have by-laws, officers, annual dues, formal meetings, etc. Though membership is voluntary for eligibles, the number of members in each association is estimated to be in the thousands.

A number of writers have noted the survival of the "psychological extended family" in the West (e.g., Sussman, 1959). The ties which bind families in the United States have been studied in terms of mutual assistance, feelings of closeness, frequency of communication, and frequency of visits, among others. We have used frequency of visiting as an index, for it can be used in modern cities and primitive villages alike. It must be recognized of course that it is only a crude index, for it ignores a myriad of factors ranging from telephone conversations as visit-substitutes to accessibility (distance, transportation, etc.). Nevertheless, it is a simple, direct measure of family interaction and thus of interest in the study of extended families that do not live together.

In the early sixties, a study of young white couples in Greensboro, North Carolina, found that 68 per cent of the wives' parents lived outside Greensboro. Of those wives whose parents lived in the city, 88 per cent reported seeing their parents (visiting them or being visited by them) at least weekly. Of those whose parents lived within 100 miles of Greensboro, 62 per cent reported seeing them at least monthly. Those with parents residing farther away naturally saw them somewhat less frequently (Adams, 1968, p. 38). Interaction with siblings was less frequent. When only the sibling nearest the respondent in age was considered, fewer than half of these Greensboro wives reported seeing him or her as often as once a month (p. 99).

Another North Carolina study, this time in a town of 5,000 inhabitants, found that about two-thirds of the women with at least one relative living in the town, spent three hours or more with those relatives each week (Mirande, 1969, p. 157).

In Goode's review of the family in the West, he notes (pp. 71-74) surveys in American cities which ascertain interaction with any relatives at least as often as once a week. The findings ranged from a low of around one-third to a high of about two-thirds who had weekly interaction with one or more relatives.

With these data from Western sources as background information, we can now turn to the visiting patterns of our Arab interviewees. Table IV-16 shows the percentage of younger wives who make visits at least once a week to their relatives and their husbands relatives, and the percentage who are visited by their relatives and their husbands relatives. While our data and Western data are not strictly comparable, it is evident that there is considerably more visiting back and forth in the Levant than in the West. Indeed, a large majority of younger wives who have parents or parents-in-law living in the same village or same city neighborhood seem to pay and receive from each at least one visit a week, with visits to and from other relatives added in! The visiting pattern is affected by proximity, as would be expected, but is as strong in the cities as in the villages, or in the upper class as in the lower class.[1]

If we examine the table for differences in frequency of visits, the only

[1] In their study of a middle class westernized area of Beirut, Khalaf & Kongstad (1973, p. 84) found that a high incidence of visiting with relatives still characterized the behavior of the inhabitants.

consistent trend to be found is a tendency to visit weekly with parents more often than with siblings. There was also a slight tendency for wives married in the 1960's to visit parents (her own or her husband's) weekly a bit more frequently than did wives married in the 1950's. On the interesting question of visits to or from wife's parents versus visits to husband's parents, there were no consistent results in the cities. In the villages, the husband's parents visited or were visited a bit more regularly than the wife's parents.

Visits to relatives were so frequent and so expected that those wives who did not report visits of at least once a week usually felt that some explanation was called for. These explanations included a wide variety of such reasons as a village or extended family feud in which one of the relatives was on the opposite side, remarriage of one of the relatives to someone the wife or husband did not like, quarrels with in-laws, inability of the wife to travel, conflict over inheritance, hard feelings because the marriage was an elopement, etc.

The overall impression that emerges from the data on visiting is that there is an enormous amount of personal contact and a strong "social and psychological extended family" indeed.

Conclusion

Perhaps the most salient of the conclusions which might be drawn from our data is that the ties of the extended family remain strong among those persons we interviewed. The preference for cousin marriage is still much in evidence. A substantial minority of the wives had lived with the husband's parents for several years, and a majority still lived in the same village or city as that of the husband's parents. There are many occasions when the extended family gathers together. In addition, a majority of the wives report visits of once a week or more to and from the husband's parents and their own parents.

There is also evidence, however, that some family ties—as reflected in endogamy and in residence patterns—have grown weaker in the past two decades. This drift away from the traditional pattern is more evident in the cities (especially Beirut) than in the villages and more in the upper than in the lower classes.

consistent trend... tendency to visit weekly with parents more often than with siblings. There was also a slight tendency for wives married in the 1960's to visit parents (her own or her husband's) weekly a bit more frequently than did wives married in the 1950's. On the question of visits to or from wife's parents versus visits to husband's parents, there were no consistent results in the cities. In the villages, the husband's parents visited or were visited a bit more regularly than the wife's parents.

Visits to relatives were so frequent and so expected that those wives who did not report visits of at least once a week usually felt that some explanation was called for. These explanations included a wide variety of such reasons as a village or extended family feud in which one of the relatives was on the opposite side, remarriage of the relatives to someone the wife or husband did not like, quarrels with in-laws, inability of the wife to travel, conflict over inheritance, hard feelings because the marriage was an elopement, etc.

The overall impression that emerges from the data on visiting is that there is an enormous amount of personal contact and strong "social and psychological extended family," indeed.

Conclusion

Perhaps the most salient of the conclusions which might be drawn from our data is that the ties of the extended family remain strong among those persons we interviewed. The preference for cousin marriage is still much in evidence. A substantial minority of the wives had lived with the husband's parents for several years, and a majority still lived in the same village or city as the husband's parents. There are many occasions when the extended family gathers together. In addition, a majority of the wives report visits of once a week or more to and from the husband's parents and their own parents.

There is also evidence, however, that some family ties—as reflected in endogamy and in residence patterns—have grown weaker in the past two decades. This drift away from the traditional pattern is more evident in the cities (especially Beirut) than in the villages, and more in the upper than in the lower classes.

TABLE IV–1

PER CENT OF WIVES MARRIED TO SON OF FATHER'S BROTHER

Year of Marriage	Before 1930				1930's				1940's				1950's				1960's			
Social Class	U	M	L	(T)	U	M	L	(T)	U	M	L	(T)	U	M	L	(T)	U	M	L	(T)
Artas				(6)				(16)				(34)				(20)				(33)
Buarij				(22)				(30)				(7)				(4)				(25)
Amman	50	0	43	(25)	17	0	0	(4)	0	0	14	(6)	0	2	10	(11)	0	5	16	(8)
Damascus	0	12	25	(14)	0	9	33	(11)	0	3	13	(4)	0	10	50	(5)	0	7	6	(6)
Tripoli	0	30	0	(17)	0	0	20	(7)	0	15	8	(11)	0	3	7	(5)	0	4	5	(5)
Beirut	13	22	0	(18)	11	19	0	(15)	4	7	0	(5)	4	6	0	(5)	0	2	3	(1)

TABLE IV–2

PER CENT OF WIVES MARRIED TO FIRST COUSINS*

Social Class	1960's				1950's				1940's				1930's				Before 1930			
Year of Marriage	U	M	L	(T)	U	M	L	(T)	U	M	L	(T)	U	M	L	(T)	U	M	L	(T)
Artas				(43)				(38)				(43)				(16)				(10)
Buarij		11	25	(37)				(15)				(14)				(30)				(22)
Amman	6	11	11	(16)	11	7	17	(11)	12	10	36	(22)	17	17	14	(16)	++	14	43	(31)
Damascus	++	11	14	(11)	00	13	++	(14)	00	6	25	(8)	++	13	++	(19)	++	18	++	(18)
Tripoli	8	7	12	(9)	5	6	8	(7)	20	15	14	(15)	++	00	40	(14)	++	40	00	(22)
Beirut	00	7	00	(4)	6	11	00	(9)	7	00		(7)	22	19	—	(21)	37	22	—	(29)

*Includes first cousins on mother's as well as father's side.

TABLE IV-3

Per Cent of Wives Married to Relatives

Year of Marriage	1960's				1950's				1940's				1930's				Before 1930			
Social Class	U	M	L	(T)	U	M	L	(T)	U	M	L	(T)	U	M	L	(T)	U	M	L	(T)
Artas				(69)				(73)				(73)				(68)				(55)
Buarij				(50)				(19)				(40)				(30)				(33)
Amman	24	34	51	(40)	33	25	57	(36)	38	43	55	(47)	33	42	43	(40)	++	43	86	(63)
Damascus	++	29	29	(29)	40	30	++	(31)	25	37	25	(33)	++	33	++	(41)	++	35	++	(41)
Tripoli	37	20	23	(23)	20	21	22	(22)	20	37	32	(34)	++	13	70	(34)	++	70	43	(57)
Beirut	6	17	11	(12)	15	31	00	(25)	15	47	20	(34)	44	56	—	(50)	50	33	—	(41)

TABLE IV-4

PER CENT OF WIVES WHO HAVE NEVER LIVED WITH HUSBAND'S PARENTS

Year of Marriage	1960's				1950's				1940's				1930's				Before 1930			
Social Class	U	M	L	(T)	U	M	L	(T)	U	M	L	(T)	U	M	L	(T)	U	M	L	(T)
Artas				(46)				(49)				(64)				(50)				(52)
Buarij				(67)				(76)				(60)				(50)				(75)
Amman	88	66	69	(70)	56	71	63	(67)	50	57	18	(39)	33	42	29	(36)	++	43	29	(31)
Damascus	++	62	50	(59)	25	45	++	(42)	71	42	33	(46)	++	27	++	(27)	++	6	++	(10)
Tripoli	75	51	45	(52)	70	39	25	(36)	40	27	19	(24)	++	27	00	(21)	++	20	00	(17)
Beirut	97	75	33	(75)	91	67	00	(69)	88	57	20	(65)	74	62	—	(69)	50	20	—	(33)

TABLE IV–5

PER CENT OF WIVES WHO LIVED WITH IN-LAWS AND
THEN ESTABLISHED SEPARATE RESIDENCE*

Locality	Year of Marriage				
	1960's	1950's	1940's	1930's	Before 1930
Artas	5	14	14	20	6
Mean No. Months +	(26)	(83)	(153)	(106)	(30)
Buarij	19	19	33	30	22
Mean No. Months	(36)	(38)	(115)	(104)	(24)
Amman	6	11	35	44	50
Mean No. Months	(23)	(48)	(141)	(129)	(190)
Damascus	9	23	31	56	64
Mean No. Months	(27)	(48)	(103)	(124)	(188)
Tripoli	9	18	20	17	11
Mean No. Months	(30)	(56)	(137)	(98)	(330)
Beirut	3	8	13	26	44
Mean No. Months	(14)	(86)	(139)	(107)	(152)

*A few wives who had lived with in-laws and then established separate residence are omitted from this table because the number of months with in-laws was not ascertained.
+ Mean No. Months is average number of months these wives lived with husband's parents after marriage.

TABLE IV–6

PER CENT OF WIVES WHO HAVE LIVED WITH IN-LAWS
CONTINUOUSLY SINCE MARRIAGE

Locality	Year of Marriage				
	1960's	1950's	1940's	1930's	Before 1930
Artas	48	22	9	12	22
Buarij	0	0	0	0	0
Amman	23	20	16	16	19
Damascus	24	20	14	7	18
Tripoli	12	16	12	7	6
Beirut	19	18	17	0	11

TABLE IV–7

Per Cent of Wives who have Never Lived with their Own Parents since Marriage

Year of Marriage Social Class	1960's				1950's				1940's				1930's				Before 1930			
	U	M	L	(T)	U	M	L	(T)	U	M	L	(T)	U	M	L	(T)	U	M	L	(T)
Artas		97	94	(86)				(92)				(93)				(93)				(100)
Buarij		97	67	(93)				(100)				(100)				(100)				(100)
Amman	100	76	66	(96)	100	93	100	(96)	100	100	91	(96)	100	83	100	(96)	++	100	86	(94)
Damascus	++	97	67	(85)	+–	88	++	(84)	57	85	+–	(74)	++	74	++	(71)	++	83	++	(82)
Tripoli	92	76	66	(74)	75	66	62	(65)	60	70	54	(62)	++	44	30	(45)	++	60	00	(39)
Beirut	100	100	78	(96)	97	98	100	(98)	100	100	80	(99)	100	87	—	(94)	100	100	—	(100)

TABLE IV-8

Per Cent of Wives who have Never Lived with Their Brothers-In-Law or Sisters-In-Law since Marriage

Year of Marriage Social Class	1960's				1950's				1940's				1930's				Before 1930			
	U	M	L	(T)	U	M	L	(T)	U	M	L	(T)	U	M	L	(T)	U	M	L	(T)
Artas				(87)				(81)				(98)				(92)				(84)
Buarij				(93)				(100)				(100)				(100)				(100)
Amman	100	98	96	(98)	100	95	83	(91)	100	90	91	(92)	83	83	71	(80)	++	100	86	(94)
Damascus	++	91	83	(90)	+-	85	++	(87)	86	86	50	(79)	++	78	++	(80)	++	64	++	(53)
Tripoli	95	74	80	(79)	90	81	87	(85)	100	77	80	(80)	++	81	50	(72)	++	70	43	(56)
Beirut	100	96	94	(97)	94	100	100	(98)	100	100	100	(100)	100	100	—	(100)	87	100	—	(94)

TABLE IV-9
PER CENT OF WIVES WHO HAVE NEVER LIVED WITH THEIR MARRIED BROTHERS AND SISTERS SINCE MARRIAGE

Year of Marriage Social Class	1960's				1950's				1940's				1930's				Before 1930			
	U	M	L	(T)	U	M	L	(T)	U	M	L	(T)	U	M	L	(T)	U	M	L	(T)
Artas				(100)				(100)				(98)				(96)				(100)
Buarij				(100)				(100)				(100)				(100)				(100)
Amman	100	100	96	(98)	100	100	++	(100)	100	100	100	(100)	++	100	100	(100)	++	100	100	(100)
Damascus	++	91	+-	(92)	+-	97	++	(92)	++	100	+-	(100)	++	92	++	(93)	++	100	++	(94)
Tripoli	79	80	79	(79)	89	84	89	(87)	80	93	97	(94)	++	81	90	(83)	++	60	57	(61)
Beirut	100	100	100	(100)	97	100	100	(99)	100	100	100	(100)	100	100	100	(100)	100	89	—	(94)

TABLE IV-10

Per Cent of Wives whose Parents-In-Law Live in the Same Neighborhood

Year of Marriage		1960's U	1960's M	1960's L	1960's (T)	1950's U	1950's M	1950's L	1950's (T)	1940's U	1940's M	1940's L	1940's (T)
Artas	%				(100)				(73)				(89)
	N				20				45				27
Buarij	%				(100)				(100)				(86)
	N				16				19				14
Amman	%	23	44	27	(34)	17	37	42	(37)	+	11	+	(15)
	N	13	34	33	80	6	40	12	58	1	9	3	13
Damascus	%	++	16	+	(19)	+	24	++	(26)	17	47	+	(40)
	N	1	38	4	43	3	35	1	39	6	17	2	25
Tripoli	%	16	64	00	(17)				(13)	+	00	11	(4)
	N	19	36	6	83	15	49	34	98	2	14	9	25
Beirut	%	16	20	00	(17)	17	35	−	(29)	+	43	+	(26)
	N	32	45	6	83	24	49	0	73	11	7	1	19

N is size of subsample

TABLE IV-11

Per Cent of Wives whose Parents-In-Law Live in Another City

Year of Marriage	1960's				1950's				1940's			
Social Class	U	M	L	(T)	U	M	L	(T)	U	M	L	(T)
Artas				(00)				(16)				(00)
Buarij				(00)				(00)				(14)
Amman	23 ++	35	33 +-	(32)	00	35	42 ++	(33)	+-	56	+-	(46)
Damascus	+-	32	+-	(30)	+-	26	++	(26)	17	18	+-	(16)
Tripoli	00	1	9	(4)	5	3	2	(3)	+-	3	00	(2)
Beirut	9	4	00	(6)	00	6	00	(4)	9	00	00	(5)

Note: Size of subsamples same as in Table IV-10

TABLE IV-12

Per Cent of Wives whose Parents Live in "the Same Neighborhood"

Year of Marriage		1960's				1950's				1940's			
Social Class		U	M	L	(T)	U	M	L	(T)	U	M	L	(T)
Artas	%				(51)				(57)				(39)
	N				39				61				43
Buarij	%				(50)				(38)				(71)
	N				16				21				14
Amman	%	18	22	36	(27)	12	16	20	(17)	40	19	28	(26)
	N	17	58	45	120	8	50	30	88	5	16	18	39
Damascus	%	++	34	57	(32)	+-	37	++	(35)	17	34	00	(27)
	N	3	53	7	63	4	54	2	60	6	29	5	40
Tripoli	%	8	12	16	(12)	25	18	15	(17)	+-	11	00	(8)
	N	24	84	44	152	16	67	61	144	2	27	22	51
Beirut	%	25	24	00	(21)	20	24	14	(22)	12	23	+-	(17)
	N	36	58	13	107	30	79	7	116	17	31	4	52

TABLE IV-13

PER CENT OF WIVES WHOSE PARENTS LIVE IN ANOTHER CITY

Social Class	1960's				1950's				1940's			
	U	M	L	(T)	U	M	L	(T)	U	M	L	(T)
Artas				(23)				(11)				(22)
Buarij				(50)				(62)				(29)
Amman	29	38	38	(37)	12	50	47	(45)	20	62	61	(56)
Damascus	++	17	14	(16)	+−	20	++	(22)	17	21	20	(20)
Tripoli	8	6	2	(5)	6	5	8	(6)	+−	8	9	(8)
Beirut	00	9.00²	00	(5)	3	3.20²	00	(3)	12	3.40²	00	(6)

Note: Size of subsamples same as in Table IV-12.

TABLE IV-14

PER CENT OF WIVES WHOSE BROTHERS-IN-LAW AND SISTERS-IN-LAW LIVE IN THE SAME NEIGHBORHOOD

Year of Marriage Social Class		1960's				1950's				1940's				1930's				1929 and before			
		U	M	L	(T)	U	M	L	(T)	U	M	L	(T)	U	M	L	(T)	U	M	L	(T)
Artas	%				(67)				(67)				(63)				(70)				(68)
	N				30				58				40				23				31
Buarij	%				(93)				(85)				(73)				(70)				(100)
	N				15				20				15				10				8
Amman	%	12	22	30	(24)	11	27	16	(22)	29	20	33	(27)	20	00	23	(15)	++	14	14	(19)
	N	16	51	40	107	9	51	25	85	7	20	21	48	5	9	6	20	2	7	7	16
Damascus	%	++	32	00	(23)	60	11	++	(15)	29	25	+-	(23)	++	14	++	(16)	++	27	++	(28)
	N	2	45	5	52	5	52	3	60	7	28	4	39	1	21	3	25	0	15	3	18
Tripoli	%	14	3	9	(6)	15	6	13	(10)	20	11	00	(4)	++	12	00	(7)	++	00	00	(00)
	N	21	79	50	150	19	78	75	172	5	32	30	67	3	14	6	23	1	10	4	15
Beirut	%	12	56	00	(10)	10	25	00	(20)	16	25	20	(22)	28	7	–	(18)	17	12	–	(21)
	N	33	16	16	105	29	84	7	120	25	44	5	74	18	5	0	33	6	8	0	14

TABLE IV-15

Per Cent of Wives whose Married Brothers and Sisters Live in the Same Neighborhood

Year of Marriage →		1960's				1950's				1940's				1930's				1929 and before			
Social Class		U	M	L	(T)	U	M	L	(T)	U	M	L	(T)	U	M	L	(T)	U	M	L	(T)
Artas	%				(53)				(42)				(43)				(36)				(18)
	N				36				62				42				25				28
Buarij	%				(53)				(38)				(57)				(50)				(75)
	N				15				21				14				10				8
Amman	%	23	11	24	(18)	22	14	00	(10)	12	14	36	(24)	00	17	00	(8)	++	14	00	(7)
	N	13	46	42	101	9	43	27	79	8	21	22	51	6	12	7	25	2	7	6	15
Damascus	%	++	34	+−	(30)	20	23	++	(21)	29	22	14	(12)	++	14	++	(15)	++	31	++	(25)
	N	2	41	4	47	5	53	4	62	7	32	7	46	1	22	3	26	1	16	3	20
Tripoli	%	4	6	6	(6)	5	6	6	(6)	40	5	6	(7)	++	13	20	(15)	++	00	00	(00)
	N	19	80	50	149	17	78	75	170	4	39	35	78	1	14	9	24	1	7	4	12
Beirut	%	5	9	6	(7)	4	18	00	(14)	19	21	00	(20)	28	29	−	(28)	00	33	−	(17)
	N	19	45	18	82	27	83	5	115	26	43	5	74	18	14	0	32	6	6	0	12

TABLE IV-16

Visiting by and to Younger Wives
(Numbers are percentages)

Place	Decade of Marriage	Wife Visits At Least Weekly to				Wife is Visited At Least Weekly by			
		Wife's Parents	Husband's Parents	Wife's Married Siblings	Husband's Married Siblings	Wife's Parents	Husband's Parents	Wife's Married Siblings	Husband's Married Siblings
Artas	1960s	74	88	66	50	70	100	58	54
	1950s	69	76	72	53	73	72	67	48
Buarij	1960s	57	100	54	93	57	100	54	93
	1950s	45	88	42	85	42	94	44	85
Amman	1960s	57	64	38	32	24	63	26	30
	1950s	49	63	27	45	33	63	21	44
Damascus	1960s	96	59	42	37	58	45	42	33
	1950s	73	58	49	23	48	42	42	23
Tripoli	1960s	63	44	39	41	52	36	41	42
	1950s	52	35	43	41	50	34	45	42
Beirut	1960s	95	90	73	66	76	77	72	29
	1950s	94	82	64	49	77	62	65	39

N's on which these percentages are based are the same as those of Tables IV-10, IV-12, IV-14 and IV-15

CHAPTER FIVE

Family Size

"Wealth and children are the ornament of this life."

SURA 18

S O HIGHLY VALUED were children in the time of Mohammed that the Quran repeatedly warned believers not to let riches and children beguile them from the remembrance of Allah. Even in those days sons were preferred to daughters, to judge from the Quranic condemnation of female infanticide and its repeated admonitions that daughters be treated with justice.

Observers and students of Arab societies since the advent of Islam have almost always noted the desire for a large number of children, especially male children, and the consequent high birth rate. In the early nineteenth century, for example, Lane wrote of Egyptians that "The estimation in which the wife is held by her husband, and even by her acquaintance, depends, in great degree, upon her fruitfulness, and upon the preservation of her children..." (p. 56). He also noted that "The women of Egypt are generally very prolific..." (p. 161). He gives no data to show how often the fertility ideal is achieved, or how many women are "very prolific." Indeed, he frequently mentions slaves, widows and other *childless* women, and his computation of annual household expenditure of a middle class family in Cairo is based on a family of four. He also refers frequently to the high child mortality rate. Consequently, we are led to suspect that, although the wives hope for many children who survive infancy, they do not regularly find these hopes realized.

The first survey of family size in a village of the Arab Levant was carried out by Granqvist in Artas between 1925 and 1931. Even before her arrival in Palestine, she had noticed in the Old Testament that the children

FORSYTH LIBRARY
FORT HAYS KANSAS STATE COLLEGE

of Abraham (who is accepted by Arabs and Jews alike as their ancestor) spoke of wanting large families but rarely fulfilled their aspirations. She attempted to obtain a complete record of all children born in Artas over a hundred year span. A summary of her data which relate to family size is presented in Table V-1. It can be seen at a glance that large families are not typical of this village, even though husbands and wives alike expressed strong desires for a large family with many sons.

The figure of 341 living children born to the 151 wives living in 1927 is probably an accurate one. Her patient and painstaking study of the village, and her acquaintance with the people of the village over several years, inspire more confidence than would any standard census-taking. In 1927 the average wife had 2 or 3 children. Of course, many wives were still of child-bearing age at the time, and it might be expected that the mean would reach something between 3 and 4 if only *completed* families were considered. Even so, these families would hardly qualify as large ones.

TABLE V–1

FAMILY SIZE IN ARTAS OVER FIVE GENERATIONS
(Data from Granqvist, 1950, pp. 88–89)

		86 Wives who Died Before 1927	151 Wives Living in 1927
Children Living to Maturity*	Total No.	249	341
	Mean per Wife	2.9	2.3
Children Died Before Maturity	Total No.	75	270
	Mean per Wife	0.9	1.7
Children Born	Total No.	324	611
	Mean per Wife	3.8	4.0
	Median of Wives	3.2	3.6

*Includes children alive in 1927 who had not yet reached adulthood.

The figure of 249 "living" children (i.e., living to adulthood) born to the wives of previous generations may be a slight underestimation. However carefully the villagers searched their memories regarding generations past, it is probable that some children grew up and died unremembered.

92

If we can assume that the number of omissions is less than 100, however, we must still grant that the average family had no more than four living children.

Child mortality was high in Artas in those days. Of all children born to wives living in 1927, 44 per cent had died. This figure is probably not an exaggeration. Even if a wife were to exaggerate the number of children who had died, Granqvist's checking with neighbors would probably have revealed it. Consequently, it can be said with some confidence that the wives of Artas living in 1927 had already borne an average of 4 children, of whom nearly sixty per cent were still alive.

The reporting of children who died in generations gone by seems to us less dependable. In spite of the Arab's interest in matters relating to family and geneology, it seems to us probable that many an infant who died three or four generations ago would not be recalled. The child mortality rate for past generations of wives was said to be 23 per cent (75 of 324 births). It seems unlikely that health conditions before 1900 were so markedly superior to those in the early twentieth century. We strongly suspect that the total number of children born, and the number who died, were greater than recorded by Granqvist. Her data show, for these women of previous generations, fewer than 4 children born per wife, with more than three-fourths of those born reaching adulthood. If these are underestimations, as we believe, then the true figure may be nearer 5 for average number born and 3 for average number surviving.

If wives have no more than 3 or 4 surviving children, it may be wondered whether the *husbands* achieved large families by having more than one wife. Certainly polygyny and serial monogamy were found in Artas. Nevertheless, there were 199 fathers recorded by Granqvist and only 590 surviving children, so this possibility for large families must be ruled out.

What can be concluded about family size in Artas? We believe the data to suggest that in the early twentieth century, and possibly in the late nineteenth century, the average completed family of Artas consisted of 3 or 4 living children even though husbands and wives alike thought of a larger number of children as ideal. One reason for the discrepancy between normative statements and actual family size was the high mortality rate, with more than 40 per cent of those born dying before reaching adulthood.

Fuller's study of Buarij in the thirties is not quantitatively oriented, and no information is given on family size. She mentions a childless wife

(p. 55) and a woman with seven children (p. 69) in contexts which suggest that these are unusual cases, but tells us nothing of usual family size. She also mentions (p. 35) that couples "expect and look forward to having children" and that a village "must have numbers," but gives no suggestion as to an ideal number. Finally, her description of medical care leads us to suspect a high rate of infant mortality, but again we have no precise evidence.

Beginning around the mid-forties, a number of social scientists conducted studies of Muslim families in the Levant (see Churchill, 1967, p. 35; Najarian, 1959, p. 41; Patai, 1958, p. 281; Williams, 1968, p. 44; Yaukey, 1961, p. 29). In these the average number of living children per nuclear family was found to be between 5 and 7. Gulick (1968, p. 153, and 1969, pp. 132-133) has summarized recent studies of household size of Muslim families of Lebanon, Syria, and Jordan, and found means ranging from 5.2 to 8.9. He argues that a large household is usually brought into being by the large number of children born to one couple rather than by an extended family living under one roof.

The Syrian census of 1960 showed median household size to be approximately 5.1 but 17 per cent of these households were made up of only one or two persons—bachelors, widowers, newly-married, etc. A better picture of completed family size can be obtained from the number of living children of older women—even though these children may now constitute elements of several households. There were 187,936 women married 30 years or more who replied to the census question on number of children living. The median number of children was 4.7. For the 172,582 women married 20 through 29 years, the median was 5.0.

The Jordanian census of 1961 reported number of children of women "ever married" even though they might have been divorced or widowed. There were 95,168 such women 50 or more years of age, and they had borne an average of 7.1 children, of whom an average of 4.1 were living. There were 55,152 women of ages 40 through 49. They reported having borne an average of 7.7 children of whom an average of 5.3 were living.

From these census data it would appear that around five living children per completed nuclear family, of women married before 1940, would be a reasonable estimate. Such an estimate would be in fair accord with the results obtained from the smaller surveys of various social scientists, as summarized above. It should be noted that fewer than 70 per cent of the children born to these women had survived, and the mean birth rate was above seven.

Goode (p. 111 ff.) mentioned several factors which contribute to the high birth rate in Arab cultures: the injunction in the Quran to express trust in Allah by having children, the high rate of infant mortality, the economic value of sons, high evaluation of sexual activity, early marriage, and the relatively high status of mothers of sons. Nevertheless, he noted evidence (p. 119) to suggest that by 1960 some effort at controlling fertility was beginning among educated urban Muslims in such advanced countries as Lebanon and Egypt.

The evidence on birth control in Lebanon was drawn from a 1959 survey by Yaukey. He interviewed 369 Lebanese Muslim women and asked what they would advise a close friend on "the convenient number of children for her." Only 192 women were willing to give an estimate, and these were predominantly those who had practiced birth control. Their median response was slightly above 4, indicating that this somewhat select group considered the rather common family of 5 or 6 children to be "inconvenient." He also asked those women who had been married more than ten years whether they had ever used any method (whether appliance, rhythm, or even abstinence) of conception control. When "educated" was defined as having completed *brevet* (about ten years of schooling), or being married to a man who had done so, there were only 35 "educated" Muslims from Beirut who replied. Of these, 83 per cent stated they had used some method of control. Of the 98 "uneducated" city women, 60 per cent stated that they had done so. In contrast, in the mixed Sunni-Shiite village surveyed, only 2 per cent of the 141 women admitted ever having used conception control. These data, fragmentary though they are, suggest that in Beirut, but not in the village, there was by mid-century some tendency to limit family size.

While one can hardly generalize from so small a sample, this study does raise the question of whether the Near East as a whole is following a pattern similar to that of the West, where reduction of family size begins first among urban educated segments of the population and then spreads to other groups. To answer this question, let us turn to the two recent census reports. The 1961 census of Jordan showed a slightly higher birth rate in rural areas, but also a higher rate of infant mortality, so the number of children living per family was as high in urban as in rural areas. In urban areas there were 849 living children under five for each 1000 women between the ages of 15 and 49, and in rural areas only 808 (p. 312). In the Syrian census the median "family" (i.e., household) size in rural areas was 5.1, which was about that of the country as a whole (p. 65). Except

95

perhaps for Beirut, then, there is no apparent tendency for cities of the Levant to be characterized by smaller families than are the villages.

The 1960 Syrian census report included information on family size as it related to occupation of husband and education of wife. Excerpts from these data are summarized in Tables V-2 and V-3. When we consider occupation of husband and family size, we find somewhat to our surprise that middle and upper class families, where the husband is a professional man, an executive, administrator or manager, have proportionately more large families (of seven or more children), than do peasant families, where the husband farms for a living. When we turn to education of the wife as related to family size, we find that illiterate women, who constitute the vast majority, have no larger families than do literate women. Even among the younger wives, married during the fifties, the literate wives already have more children than do the illiterate wives.

Only among the small group of university graduates can one see evidence that more highly educated women have smaller families. Of the 405 wives with university degrees, only four of them, all married before 1930, had seven or more living children. A majority, even of those married long enough to have completed families, had fewer than four children.

On the whole, the census reports offer little evidence that urban educated women of the Levant had by mid-century begun leading a trend toward smaller families. Only among the most highly educated few is any such trend perceptible.

In summarizing our knowledge about changing family size in the Levant, we must admit the incompleteness and even inadequacy of the data available. Nevertheless, the few pioneer studies cited above, the more numerous recent investigations, and the two census reports, have provided us with some facts. If we were to use these facts to guess at the general situation regarding family size in the Levant in the twentieth century, we would describe it as follows. At the turn of the century, Arabs maintained the tradition of hoping for large families, with many sons. These hopes were pretty generally frustrated by poor health conditions, and consequent high rate of infant and child mortality. The average completed family contained not more than four children. By the nineteen forties, the situation in the Levant had changed. Completed Muslim families averaged about five children, and the large family ideal was fairly often realized in practice. By mid-century however, the large family ideal had begun to weaken, at least among the more highly educated, and some interest in limiting family size had become discernible, particularly in the cosmopolitan city of Beirut.

In an effort to get more information on these matters, our interviewers posed questions on a number of issues related to fertility: size of wives' families, size of husbands' families, number of living children, ideal family size, birth control practices, and number of children who died. The replies of the interviewees are summarized in Tables V-4 through V-15.

Families of Orientation. Each wife was asked the number of brothers she had, and the number of sisters. She was later asked for the same information about her husband's family. From these replies we were able to obtain information on the size of families of the preceding generation.

An examination of these data on family size (Tables V-4 and V-5) reveals no general tendency for younger wives or husbands to come from smaller families than do older wives or husbands. On the contrary, if we ignore Beirut, we find that persons married before 1940 report *fewer* siblings on the average than do those married after 1949. Similarly, the older wives and husbands were more likely to have come from small families (of fewer than four children) than were the younger husbands and wives (Tables V-6 and V-8). These differences are probably attributable to higher infant mortality rates in the early part of the century, and a tendency not to report brothers and sisters so little known and long deceased. In Beirut, where health services have long been better than those of the other cities, there is no time trend in family size. From the decade of the 30's through the decade of the 60's, the mean number of children per Beirut family was always between 5 and 6. We must conclude that our data on more than 3000 families of orientation show no indication that the older generation as a whole had begun to adopt the modern concept of planning for small families. On the contratry, family size for the "older generation" *increased* during this century (Table V-5).

Some evidence of differential fertility patterns is found in the data reported by younger wives and husbands (married after 1949) from Beirut. In this group only, those rated as upper class came from smaller families than did those rated as middle or lower class. The average number of children in these upper class families of orientation was between 4 and 5. This suggests that upper class urban Muslims of Beirut had begun to limit family size during the second quarter of this century.

Families of Procreation. When we turn to the number of children in the families of our interviewees (Table V-10), we find no evidence of a *general* decrease in size of family from one generation to the next. If we assume that wives who were married some time before 1950 have completed their families, and compare for these women the size of the family of procreation

97

and the family of orientation, we find no consistent differences. The wives married before 1950 had families as large as the families of their mothers—or their mothers-in-law (husband's family of orientation). The only exception to this generalization was the upper class group from Beirut. This group had markedly fewer children than did their mothers or mothers-in-law. Again we are led to the conclusion that *upper class Muslims of Beirut began a trend toward smaller families some time before mid-century.*

There was a definite class difference in number of children reported by the interviewees. Upper class mothers had fewer children than did middle and lower class mothers. This difference was most marked among younger wives of Tripoli and Beirut, but not limited to that group. The class difference which, among the older generation, was found only in Beirut, is, for the current generation, found in all four cities.

Ideal Family Size. Each interviewee was asked to give her opinion on the ideal number of children in a family (Table V-11), and then asked the ideal number of each sex.

There is a large, consistent difference between younger and older wives in opinions on ideal family size. Those married before 1930 generally thought that 5 to 7 children would be ideal. They consistently asserted that the ideal number was *greater* than the average number of living children in their families of procreation, and greater than the number in their families of orientation. These older wives held to the traditional ideal of large families. In contrast, those women married since 1960 thought that the ideal family should contain around 3 or 4 children. The ideal numbers given by them were consistently smaller than the number of children in their own families of orientation, or their husbands' families of orientation. Among all social classes, these younger wives had broken with the large-family ideal.

This trend toward preference for smaller families was found in all localities. In Buarij, where the older wives spoke of more than 8 as the ideal, the youngest wives held to an ideal of less than 5, on the average. Even in Beirut, where older wives had an ideal on the average of only 4.5 children, the average among younger wives (married in the sixties) dropped to 3.2.

There were significant and consistent class differences in ideal family size. Among younger wives and older wives, in all four cities, the upper class mothers described the ideal family as smaller than did the other mothers (cf. Hirabayashi & Ishaq, 1958). A family of 2 or 3 children was usually described as ideal by those upper class wives married in the sixties, and a family of 4 or 5 by those married before 1940. These interviews cannot tell us *when* it was that upper class women began to turn away from the large family ideal. What they do tell us is that in the sixties, upper class women of *all ages* from all four cities had done so.

Sex Composition of the Ideal Family. In reply to the question about the number of boys and girls in an ideal family, a majority of the wives said either that there should be an equal number of each, or that there should be one more male child than female. In no city or village was the average ratio of males to females greater than 3 to 2 (cf. Yaukey, 1961, p. 193). The consistency with which wives stated that an ideal family should have a large proportion of girls raises some question about the widely-held belief that "Arabs prefer male offspring." For Arab women, sons are important, but daughters are also necessary to round out an ideal family.

Husbands' Views on Family Size. Each wife was asked to estimate her husband's opinion on how many children the ideal family should contain (Table V-12). This is a far cry from interviewing husbands, but it does give—at the very least—some indication of how wives perceive their husbands. In most instances, the wives said that their husbands agreed with them or thought the ideal family was one child larger than the wife's ideal. In very few cases did the wife think the husband preferred *fewer* children than she. This pattern of response, reporting general agreement with the spouse, is a fairly common one among non-Arabs. Only occasionally, as among the younger women of Buarij, was there notable disharmony between the ideals of the wives and of their husbands. In these cases, the husbands still held to the old ideal of large families, while the wives preferred smaller ones.

Birth Control. At the end of each interview, after a number of subjects had been discussed and some degree of rapport established, the interviewee was asked whether she used any technique of birth control (Table V-13).

More than 98 per cent replied to the question. Perhaps the most striking thing about the replies is the large differences between groups. In one group, more than 80 per cent practice birth control. In another group of the same religion, living a few miles away, *not one* says she or her husband practices birth control.

Younger wives answered in the affirmative far more often than did the older wives. This was the case in every place studied except Artas, where birth control was denied by young and old alike. In every city, a majority of those married since 1940 reported that they had practiced birth control.

There was also a class difference, with the upper class fairly consistently having a high percentage of affirmative answers and the lower class equally consistently having a lower percentage (cf. Abu-Lughod, 1965).

There were also differences from one city and village to another. The wives of Amman and Damascus more often said they had practiced birth control than did those of Beirut and Tripoli, and the wives of Beirut and Tripoli more often than those of Buarij and Artas. Only four Artas wives— all with more children than they thought "ideal"—reported any effort at preventing conception.

Most of the younger wives not practicing birth control said the reason was that they wanted more children (Table V-14). If we can assume that a number of these will eventually complete their families and then begin such practices, then we might predict that the number practicing birth control in the cities may soon equal the level in Western countries.

Among the older wives not practicing, or having practiced, birth control, the most common explanation given was that it was contrary to religious teachings or contrary to God's will. Some quoted Sura 42: "He creates what He will. He gives daughters to whom He will and sons to whom He pleases. To some He gives both sons and daughters, and to others He gives none at all. Mighty is Allah and all-knowing."

Another fairly frequent comment of older wives was "we didn't know about such things in those days" or "that was not the custom at that time." These women were conscious of the change in knowledge and practice that occurred between the 1930's and the 1950's.

It is interesting to note that only 39 wives—all from cities—stated that the objection or refusal of the husband was the reason they abstained from any effort at controlling conception. If we can accept their statements at face value, there is little overt conflict between "non-controlling" husbands and wives on this issue. On the other hand, some wives practicing birth control did report seeking a method which might be kept secret from the husband.

Infant Mortality. When the mothers were asked about the number of infants who had died before age six there was a significant difference between the replies of younger and older mothers. In every city and village, the older mothers reported a much higher rate of infant mortality than did the younger ones (Table V-15).

Health conditions seem to have improved less over the years in Artas than in any of the other places. Mothers there married before 1930 reported infant mortality at a rate of 28 per cent, which was no worse than any of the other places except Beirut. Mothers married during the 1950's reported a rate of 24 per cent. Even those married after 1959, some of whom had children not yet five years of age, reported that 14 per cent of children born had died before age 6. These data, taken with the comparatively high child mortality rate in Amman, reveal the poor health conditions in war-torn Jordan.

Class differences in infant mortality existed, but these were much smaller, and less consistent, than the differences over time, or the differences between Beirut and the other localities.

In most instances, the interviewers ascertained the sex of the infant reported as having died. Of those infants, 482 were male and 455 female. The higher mortality rate of males is the usual finding in Europe and North America. To find it in the Islamic world, however, argues against serious neglect of females so frequently thought to exist there (cf. Goode, p. 123). These data bear out the implication of the data on the ideal family—while males may be preferred, females are also valued and protected.

Trends in Family Size. Our data suggest an *increase* in family size between the beginning and the middle of this century, particularly in the less modern areas. In the village of Artas, it is possible to make direct comparisons between families of 1927 and 1967. In 1927 there were 151 wives in the village. They had borne an average of 4 children each, and an average of 2.3 children were alive, or had lived to adulthood. By 1967 there were 208 wives in Artas. These had borne an average of 5.1 children, and an average of 3.8 were living. Evidently, both family size and rate of child survival had increased susbstantially in forty years.

The Muslim families of Beirut were an exception to the general growth trend. These families were already large by the first decades of this century, to judge from the families of orientation of the older wives. They were no larger at mid-century. Indeed, evidence from several sources indicates that *upper class* families in Beirut had before mid-century begun a trend toward smaller families.

The ideal of a large family with many sons, so long reported as characteristic of Arab value systems, is typical of our more traditional respondents—the older women of the lower class. The younger the woman, and the higher her social class, the smaller the number she gave as constituting an ideal family. On the average, lower class wives married before 1930 thought of a family of 7 as ideal; upper class wives married after 1959 thought of 3 children as ideal. Moreover, there were indications that the wives who preferred smaller families were taking steps to realize their ideal. A substantial majority of city wives, particularly of the upper class, reported having practiced some method of birth control.

The "small family" ideal was more common in those groups with lower rates of infant mortality, as would be expected. As health conditions in the area continue to improve, we can expect the emphasis on fecundity to decline.

We believe the data point toward a future decrease in family size of Muslims of the Levant. Indeed, among those Arabs most attuned to the modern world, the trend has already begun.[1]

[1] A national fertility sample survey was carried out in Jordan in 1972, among women of the East Bank under the age of 50. A preliminary report of some of the findings was published (Rizk, 1973) after this manuscript had gone to press. This report reveals that families in Jordan are still large, and urban-rural differences continue to be insignificant. On the other hand, upper class women and women with secondary or university education now have fewer children than do other women. Evidently, the trend toward the smaller family has begun among women of the East Bank.

TABLE V–2

OCCUPATION OF HUSBÀND, YEAR OF MARRIAGE AND THE NUMBER OF
LIVING CHILDREN REPORTED BY WIVES IN THE 1960 SYRIAN CENSUS

Occupation of Husband	Year of Marriage	Per Cent of Women Reporting			Number of Women Reporting
		0-3 children	4-6 children	7 or more children	
Professional	1930 or before	31.4	41.1	27.5	1,610
and	1931–1940	28.1	48.2	23.7	2,226
Technical	1941–1950	39.8	55.7	4.6	1,715
	1951–1955	76.7	23.1	0.2	2,867
Administrative	1930 or before	25.1	38.5	36.4	1,033
Executive	1931–1940	25.9	44.6	29.6	1,404
and	1941–1950	35.8	58.8	5.4	923
Managerial	1951–1955	78.5	21.4	0.1	1,104
Farmers	1930 or before	25.8	46.1	28.1	81,245
and	1931–1940	25.4	56.3	18.3	83,377
Farm Workers	1941–1950	46.9	50.6	2.4	66,290
	1951–1955	87.9	11.8	0.3	69,107
All	1930 or before	30.5	43.3	26.3	187,036
Occupations*	1931–1940	25.1	52.3	22.6	171,879
and	1941–1950	43.6	53.1	3.3	129,574
Unemployed	1951–1955	83.9	15.9	0.2	147,837

*Includes, in addition to the three categories shown, clerical, sales, transport, communications, recreation and manufacturing workers as well as workers not classified in the census.

TABLE V–3

EDUCATIONAL LEVEL, YEAR OF MARRIAGE AND THE NUMBER OF
LIVING CHILDREN REPORTED BY WIVES IN THE 1960 SYRIAN CENSUS

Educational Level	Year of Marriage	Per Cent of Wives Reporting			Number of Wives Reporting
		0-3 children	4-6 children	7 or more children	
Illiterate	1930 or before	30.6	43.3	26.1	177,790
	1931–1940	25.3	52.5	22.2	155,357
	1941–1950	44.5	52.5	3.0	116,608
	1951–1955	84.9	14.8	0.3	127,691
Read only	1930 or before	28.2	41.8	29.9	8,386
or	1931–1940	21.9	50.2	28.0	13,701
Read and	1941–1950	33.1	61.2	5.7	9,806
Write	1951–1955	76.1	23.7	0.2	13,218
Elementary,	1930 or before	32.5	44.8	22.7	831
Primary or	1931–1940	29.4	51.4	19.2	2,759
Secondary	1941–1950	42.0	53.9	4.2	3,067
Certificate	1951–1955	79.0	20.8	0.1	6,707
University	1930 or before	65.5	20.7	13.8	29
Degree	1931–1940	71.0	29.0	0.0	62
	1941–1950	78.5	21.5	0.0	93
	1951–1955	91.9	8.1	0.0	221
All Levels	1930 or before	30.5	43.3	26.3	187,036
	1931–1940	25.1	52.3	22.6	171,879
	1941–1950	43.6	53.1	3.3	129,574
	1951–1955	83.9	15.9	0.2	147,837

TABLE V-4

Size of Wives' Families of Orientation

Year of Marriage →	1960's				1950's				1940's				1930's				Before 1930			
Social Class →	U	M	L	(T)	U	M	L	(T)	U	M	L	(T)	U	M	L	(T)	U	M	L	(T)
Artas M				(6.5)				(6.5)				(6.1)				(6.0)				(4.8)
Artas N				(42)				(65)				(44)				(25)				(32)
Buarij M				(6.8)				(7.0)				(5.8)				(4.8)				(4.7)
Buarij N				(16)				(21)				(15)				(10)				(9)
Amman M	6.6	6.8	7.4	(7.0)		6.8	7.1	(6.9)	6.2	6.1	6.4	(6.2)	5.8	5.1	6.7	(5.7)	8.5	6.3	5.7	(6.4)
Amman N	17	61	51	(129)		55	30	(94)	8	21	22	(51)	6	12	7	(25)	2	7	7	(16)
Damascus M	4.3	6.0	7.9	(6.1)	4.0	5.6	5.0	(5.5)	4.8	6.5	5.6	(6.1)	3.0	5.5	3.3	(5.2)	3.0	5.7	4.2	(5.3)
Damascus N	3	56	7	(66)	5	61	4	(70)	8	33	8	(49)	1	23	3	(27)	1	17	4	(22)
Tripoli M	5.7	7.5	6.9	(7.0)	5.8	6.8	6.8	(6.7)	4.8	6.2	6.1	(6.1)	3.7	6.1	5.7	(5.7)	9.0	4.6	2.9	(4.2)
Tripoli N	24	101	64	(189)	20	90	85	(195)	5	40	37	(82)	3	16	10	(29)	1	10	7	(18)
Beirut M	4.2	5.2	6.6	(5.1)	4.1	5.8	4.9	(5.3)	4.8	5.0	5.5	(5.0)	6.0	5.4	–	(5.7)	8.2	6.2	–	(7.2)
Beirut N	35	60	17	(112)	34	90	7	(131)	26	47	4	(77)	19	16	0	(35)	8	9	0	(17)

M is mean number of children in the families of orientation of the women interviewed.
N is number of women responding to this question.

TABLE V–5

Size of Husbands' Families of Orientation

Year of Marriage Social Class	1960's				1950's				1940's				1930's				Before 1930			
	U	M	L	(T)	U	M	L	(T)	U	M	L	(T)	U	M	L	(T)	U	M	L	(T)
Artas M				(5.8)				(6.0)				(5.1)				(5.3)				(5.8)
Artas N				(40)				(65)				(43)				(25)				(31)
Buarij M				(6.2)				(6.1)				(5.3)				(4.9)				(4.8)
Buarij N				(16)				(21)				(15)				(10)				(9)
Amman M	7.8	7.3	7.0	(7.2)	6.9	6.6	6.5	(6.6)	7.0	6.0	6.3	(6.3)	7.0	5.6	6.7	(6.2)	5.0	7.0	7.7	(7.1)
Amman N	17	61	51	(129)	9	55	30	(94)	8	21	22	(51)	6	12	7	(25)	2	7	7	(16)
Damascus M	4.0	6.4	4.6	(6.1)	5.0	6.1	3.5	(5.9)	6.1	5.9	3.4	(5.6)	5.0	5.3	4.0	(5.1)	1.0	5.4	3.5	(4.8)
Damascus N	3	56	7	(66)	5	61	4	(70)	8	33	8	(49)	1	23	3	(27)	1	17	4	(22)
Tripoli M	5.5	6.8	6.8	(6.6)	5.5	5.7	5.5	(5.6)	4.8	4.5	4.8	(4.7)	6.0	4.7	3.2	(4.3)	4.0	4.4	3.0	(3.8)
Tripoli N	24	101	64	(189)	20	90	85	(195)	5	40	37	(82)	3	16	10	(29)	1	10	7	(18)
Beirut M	4.9	5.4	7.6	(5.7)	4.2	5.8	7.1	(5.6)	5.9	5.5	9.8	(5.8)	5.8	5.1	–	(5.5)	7.2	5.2	–	(6.1)
Beirut N	36	60	18	(114)	34	90	7	(131)	26	46	4	(76)	19	16	0	(35)	8	10	0	(18)

TABLE V-6

PER CENT OF WIVES COMING FROM SMALL* FAMILIES

Year of Marriage	1960's				1950's				1940's				1930's				Before 1930			
Social Class	U	M	L	(T)	U	M	L	(T)	U	M	L	(T)	U	M	L	(T)	U	M	L	(T)
Artas				(10)				(9)				(10)				(4)				(25)
Buarij				(12)				(24)				(20)				(40)				(44)
Amman	18	7	10	(9)	22	11	7	(11)	12	19	18	(18)	17	33	00	(18)	++	29	14	(19)
Damascus	++	16	14	(11)	40	21	++	(23)	25	9	25	(14)	++	30	++	(37)	++	11	++	(23)
Tripoli	17	13	6	(11)	10	10	12	(11)	20	20	19	(20)	++	31	30	(34)	++	30	71	(44)
Beirut	43	23	00	(26)	29	13	++	(19)	35	19	+-	(25)	21	37	-	(29)	00	11	-	(6)

*Three children or less.

TABLE V-7

PER CENT OF WIVES COMING FROM LARGE* FAMILIES

Year of Marriage	1960's				1950's				1940's				1930's				Before 1930			
Social Class	U	M	L	(T)	U	M	L	(T)	U	M	L	(T)	U	M	L	(T)	U	M	L	(T)
Artas				(54)				(52)				(45)				(36)				(25)
Buarij				(44)				(57)				(40)				(20)				(22)
Amman	53	57	67	(60)	56	49	53	(51)	37	38	45	(41)	50	25	71	(44)	++	57	43	(50)
Damascus	++	32	74	(35)	00	38	++	(34)	25	48	25	(41)	++	35	++	(33)	++	35	++	(32)
Tripoli	21	57	53	(52)	20	46	42	(42)	20	42	41	(40)	++	31	30	(31)	++	10	00	(11)
Beirut	3	27	53	(23)	6	32	43	(26)	23	17	+−	(21)	26	25	−	(26)	50	33	−	(41)

*Seven children or more.

TABLE V-8

PER CENT OF HUSBANDS COMING FROM SMALL* FAMILIES

Year of Marriage	1960's				1950's				1940's				1930's				Before 1930			
Social Class	U	M	L	(T)	U	M	L	(T)	U	M	L	(T)	U	M	L	(T)	U	M	L	(T)
Artas				(10)				(6)				(26)				(26)				(29)
Buarij				(12)				(10)				(20)				(30)				(33)
Amman	6	5	10	(7)	33	16	13	(17)	00	14	14	(12)	00	25	14	(16)	++	43	14	(25)
Damascus	++	7	29	(11)	60	18	++	(23)	00	21	37	(20)	++	30	++	(30)	++	24	++	(32)
Tripoli	17	16	12	(15)	25	21	25	(23)	40	45	32	(39)	++	37	40	(34)	++	50	71	(56)
Beirut	19	12	00	(12)	35	13	00	(18)	15	15	+−	(14)	21	19	−	(20)	12	40	−	(28)

*Three children or less.

TABLE V–9

PER CENT OF HUSBANDS COMING FROM LARGE* FAMILIES

Year of Marriage	1960's				1950's				1940's				1930's				Before 1930			
Social Class	U	M	L	(T)	U	M	L	(T)	U	M	L	(T)	U	M	L	(T)	U	M	L	(T)
Artas			53	(32)				(42)				(35)				(26)				(32)
Buarij			14	(50)				(24)				(27)				(10)				(22)
Amman	47	59	53	(55)	56	47	40	(49)	37	38	45	(45)	50	50	43	(48)	++	57	57	(50)
Damascus	++	48	14	(42)	00	41	++	(37)	12	39	00	(27)	++	22	++	(19)	++	24	++	(18)
Tripoli	17	46	53	(44)	30	37	33	(34)	40	17	16	(18)	++	25	00	(17)	++	10	14	(11)
Beirut	14	32	56	(32)	12	38	71	(33)	38	35	+–	(39)	42	25	–	(34)	50	30	–	(49)

*Seven children or more.

TABLE V-10

AVERAGE SIZE OF INTERVIEWEE'S FAMILIES OF PROCREATION
(number of children living)

Year of Marriage		1960's				1950's				1940's				1930's				Before 1930			
Social Class		U	M	L	(T)	U	M	L	(T)	U	M	L	(T)	U	M	L	(T)	U	M	L	(T)
Artas	M				(1.4)				(3.3)				(5.0)				(5.4)				(5.2)
	N				(42)				(65)				(44)				(25)				(32)
Buarij	M				(1.6)				(4.3)				(6.8)				(7.1)				(4.0)
	N				(16)				(21)				(15)				(10)				(9)
Amman	M	1.5	1.8	1.8	(1.8)	4.5	4.2	4.3	(4.3)	5.1	7.2	6.6	(6.2)	6.3	6.6	6.0	(6.4)	4.5	5.6	6.7	(5.9)
	N	15	43	44	(102)	8	51	30	(89)	8	20	22	(50)	6	12	7	(25)	2	7	7	(16)
Damascus	M	2.0	1.2	1.0	(1.2)	2.2	2.9	5.8	(3.0)	3.9	4.5	6.1	(4.7)	2.0	5.5	6.3	(5.5)	4.0	4.9	5.2	(5.0)
	N	3	56	7	(66)	5	61	4	(70)	8	33	8	(49)	1	23	3	(27)	1	17	4	(22)
Tripoli	M	1.3	2.0	2.1	(1.9)	3.6	4.5	5.2	(4.7)	4.6	6.2	7.1	(6.5)	5.0	7.2	6.4	(6.7)	8.0	6.5	6.3	(6.5)
	N	24	101	64	(189)	20	90	85	(195)	5	40	37	(82)	3	16	10	(29)	1	10	7	(18)
Beirut	M	1.4	1.8	2.5	(1.7)	2.8	3.5	5.3	(3.4)	3.5	4.1	6.0	(4.0)	4.1	5.3	—	(4.6)	4.6	5.2	—	(4.9)
	N	32	47	14	(93)	34	87	7	(128)	26	46	4	(76)	19	15	0	(34)	8	9	0	(17)

TABLE V–11

WIVES' OPINIONS ON NUMBER OF CHILDREN IN AN IDEAL FAMILY

Year of Marriage		1960's				1950's				1940's				1930's				Before 1930			
Social Class		U	M	L	(T)	U	M	L	(T)	U	M	L	(T)	U	M	L	(T)	U	M	L	(T)
Artàs	M				(4.4)				(4.5)				(4.9)				(5.8)				(5.8)
	N				(39)				(61)				(42)				(22)				(27)
Buarij	M				(4.7)				(7.4)				(9.5)				(8.8)				(8.4)
	N				(13)				(20)				(15)				(10)				(7)
Amman	M	2.8	3.4	3.6	(3.4)	4.2	4.0	4.3	(4.0)	4.4	5.2	5.0	(5.0)	6.7	5.0	5.6	(5.6)	4.5	7.1	7.1	(6.8)
	N	17	61	51	(129)	9	55	30	(94)	8	21	22	(51)	6	12	7	(25)	2	7	7	(16)
Damascus	M	2.0	2.8	2.5	(2.8)	3.3	3.3	4.7	(3.4)	3.7	4.0	4.4	(4.0)	4.0	5.7	4.0	(5.5)	4.0	5.6	7.2	(5.7)
	N	3	55	7	(65)	5	61	3	(69)	8	33	7	(48)	1	23	3	(27)	1	17	3	(21)
Tripoli	M	3.0	3.4	3.5	(3.4)	4.0	4.6	5.1	(4.7)	4.4	5.7	5.4	(5.5)	4.7	6.2	6.3	(6.1)	6.0	6.3	7.3	(6.7)
	N	24	101	64	(189)	20	90	84	(194)	5	40	37	(82)	3	15	10	(28)	1	10	7	(18)
Beirut	M	3.0	3.2	4.0	(3.2)	3.3	3.9	5.1	(3.8)	4.0	4.0	5.2	(4.1)	4.0	4.7	–	(4.3)	4.2	5.2	–	(4.8)
	N	36	60	18	(114)	34	90	7	(131)	26	47	5	(78)	19	16	0	(35)	8	10	0	(18)

TABLE V-12

AVERAGE FAMILY SIZE IDEAL OF HUSBANDS, AS ESTIMATED BY WIVES
(number of children)

Year of Marriage / Social Class		1960's				1950's				1940's				1930's				Before 1930			
		U	M	L	(T)	U	M	L	(T)	U	M	L	(T)	U	M	L	(T)	U	M	L	(T)
Artas	M				(4.0)				(4.6)				(5.0)				(5.5)				(5.7)
	N				(41)				(63)				(43)				(23)				(29)
Buarij	M				(7.9)				(10.5)				(11.5)				(8.4)				(9.8)
	N				(14)				(19)				(14)				(9)				(9)
Amman	M	3.4	3.3	3.8	(3.5)	3.8	4.1	4.3	(4.1)	4.4	5.2	5.4	(5.1)	6.5	5.5	5.3	(5.7)	5.0	7.1	7.4	(7.0)
	N	17	61	51	(129)	9	55	30	(94)	8	21	22	(51)	6	12	7	(25)	2	7	7	(16)
Damascus	M	2.0	3.9	6.2	(4.0)	3.0	4.7	4.2	(4.5)	4.4	7.0	8.8	(6.9)	4.0	6.5	9.3	(6.7)	4.0	8.6	10.2	(8.6)
	N	3	54	5	(62)	5	59	3	(67)	7	31	8	(46)	1	22	3	(26)	1	17	3	(21)
Tripoli	M	3.5	3.6	3.9	(3.7)	4.2	5.3	6.0	(5.5)	5.6	6.5	7.1	(6.7)	5.0	7.7	7.5	(7.4)	8.0	7.1	8.4	(7.7)
	N	24	101	64	(189)	20	90	84	(194)	5	40	37	(82)	3	15	10	(28)	1	10	7	(18)
Beirut	M	3.1	3.3	4.1	(3.4)	3.2	4.3	6.0	(4.1)	3.6	4.6	5.2	(4.3)	3.8	5.5	–	(4.6)	5.5	5.6	–	(5.5)
	N	36	57	18	(111)	32	88	7	(127)	25	43	5	(73)	18	16	0	(34)	8	7	0	(15)

TABLE V–13

Per Cent of Wives who Practice Birth Control

Year of Marriage		1960's				1950's				1940's				1930's				Before 1930			
Social Class		U	M	L	(T)	U	M	L	(T)	U	M	L	(T)	U	M	L	(T)	U	M	L	(T)
Artas	%				(00)				(00)				(9)				(00)				(00)
	N				(42)				(64)				(43)				(24)				(30)
Buarij	%				(29)				(28)				(27)				(10)				(11)
	N				(17)				(18)				(15)				(10)				(9)
Amman	%	94	87	69	(81)	67	75	73	(73)	88	67	41	(59)	83	33	43	(48)	0	00	14	(6)
	N	17	61	51	(125)	9	55	30	(94)	8	21	22	(51)	6	12	7	(25)	2	7	7	(16)
Damascus	%	67	89	43	(83)	100	90	50	(89)	100	87	50	(83)	–	87	67	(85)	100	69	0	(57)
	N	3	56	7	(66)	5	61	4	(70)	8	32	8	(48)	0	23	3	(26)	1	16	4	(21)
Tripoli	%	87	65	35	(58)	90	70	52	(64)	100	60	59	(62)	100	31	30	(38)	0	00	00	(00)
	N	23	101	63	(187)	20	90	85	(195)	5	40	37	(82)	3	16	10	(29)	1	10	7	(18)
Beirut	%	81	59	56	(65)	69	41	71	(50)	31	38	60	(37)	17	6	–	(12)	25	10	–	(17)
	N	36	59	18	(113)	32	87	7	(126)	26	45	5	(76)	18	16	0	(34)	8	10	0	(18)

TABLE V–14

Reasons for not Practicing Birth Control

(Numbers in table show per cent of those not practicing birth control
who cite each of those reasons as the chief one)

Year of Marriage / Reason Cited*	1960's H	W	R	1950's H	W	R	1940's H	W	R	1930's H	W	R	Before 1930 H	W	R
Artas	–	67	29	–	38	48	–	20	63	–	11	53	–	4	40
Buarij	–	82	18	–	42	50	–	11	56	–	–	–	–	0	20
Amman	12	64	24	32	24	24	24	5	38	8	8	31	0	0	27
Damascus	0	80	10	0	50	16	0	25	12	–	–	–	0	0	50
Tripoli	16	66	3	24	25	21	11	18	32	0	31	38	11	22	44
Beirut	0	80	10	11	67	11	0	80	20	12	0	37	–	–	–

*H – husband objects; W – wife wants more children; R – religious reasons.

TABLE V–15

Infant Mortality

Year of Marriage of Mothers	1960's				1950's				1940's				1930's				Before 1930			
	M	F	T	(%)	M	F	T	(%)	M	F	T	(%)	M	F	T	(%)	M	F	T	(%)
Artas	5	4	10	(14)	31	30	67	(24)	44	38	93	(30)	26	25	51	(28)	32	27	65	(28)
Buarij	0	1	1	(4)	7	7	15	(14)	6	12	18	(15)	16	15	31	(30)	11	10	21	(37)
Amman	18	10	28	(13)	38	33	71	(16)	25	21	46	(13)	20	19	39	(20)	15	8	23	(20)
Damascus	1	1	2	(2)	4	3	7	(3)	8	9	17	(7)	10	14	24	(14)	19	24	43	(28)
Tripoli	11	8	19	(5)	57	48	105	(10)	35	46	81	(13)	14	16	30	(13)	18	20	38	(25)
Beirut	3	0	3	(2)	1	0	1	(0)	1	2	3	(1)	2	4	6	(4)	4	0	4	(6)
Totals	38	24			138	121			119	128			88	93			99	89		

M is number of male children who died before the age of 6; F is number of females who died before age 6; T is the total number who died before 6, and includes some children for whom our records do not show the sex. The columns of percentages(%) show the per cent of children who were born alive but died before reaching the age of 6.

CHAPTER SIX

Modesty and the Role of Women

*Men have authority over women because Allah has made the one superior to the
other, and because they spend their wealth to maintain them. Good women are
obedient. They guard their unseen parts because Allah has guarded them.*

SURA 4

T HE QURAN makes clear that women of Islam may enter Paradise,
that Allah rewards their good deeds, that they have rights of inheritance and that they should be treated with justice. At the same
time it recognizes the special status and special responsibilities of women.
They should be obedient to father and husband, they inherit only half
as much as do males, their testimony is less weighty than that of males,
and they must make special efforts both to turn their eyes from sexual
temptation and to avoid tempting men.

Students of early Islam seem generally agreed that, by condemning
female infanticide and spelling out rights of women, Mohammed brought
about in a fairly short time a considerable improvement in the status of
the women of Arabia (Levy, 1962, p. 92). Soon after, however, the ideal of
tribal honor was enhanced and stimulated by the conquests of Islam, and
woman's status ceased improving and in some areas even deteriorated
(Gordon, 1968, p. 9).

Islamic culture has traditionally used "avoidance and segregation of
social spheres" as a means of accommodating to, and possibly of perpe-
tuating, perceived differences between the sexes (cf. Gulick, 1968, p. 149).
Important pillars of this pattern of avoidance and segregation are the
codes of honor and of modesty. The honor of the males of the family
requires that the females conform to the modesty code. This code is more
easily observed when there are well-established patterns of male-female
avoidance, and of segregation. Thus, honor and modesty and male-female
avoidance patterns and beliefs about characteristics of the sexes are all

117

aspects of an interwoven and interlocking cultural Arabesque (Antoun, 1968; Dodd, 1970 and 1973).[1]

When we study changes in the role of women in the Arab Levant, we are studying changes in the definition of modesty, of behavior that is compatible with honor. The woman who discards the face veil does not do so because she has chosen immodesty, but because she and her male relatives have redefined modest and honorable dress. Such a redefinition involves changed beliefs about impulse control and susceptibility to temptation of both males and females, and about the degree of avoidance necessary to prevent disruptive behavior. In short, changes in such specific behavior as veiling are a symptom (and a cause) of changes in the general Islamic pattern of beliefs about the natures of men and women and in judgments about proper codes of modesty and honor.

In this study we asked the wives about a number of items of behavior which we felt were significant aspects of the role of women in Islamic society. Changes in these items are not only important in themselves, but they also bespeak broader changes in woman's role.

Veiling

In Western eyes at least the veiling of Muslim women is a major symbol of their secluded and inferior status, and the gradual disappearance of the custom in this century is evidence of progress toward emancipation. As a Western feminist remarked in 1936, "the barometer of social change in the Muslim world is the veil" (Woodsmall, p. 40). We would agree that the discarding of the face veil is indeed an event of major importance in the Arab Levant of the twentieth century, and is a sign of modernization, though we recognize that veiling was never practiced in many traditional and conservative Islamic communities.

In pre-Islamic Arabia, only city women were veiled. In the time of Mohammed, veiling was the rule among the women of his own tribe, the Quraysh (Levy, 1962, p. 124). The Quran (Sura 33) enjoins wives of true believers to draw their veils or cloaks close about them when going out, but there has been considerable disagreement among interpreters as to precisely what this requires. Nevertheless, because the female members

---

[1] Emphasis on honor and modesty has been recognized by a number of scholars as a circum-Mediterranean trait (e.g., Peristiany, 1965, and Schneider, 1971) and Quigley (1973) has pointed out that this concern has been carried into Latin America as well.

118

of the Prophet's own family were veiled, and because veiling fitted into the larger context of modesty and seclusion and guarding of women, the practice became or continued widespread, particularly in the cities, throughout most of the Islamic world.[1]

In the first third of the twentieth century, veiling was the norm in towns and cities, but not the villages, of the Arab Levant. In Beirut, Tripoli, and Damascus there was talk of "lifting the veil," but only a small minority dared to do so. Amman, with its strong Bedouin influence, was somewhat more "modern" than the larger cities on this score (Woodsmall, 1936, pp. 50 ff.). The peasant women of the area, compelled by necessity to work in the fields, and protected by the rarity of strangers in the villages, generally left their faces unveiled (Bliss, 1917, pp. 282 ff. and Patai, 1969, p. 117). Fuller reported that the women of Buarij in 1937-38 "always" covered their heads with a shawl (1961, p. 95), but did not cover the face. Granqvist (1947, pp. 125 and 162) noted that the women of Artas in the late twenties wore a head cloth which could be drawn over the face temporarily when passing a group of men.

Our data (Tables VI-1 and VI-2) show the steady decline in the use of the veil in every locality studied. The most dramatic change occurred in Beirut. A majority of those married before 1930 veiled before marriage, and continue to veil, while not one woman married in the sixties now wears the veil (cf. Churchill & Sabbagh, 1968, p. 50). The change in Damascus and in Amman is almost as great as in Beirut. A majority of the women of Tripoli still veil, as Gulick found by counting faces one feast-day morning in 1962 (1967, p. 56), and this is especially true of unmarried girls past puberty. Nevertheless, the practice is dying out, and only a third of the women married in the sixties still veil. In Artas, where the head scarf also serves as a veil, few of the younger women wear it. Only in Buarij, where the scarf simply covers the hair, and is more often useful or decorative than inconvenient, do the younger women still wear it.

There is a definite class difference in veiling, and this difference is especially marked among those women married after 1940. In every city it is the upper class which most often discards the veil and the lower class which most often retains it (cf. Hirabayashi & Ishaq, 1958, p. 39). As Sayigh (1968, p. 20) has said "The seclusion of women seems always to

[1] As Tillion (1966) has observed, veiling has served endogamy in the Mediterranean littoral for thousands of years, among many peoples of many religions. See also Stern (1939, p. 109).

have been a status symbol, permeating downward from the wealthy to the poor. Now emancipation is following the same course."

Religious Observances

In Western societies women are more active than men in the various rituals and observances of organized religion (Berelson & Steiner, p. 392). It therefore comes as a surprise to Westerners to learn that in the Levant generally women are not to be found at the daily prayers at the mosque, do not attend the Friday services, and are not even present in the mosque at funerals of close relatives. There were exceptions, as in Mecca, but general tradition in Islam was against permitting women to worship in the mosque. Since 1971, however, women of Egypt have been allowed to attend Friday prayers under certain conditions, and the practice can be expected to grow in the Levant.

This restriction is sometimes explained as avoiding the possibility that the mosque be defiled by a woman who is ritually unclean or impure (e.g., if she is menstruating). A more likely explanation is that exclusion from services at the mosque was a part of the general seclusion of women and a confirmation of their inferior status. It should be noted that attending services at the mosque is not one of the five fundamental requirements of a good Muslim, and that all of these requirements (or duties) are permitted and encouraged of women. The five basic tenets or duties are:
1. Witnessing that there is but one God, and that Mohammed is His Prophet.
2. Praying five times a day.
3. Giving alms to the poor and needy, to wayfarers, and for advancing the cause of God.
4. Fasting during the daylight hours of the month of Ramadan, or (if one is ill or traveling during Ramadan) on other equivalent days.
5. Making the pilgrimage to the Mecca, if possible.

In studying changes in religious behavior of women, we chose to ask our respondents about praying and fasting because preliminary observation had led us to believe that the other duties were either unanimously professed (as is almsgiving) or rather rare (as is making the pilgrimage).

It is impossible to generalize with any confidence on the degree to which the women of the Levant have, in the past, conformed to or fallen short of the Islam ideal on such basic matters as praying and fasting. One writer, in discussing religious behavior in Jordan, stated that "every devout Moslem observes the Koranic injunction to pray five times a day" and that "women usually pray in the seclusion of the home" (Harris, 1958, pp. 36-37), leaving it to the reader to guess how many women were devout. He did make clear, however, that "westernized elements" and Bedouins were guilty of breaking the fast of Ramadan. Another scholar said as recently as 1969 that, to the "average Middle Easterner," religion without such formal observances as the fast and the prayers is "unthinkable " (Patai, 1969, p. 403).

Praying and fasting were apparently the rule in Artas in the twenties. Granqvist mentions in a footnote that "Very disturbing to my work were the five daily prayers which my women had to say regularly and also periods of fasts when the people were especially weak and weary" (1931, p. 20). But a more recent study (1956 and 1960) of another Palestinian Sunni village gave a quite different picture. Lutfiyya found that very few of the villagers prayed regularly or fasted rigorously, although they "attempt to convey the impression that they are practicing their religious duties assiduously" (1966, p. 43).

Other observers have also questioned the generality of praying and fasting, especially among women. Lane, after mentioning the fact that women were not allowed in the mosque, observed flatly that "Very few women in Egypt even pray at home" (p. 83). He then noted that fasting was apparently considered more important than praying, for everyone either fasted, or pretended to do so, or had a legitimate excuse (pregnancy, nursing a child, illness, *et al*).

More than a century later, Fuller noted that the villagers of Buarij did not pray regularly, but did observe the fast of Ramadan. Williams (1968, p. 14) found the same pattern in nearby Haouch el Harimi. The Buarij women seemed to turn more toward "folk religion" or local superstitions than to the rituals of Islam (pp. 81-83). Gulick's anthropological survey led him to the conclusion that most Arab Levantines are more committed to folk beliefs and rituals (e.g., fear of the Evil Eye or votive offerings at local shrines) than to the dogma and practices of formal religion (1968, p. 188).

There are no firm data on the praying and fasting of urban women of the Levant. One recent study of Tripoli (Gulick, 1967, pp. 166 ff.) seemed to imply that fasting is widespread, but gave no data on praying.[1] A 1959 survey of more than 600 Middle Eastern Muslim female students, most of them from cities, found that only 25 per cent claimed to abide by the rules and practices of their religion (Mùhyi, p. 51).

[1] The book opens with the call to prayer, but nowhere mentions the response.

From the sparse information available we are led to surmise that the Fast of Ramadan is observed more widely than is the duty of praying regularly, and that the women of the Levant (unlike those of Egypt, if Lane is correct) formerly observed their religious duties more faithfully than they do today.

We asked each woman in our sample whether she had prayed regularly before marriage and whether she did so now. We then asked the same two questions about fasting during Ramadan. The replies are summarized in Tables VI-3, VI-4, VI-5, and VI-6.

With respect to the duty of prayer, there is an unmistakable time trend. The later the year of marriage, the less the likelihood that the wife say she prayed regularly—whether before or after marriage. In each age group in every locality, about as many stated they prayed now as stated that they had done so before marriage. Consequently, we have no evidence that women who had once prayed regularly are now giving up the practice. Rather, it seems that the younger generation differs from the older generation.

No attempt was made to check the accuracy of the statements about praying and the interviewers did not say that fulfilling the duty of praying required all five prayers daily. Even so, a minority of the women married in the sixties in any locality claimed to pray regularly. We are therefore inclined to believe that during this century regular praying has ceased to be the custom for women in the Levant.

There are no consistent class differences in praying. Whether one claims she prays regularly or not depends on age, not on social class.

There were large differences between one locality and another. The women of Damascus were most likely to say that they prayed, and those of Artas were next.[1] At the opposite end of the scale were the women of Buarij and Beirut, where few of the youngest wives and only half the oldest say that they pray.

When we turn to the data on observing the Fast of Ramadan, in Tables VI-5 and VI-6, we find a totally different pattern of responses. The vast majority of women in every class and every locality say that they observe the Fast. Unlike veiling or praying, fasting is the norm.

To say that fasting is the norm is not to say that every woman fasts rigorously from daylight to sundown. Women may postpone a fast day if

---

[1] Almost all of the women of Artas who were old enough to have known Granqvist said that they prayed regularly.

they are pregnant, nursing an infant, menstruating, ill, or on a journey. Moreover, it is recognized in many communities (e.g., Fuller, p. 80) that one should not fast to the point of preventing urgent and necessary work. Finally, we have noticed that some people, whether Muslims in Ramadan or Christians in Lent, will say that they are fasting even if there are occasional lapses.

It is significant that many women who do not pretend to pray regularly, or even to abstain from alcohol, state that they observe the Fast of Ramadan. One explanation for this is that Ramadan has deep social significance in Islamic communities, and is the annual occasion of several important ceremonies, rituals, exchanges, and festivals (Antoun, 1968 b). Thus the observing of Ramadan is woven into the whole fabric of the social life. Moreover, public life in an Islamic community (and in Muslim sectors of mixed communities) is altered during Ramadan. Work is curtailed during the day, and there is far more activity—commercial and social—in the night (Gulick, 1967, p. 168). Nocturnal feasting and visiting and other pleasures often follow a day of fasting. Thus there are many external supports and reminders for observing the Fast.

Education

We mentioned in Chapter II that husbands of women interviewed more often had at least a primary school education than did the women themselves. Tables VI-7 through VI-10 show that the differences were as great or greater in the preceding generation. Among parents of our respondents, and among parents of respondents' husbands, a primary education or more was in all localities more likely to be the privilege of males.

Nevertheless, a comparison of generations shows that women have made progress, and the trend is definitely toward education for women as well as for men. The lower class women of the cities and the women of the villages are lagging behind, but some of them have completed primary school of late. The significance of the time trend is put into relief if we notice that younger wives (married 1950 or after) had a primary education more often than did their fathers or their husbands' fathers. The females of one generation are better educated than the males of the preceding generation.

Given the fact that educational opportunities are limited in the Middle East, that the society is patrilineal, and that woman's role centers on the

123

home, it is hardly surprising that boys receive more education than do girls. There is, however, another element involved in parents' attitudes toward the education of girls—that of modesty. The girl who attends school is to some degree exposed and unguarded. For this reason some parents prefer that their daughters drop out of school before puberty, and others insist that they attend a girls' school after puberty.

In order to test the hypothesis that the modesty code was involved in the attitude toward education, we asked the mothers whether they would be willing for their daughters to attend a woman's college and then asked whether they would be willing for them to attend a coeducational college. In the Middle East, as in much of Europe, the term "college" is used for a school at the level of an American senior high school or junior college, attended by persons in their teens. The attitudes of our respondents are reflected in Table VI-11.

It can be seen that most of the women in the cities, and a substantial number of those in the villages, would approve of their daughter attending a college for girls. What is more surprising is that most of the city women would also approve their daughters attending a coeducational school. The traditional idea of protecting girls by keeping them at home is held by only a few women interviewed, principally from Artas. The idea of protecting them by segregation at school (girls' colleges) seems to be held by the women of the two villages, and by the oldest women of the cities. Obviously the modern mothers place a high value on education, and their modesty code has been modified to accommodate the desire for educated daughters. As one city mother put it: "Can a doctor (i.e. an educated man) be happy with a wife who can't even read?"

In the villages, many mothers do not see education as a marriage asset. They would like their daughters to marry young rather than continue in school. In Artas, two girls in the sixth grade and one in the fifth were already engaged. Also, mothers of large families expect their older daughters to leave school to work at home. In Buarij there is no school which offers the elementary certificate, and the mothers are reluctant for their daughters to walk the 3 kilometers to school in nearby Mourayjat. Finally, some families are distrustful of male teachers. The observations of Williams in Haouch el Harimi, a few kilometers away, suggest that their wariness is at least sometimes justified (1968, pp. 52-53).

Employment Outside the Home

In the villages of the Levant, women have traditionally worked in the field as well as at home (Harris, 1958, p. 126; Fuller 1961, p. 73; Granqvist, 1931, p. 20; Williams, 1968, p. 63). In the cities, women were more secluded and if their household tasks were supplemented at all it was usually by such handicrafts (e.g. embroidery) as could be done at home. Even as recently as the late thirties, very few women of Syria, Lebanon, or Jordan were employed in industry or commerce (Patai, 1969, pp. 131-133) and these often worked in a secluded or segregated room, or in the company of male relatives (Woodsmall, 1936, pp. 264 ff.). They were usually unmarried, and quit working when they married.

A change seems to have occurred some time after the thirties. A 1955 industrial census showed that 23 per cent of Beirut employees and 12 per cent of Tripoli employees were women—mostly unmarried women. (Gulick, 1967, pp. 111 and 144-145). A 1955 survey of Amman showed that a majority of women with at least primary education were in favor of women working (Hirabayashi & Ishaq, 1958, p. 39). A survey of Middle Eastern students made about the same time found that almost all students thought women should be allowed to work outside the home *before* marriage, and a majority (both of males and females) even favored such work *after* marriage (Najarian, 1959, p. 38).

The Syrian census of 1960 found that at that time nearly nine per cent of wage and salary earners were female. In Damascus the figure was 12.5 per cent. In 1961, according to the official census, 5.5 per cent of all Jordanian employees and 6.2 per cent of all employees in Amman were female. In both countries farming, usually for a relative, was one of the most commonly cited occupations of women. Others fairly often mentioned, in order of frequency in Syria, were: dressmaker or tailor, building cleaner or caretaker, teacher, spinner or weaver or knitter, nurse or midwife and housekeeper or maid. Contrast with Western employment patterns, which probably reflects reluctance for women to meet with male strangers in situations where supervision may be lax, is seen in the fact that in Syria less than seven per cent of all clerical workers (including stenographers, typists, cashiers, bookkeepers, etc.) and less than one per cent of all sales persons are female.

Even though there has been of late some increase in the number of women working, employment in nonagricultural activities is still much rarer than in the West or even in Latin America. Youssef compared

125

census data from the Middle East and Latin America and argued that the low participation of Arab women in nonagricultural labor was caused not only by high incidence of early marriage and high fertility, but also by the emphasis on honor which results in kinship institutions providing economic support for secluded women (1972, p. 152). Her discussion focused on the time period of the sixties and did not consider any changes which may be occurring in the Middle East.

Our interview data confirm the trend toward greater incidence of city women working outside the home, and greater approval of such employment. Table VI-12 shows a fairly consistent increase over time in the number of city wives who worked before marriage. Of the wives married in the sixties, about half of those from Amman and Damascus and a fourth of those from Beirut and Tripoli had worked full time before marriage. Of those married before 1930, only three (all from Tripoli) had worked full time before marriage. A similar time trend holds for employment *after* marriage, although the proportion of those working after marriage is in general smaller than the proportion working before marriage.

In the villages, full time employment outside the home was, and continues to be, a rarity for women. Their labor outside the home is restricted to work in the fields with their fathers and brothers or with their husbands.

There are no consistent class differences in frequency of employment in the cities. Apparently greater need counteracted the greater conservatism of the poor.[1] As might be expected, there were class differences in type of employment. The upper and middle class women most often engaged in teaching and clerical work, and lower class working women were usually maids or dressmakers. Some of the middle and of the lower class were nurses. There were a number of other types of employment listed, in almost all cases by upper or middle class women: tourist guide, airline hostess, saleswoman, journalist, social worker, interior decorator, research assistant, doctor, business owner, travel agent, lawyer, and others.

Women who had worked after marriage (either full time or part time) were asked their husbands' attitude toward such work. A large majority in every locality thought their husbands approved. In Beirut *all* working wives thought their husbands approved. These are presumably the modern husbands, who accept in principle and in fact the employment of their wives.

---

[1] In a study of Egyptian secondary school boys, Dodd (1968, p. 167) found that middle class boys endorsed the idea of a working wife more often than did lower class boys.

Women who had not worked after marriage, either full time or part time, were asked how they and their husbands felt about women working outside the home either before marriage or after marriage (assuming that the children could be cared for properly). Tables VI-13 and VI-14 show the frequency of approval. Except in Artas, and to a lesser degree Amman, only a minority of the wives oppose all employment for women, before and after marriage. There is not much difference between younger and older wives on this issue. There is some tendency for the upper class women to be less disapproving and for the lower class women to be more disapproving.

The husbands, on the other hand, are described as generally opposed to woman's employment outside the home. In the opinion of these women who do not work, it is husbands more often than wives who disapprove of women working. Only in Beirut are a majority of husbands seen as approving. Again there is little time trend, but it must be kept in mind that Tables VI-13 and VI-14 exclude women who have worked after marriage, and thereby exclude many younger husbands and wives with a modern viewpoint on this question.

To summarize, there is an increasing tendency for women to be employed outside the home, especially before marriage, and for husbands of women so employed to favor the idea, at least conditionally. The majority of women interviewed, however, had never worked outside the home. If we exclude Artas, we can say that most of these "non-working" women felt it would be all right for women to work, particularly before marriage, but that more than half of them believed their husbands were opposed.

Recreation

One observer, speaking of the life of Muslim women of Lebanon and Syria in the early twentieth century, said that seclusion "so cuts women off from the outside world that a weekly excursion to sit in a cemetery closely veiled may be eagerly anticipated as a diversion and a relief" (Bliss, 1917, p. 280). On the other hand, Lane asserted that within the nineteenth century upper class harem, there was much pipe smoking, story telling and indulgence "in easy gaiety, and not infrequently in youthful frolic" (p. 194).

From several twentieth century studies of Muslim villages in the Levant, one gains the impression that there is much work to be done and little opportunity for recreation. Even when a girl has free time, she should

127

not be seen outside the house, or appear frivolous (Williams, 1968, p. 77). Exceptions are on special festivals. Some of these do indeed require a visit to the cemetery of one's male ancestors. Other occasions call for singing and dancing, and in some villages the sexes may be mixed, though chaperoned, at such events (Fuller, 1961, p. 86; Sweet, 1960, p. 195). In other places the males and females both dance, but out of sight of each other (Granqvist, 1950, p. 185, and 1935, p. 37).

Recreation, like other aspects of social life, is changing. In the modern city of Beirut young women of 1965, as compared with those of 1952, were found by one sociologist to "have more freedom to go out for recreation even alone but still more usually in groups" (Churchill, 1968, p. 50). In relatively conservative Tripoli, however, the only noticeable recreations of women seemed to be (in 1962) promenades with a group of female friends or relatives, attending the cinema, and exchanging visits *en famille* (Gulick, 1967, pp. 162 ff.).

We asked the women in our samples about cinema attendance, tobacco smoking, dancing, drinking alcoholic beverages, and swimming, for themselves and their children. Their replies revealed some areas of change and other areas of resistance to change in the recreational sphere.

CINEMA. The number of wives who before marriage went to the movies, either alone or with other women (i.e., without an agnate) is shown in Table VI-15. There is a definite and consistent time trend in each city. The later the time of marriage, the greater the likelihood that the wife had gone to the movies, unaccompanied by males of the family, before marriage. Even in Buarij, where there is no movie theater, a few younger wives had attended movies before marriage. Only in Artas, which also has no movie theater, and where travel and spending money for women are rarest, did none of the women report movie attendance. There is also the expected class trend, with the lower class women a little less likely than others to attend before marriage.

It is also common in the cities for married women at least occasionally to go to the movies without their husbands (Table VI-16). Obviously the modesty code no longer requires a respectable woman to remain at home, or to go out only if accompanied by her father, brother or husband.

At another point in the interview, after asking the mother about her own behavior, we asked her opinion about her own daughters attending movies. The majority had no objection, provided that the daughter be accompanied by a trustworthy person, such as an elder brother or other adult relative (Table VI-17). The exception was this time not Artas, but

Buarij. In Beirut, a majority of the wives said they would permit their daughters to go to the movies even if not chaperoned (Table VI-18). Elsewhere only a minority approved such freedom. Both age and social class were related to this kind of approval. More permissiveness was expressed by younger and upper class wives than by others.

Mothers in the cities were also asked about their sons attending movies, and more than 90 per cent approved without further qualification. The few who objected were older mothers who disapproved of the lax morals depicted in European and American films. The contrast between these replies and those relating to daughters is sharp.

SMOKING. The use of tobacco is quite widespread among the women of Beirut and Amman, a little less so among those of Damascus and Tripoli, but quite rare in Buarij and Artas (Table VI-19). Older wives in every locality say they smoke about as often as do younger wives. Smoking was less common among women of the lower class than among other women.

When we asked about smoking before marriage, we found that many who smoked after marriage had not done so before. This difference was particularly great among the older women (Table VI-20). This may mean that smoking has become more common in recent years among younger and older women alike, that smoking by unmarried girls was frowned upon in the old days and is now accepted, or that the older women were so young at marriage that they had not yet had a chance to cultivate the habit.

We also asked whether they approved of smoking by a son or a daughter. A majority in every place opposed smoking by sons as well as by daughters! Predictably, those wives that smoked were more permissive than those who did not, so that younger, upper class city wives were least disapproving. Also, mothers were a little more likely to accept smoking by a son than by a daughter. The son-daughter differences are so small, however, that we are led to think that smoking, under some circumstances at least, may not be closely tied in with the modesty code. Pipe smoking could, and did, occur in well-secluded harems of the past.

Unfortunately we did not ask about circumstances in which smoking was acceptable. Many mothers, we suspect, might object to smoking of daughters in public even though they accepted it in private. That is, public smoking might be related to modesty. Furthermore, smoking—like casual appearance and demeanor—may be considered as showing lack of respect for those in authority. In traditional homes a son may never smoke before his father, even though he is aware that his father knows him to be a regular smoker.

DANCING. There are traditional Middle Eastern dances which involve groups of men, or of women. There are traditional solo dances. Mixed dancing, whether waltz or rhumba or rock, is definitely a Western import. Involving, as it does, contact between the sexes in a mood of gaiety, mixed dancing is naturally something of a threat to the modesty code. We therefore attempted to determine the number of women who had done such dancing, and the number who approved of dancing by their own sons and daughters.

Few of our respondents said they had ever done any mixed dancing (Tables VI-22 and VI-23). Such dancing seems to have been limited to some of the younger city wives of the upper and middle class. The respondents also disapproved of the idea of one of their daughters going dancing without a chaperone. This disapproval was almost unanimous, except among the upper class women of Beirut (Table VI-24). Going to a chaperoned dancing party was also condemned by village mothers and lower class city mothers (Table VI-25). Such dancing was considered permissible by a majority of upper class mothers, not only in Beirut but in the other cities as well (cf. Muhyi, 1959, p. 53). Here again we find modern trends beginning in the Beirut upper class, followed by the upper class of other cities, and then spreading to the middle class. The future of the lower class and the villagers may be conjectured.

SWIMMING. Appearing at a public pool or beach in swimming costume is almost as far as one can get from the practice of veiling and seclusion. Consequently, changes in numbers of women who go swimming are of considerable significance. At the same time, swimming does depend on facilities, so one can hardly compare the women of a village where water is scarce with those who live in a town on the seacoast.

The women of the villages have never gone swimming, and they would not approve of their daughters appearing at a public beach, even if chaperoned (Tables VI-26, VI-27, and VI-28). Only a minority of the city women had ever gone swimming, and these were mostly younger women from the upper class. A somewhat larger group, however, would be willing for their daughters to appear at a public beach if she were chaperoned. Here too there is a strong class difference. There is also some tendency for the younger wives to be a little more often permissive. Very few mothers would permit their daughter to go to the beach unchaperoned. The upper class mothers of Beirut are the exception. A majority of them—young and old alike—would have no objection.

ALCOHOL. When asked about drinking, all of the village women and most

130

of the city women denied having drunk alcoholic beverages. Those who admitted having imbibed were usually upper class (Table VI-29). There was a slight tendency for younger mothers to admit drinking more often than did older mothers. Apparently this practice is only beginning to catch on in the Levant, and the innovators are as usual the younger upper class city mothers.

Decision Making

One anthropologist has pointed out that women may hold the real power within the family even though the men have the position of status and esteem (Friedl, 1967). Sociologists have also recognized the difficulties of assessing accurately the power structure within a family (e.g., Safilios-Rothschild, 1970). In an effort to get some insight into the interactions between husbands and wives, we asked the wife about how decisions were arrived at on a number of possible issues: choice of place of residence, naming a baby, marriage of children, whom to visit, how the wife dresses, etc. Most of the city wives spoke of cooperation between husband and wife on most of these issues. Some of the village women spoke of cooperation, but most of them said the husband made the decisions.

Responses to four of the questions are described in Tables VI-30 through VI-33. When the issue is choice of the place of residence, it is usually the husband who decides in the villages and in Tripoli. Among the younger women of Amman, Damascus and Beirut, wives say the decision is made jointly by them and their husbands. There is a class difference, with lower class wives claiming least often to participate in this decision and upper class wives claiming most often that they do so.

When queried about the final decision in the marriage of their children, a few wives said the final decision had been or would be theirs, but many more said they had cooperated with their husbands in making the decisions, or expected to do so. Both of these types of replies were classed as "involved in the final decision," and the proportion of such replies is shown in Table VI-31. In Amman and in Beirut most wives participate or expect to participate in decisions on the marriage of their children. In Damascus, Tripoli and Artas roughly half do so, and in Buarij about one-third do.

When the husband and wife decide to pay a social call, the decision is often made by the husband alone, if we are to judge from the statements of the wives as summarized in Table VI-32. Somewhat unexpectedly more of the women of Damascus and Buarij say they participate in such

131

decisions than do those of any of the other localities. Class differences were not consistent, but generally it was the upper class women who said more often than others that they influenced visiting decisions.

The question on who makes the final decision about how the wife dresses obviously has different meanings in Beirut and Artas. It could refer to miniskirts in one instance and the veil in another. Yet in either case it would relate to decision making in the home, and on a subject where women would assert both knowledge and interest. From Table VI-33 it is evident that most wives, even in Artas, make these decisions.

It is interesting to note that our data reveal little time trend. The older wives report about as large a role in the decision-making process as do the younger. It seems to us likely that younger wives have more authority, more ability to influence family decisions, than did young wives of fifty years ago. The older wives, however, have gained in authority with age (and perhaps with the senescence of the much older husbands), so that our data give no clear indication of changes over the decades.

Whether or not one feels that the statements of these women give an accurate picture of the interaction which goes on in these families, one must admit that the large majority of these city women do not describe themselves as helpless persons, or as chattel, but as persons with the power to decide, or to assist in deciding, issues which concern them and their families. Only in Artas would the women's statements suggest low status and little (declared) authority.

Other Aspects of Women's Role in the Villages

In a supplementary interview, a number of the village women were asked specific questions which related to traditional features of the Arab women's role as previously described by anthropologists (e.g., Antoun, 1968 a, pp. 671-697). Their replies are summarized in Table VI-34.

In Artas the women usually rise when their husbands enter a room and give him the place of honor in seating arrangements. If they appear outside the home with their husbands, they usually walk behind him and never touch him. They do not join husbands at dinner when male guests are present. A majority refrain from arguing with the husband, not because he is recognized as superior but because it is useless ("he won't listen") or because it might lead to blows, a second wife or even divorce. Most of the older wives and about a third of the younger ones call the husband by teknonym ("father of so-and-so") rather than by his first name. Most wives were not consulted about their own marriages. Their husbands were chosen for them. The older women had done the same for their own daughters. Of the mothers with young unmarried daughters, about three-fourths said they intended to consult daughters before arranging their marriages.

The general pattern in Buarij is a little less traditional than in Artas. Women do not rise for their husbands, nor do they usually assign him seating priority. They join the dinner when guests are present. They usually consult their daughters before arranging their marriage.

The younger wives are a little less traditional on almost all items than are the older ones. In some cases the difference is slight, in others it is large. The trend, however, is consistent and unmistakable.

The women were also asked about leaving the house to pay visits. Most of them said they attended family gatherings fairly often, and in Artas they usually specified gatherings of female relatives. More than a quarter of the women of Artas, but none from Buarij, said that they rarely went out. Some added that they were too tired or too busy to go out. In Buarij, 25 per cent of the younger women and 14 per cent of the older women said they would feel free to attend *any* social, business, political, or other gathering that their husband attended, unless it was forbidden because in the mosque or some such reason. Only two women in Artas claimed such liberty.

The village women are aware of social changes all around them, and consider the changes a mixed blessing. They approve of more education for the villagers, greater independence of women, and some even mention later age at marriage. At the same time they note with disapproval changes in morals, values, and customs. Many are concerned over the selfishness and disrespect shown by the younger generation. In Artas a good number dislike movies and modern dress. On one subject, however, there is general agreement: modern technology has eased the burden of existence.

The Changing Role of Arab Women

In the early twentieth century, women of the Arab Levant were generally segregated, and there was a broad pattern of avoidance between the sexes, especially among non-relatives. Women were expected to behave with modesty so that they would neither tempt men nor give the appearance of wanting to do so. The honor of men required them to enforce the code, compelling their daughters and sisters to adhere to it. Violation of the modesty code by a female brought dishonor to all her male relatives. Consequently, the role of Arab women was interwoven with considerations of modesty and honor.

In the Levant of today there is still much concern with questions of modesty and honor. The daily press, even in Beirut, carries regular reports of "crimes of honor" in which a girl is murdered by a father or a brother for "notorious" (i.e., immoral and widely-known) behavior. Yet the role of women has changed drastically since World War II. There has been a reassessment of what can be accepted as modest behavior. In 1925 an unmarried girl of the upper class in Beirut would have met serious objections from her father and brothers if she had gone out with her face and hair uncovered, but in 1955 her daughter could go (chaperoned) to a public beach and appear in a bikini with less critism.

Changes have occurred at different rates in different aspects of behavior. The veil is everywhere disappearing, even in conservative Tripoli. Regular prayers are becoming rarer, though observing the Fast of Ramadan remains nearly universal. More and more girls leave the home during the day to attend school, and in the cities mothers even approve of coeducation for teenagers.

Employment of city women is increasing, especially before marriage. Of those who had worked, a majority said their husbands approve of an unmarried girl working for pay outside the home. Of those women who had never worked, most approved of women's employment but thought their husbands did not approve.

In the area of recreation, change is most evident in cinema attendance without chaperone. Mixed dancing and swimming were rare among these mothers, but there was a growing trend in the cities to approve them for daughters if the acitivity were chaperoned. Use of alcohol was generally disapproved by young and old alike.

Women in the cities said they cooperated with their husbands in making decisions about family life, but women in the villages said their husbands made most of the decisions. Even in the villages, there was some hint of change in a wide variety of behavior, ranging from addressing the husband by his first name to sitting with the guests at dinner.

The changing role of women in the Arab Levant is unmistakable, as is the order in which changes occur. Beirut usually changes first, then the other cities, then Buarij and finally Artas. On most items, though by no means all, the upper class changes first and the lower class changes last.

The general trend is toward greater liberty for women, and this emancipation is generally desired by our respondents even though they are concerned by the loosening of moral restraints on youth.

TABLE VI-1

WOMEN WHO VEILED* BEFORE MARRIAGE

Year of Marriage Social Class		1960's				1950's				1940's				1930's				Before 1930			
		U	M	L	(T)	U	M	L	(T)	U	M	L	(T)	U	M	L	(T)	U	M	L	(T)
Artas	%				(19)				(15)				(43)				(48)				(52)
	N**				(42)				(65)				(44)				(25)				(31)
Buarij	%				(69)				(81)				(87)				(90)				(100)
	N				(16)				(21)				(15)				(10)				(8)
Amman	%	0	2	12	(5)	0	9	30	(15)	0	38	68	(45)	50	50	29	(44)	50	43	57	(50)
	N	17	61	51	(129)	9	55	30	(94)	8	21	22	(51)	6	12	7	(25)	2	7	7	(16)
Damascus	%	0	6	50	(11)	0	41	100	(42)	88	55	88	(65)	0	70	67	(67)	0	88	100	(86)
	N	3	48	6	(57)	4	56	3	(63)	8	33	8	(49)	1	23	3	(27)	1	17	4	(22)
Tripoli	%	30	50	67	(51)	45	80	92	(81)	80	100	97	(97)	100	100	100	(100)	100	100	100	(100)
	N	23	98	64	(185)	20	90	84	(194)	5	39	37	(81)	3	16	10	(29)	1	10	7	(18)
Beirut	%	0	0	6	(1)	0	7	43	(7)	0	17	80	(16)	5	44	–	(23)	62	100	–	(83)
	N	32	51	18	(101)	31	84	7	(122)	23	46	5	(74)	19	16	0	(35)	8	10	0	(18)

*In the cities the veil was a face veil; in the villages the veil covered the hair but could be drawn over part of the face.

**N is number of women replying.

TABLE VI–2

MARRIED WOMEN WHO VEIL

Year of Marriage		1960's				1950's				1940's				1930's				Before 1930			
Social Class		U	M	L	(T)	U	M	L	(T)	U	M	L	(T)	U	M	L	(T)	U	M	L	(T)
Artas	%				(18)				(17)				(43)				(40)				(52)
	N				(38)				(63)				(44)				(25)				(31)
Buarij	%				(75)				(86)				(87)				(90)				(89)
	N				(16)				(21)				(15)				(10)				(9)
Amman	%	0	2	10	(5)	0	13	40	(20)	0	43	77	(51)	100	75	29	(68)	100	100	86	(94)
	N	17	61	51	(129)	9	55	30	(94)	8	21	22	(51)	6	12	7	(25)	2	7	7	(16)
Damascus	%	0	9	67	(15)	0	24	75	(25)	38	25	88	(38)	0	26	100	(33)	0	59	100	(64)
	N	3	46	6	(55)	4	55	4	(63)	8	32	8	(48)	1	23	3	(27)	1	17	4	(22)
Tripoli	%	5	29	55	(36)	11	55	76	(60)	40	82	86	(81)	33	75	100	(79)	100	100	100	(100)
	N	19	95	64	(178)	19	83	84	(186)	5	39	37	(81)	3	16	10	(29)	1	9	7	(17)
Beirut	%	0	0	0	(0)	0	4	14	(4)	0	9	60	(10)	0	19	–	(10)	38	100	–	(72)
	N	29	43	18	(90)	25	81	7	(113)	18	44	5	(67)	15	16	0	(31)	8	10	0	(18)

TABLE VI–3

WOMEN WHO PRAYED REGULARLY BEFORE MARRIAGE

Year of Marriage Social Class		1960's				1950's				1940's				1930's				Before 1930			
		U	M	L	(T)	U	M	L	(T)	U	M	L	(T)	U	M	L	(T)	U	M	L	(T)
Artas	%				(24)				(18)				(75)				(68)				(90)
	N				(42)				(65)				(44)				(25)				(31)
Buarij	%				(0)				(0)				(0)				(10)				(25)
	N				(16)				(21)				(15)				(10)				(8)
Amman	%	0	5	16	(9)	0	18	30	(20)	13	52	64	(51)	83	75	100	(84)	50	100	100	(94)
	N	17	61	51	(129)	9	55	30	(94)	8	21	22	(51)	6	12	7	(25)	2	7	7	(16)
Damascus	%	0	56	50	(54)	75	70	100	(71)	63	76	88	(76)	100	65	67	(67)	100	71	100	(77)
	N	3	48	6	(57)	4	56	3	(63)	8	33	8	(49)	1	23	3	(27)	1	17	4	(22)
Tripoli	%	22	24	22	(23)	35	33	32	(33)	80	56	49	(54)	100	56	70	(66)	100	100	100	(100)
	N	23	98	64	(185)	20	90	84	(194)	5	39	37	(81)	3	16	10	(29)	1	10	7	(18)
Beirut	%	9	20	17	(16)	32	40	14	(37)	39	61	60	(54)	47	56	–	(51)	63	70	–	(67)
	N	32	51	18	(101)	31	84	7	(122)	23	46	5	(74)	19	16	0	(35)	8	10	0	(18)

TABLE VI-4

MARRIED WOMEN WHO PRAY REGULARLY

Year of Marriage Social Class		1960's U	1960's M	1960's L	1960's (T)	1950's U	1950's M	1950's L	1950's (T)	1940's U	1940's M	1940's L	1940's (T)	1930's U	1930's M	1930's L	1930's (T)	Before 1930 U	Before 1930 M	Before 1930 L	Before 1930 (T)
Artas	%				(24)				(21)				(75)				(60)				(90)
	N				(38)				(63)				(44)				(25)				(31)
Buarij	%				(0)				(14)				(40)				(40)				(44)
	N				(16)				(21)				(15)				(10)				(9)
Amman	%	0	5	16	(9)	0	16	33	(20)	13	48	64	(49)	67	83	100	(84)	100	86	100	(94)
	N	17	61	51	(129)	9	55	30	(94)	8	21	22	(51)	6	12	7	(25)	2	7	7	(16)
Damascus	%	0	46	33	(42)	75	65	75	(67)	50	72	88	(69)	100	78	100	(81)	100	100	100	(100)
	N	3	46	6	(55)	4	55	4	(63)	8	32	8	(48)	1	23	3	(27)	1	17	4	(22)
Tripoli	%	21	21	20	(21)	21	35	36	(34)	80	51	57	(56)	100	63	100	(79)	100	100	100	(100)
	N	19	95	64	(178)	19	83	84	(186)	5	39	37	(81)	3	16	10	(29)	1	9	7	(17)
Beirut	%	7	12	6	(9)	28	27	0	(26)	28	43	60	(40)	40	50	–	(45)	38	70	–	(56)
	N	29	43	18	(90)	25	81	7	(113)	18	44	5	(67)	15	16	0	(31)	8	10	0	(18)

TABLE VI-5

WOMEN WHO FASTED* before MARRIAGE

Year of Marriage Social Class		1960's				1950's				1940's				1930's				Before 1930			
		U	M	L	(T)	U	M	L	(T)	U	M	L	(T)	U	M	L	(T)	U	M	L	(T)
Artas	%				(98)				(97)				(100)				(92)				(100)
	N				(42)				(65)				(44)				(25)				(31)
Buarij	%				(100)				(100)				(100)				(100)				(100)
	N				(16)				(21)				(15)				(10)				(8)
Amman	%	53	74	94	(98)	67	80	100	(85)	88	90	95	(92)	100	92	100	(96)	100	100	100	(100)
	N	17	61	51	(79)	9	55	30	(94)	8	21	22	(51)	6	12	7	(25)	2	7	7	(16)
Damascus	%	100	98	100	(98)	100	96	100	(97)	88	97	100	(96)	100	100	100	(100)	100	100	100	(100)
	N	3	48	6	(57)	4	56	3	(63)	8	33	8	(49)	1	23	3	(27)	1	17	4	(22)
Tripoli	%	96	99	98	(98)	95	98	100	(98)	100	100	100	(100)	94	94	100	(97)	100	100	100	(100)
	N	23	98	64	(185)	20	90	84	(194)	5	39	37	(81)	3	16	10	(29)	1	10	7	(18)
Beirut	%	100	100	100	(100)	97	99	100	(98)	100	98	100	(99)	100	94	–	(97)	100	100	–	(100)
	N	32	51	18	(101)	31	84	7	(122)	23	46	5	(74)	19	16	0	(35)	8	10	0	(18)

*The Fast of Ramadan

TABLE VI-6

MARRIED WOMEN WHO FAST*

Year of Marriage / Social Class		1960's				1950's				1940's				1930's				Before 1930			
		U	M	L	(T)	U	M	L	(T)	U	M	L	(T)	U	M	L	(T)	U	M	L	(T)
Artas	%				(97)				(98)				(100)				(100)				(100)
	N				(38)				(63)				(44)				(25)				(31)
Buarij	%				(100)				(100)				(100)				(100)				(100)
	N				(16)				(21)				(15)				(10)				(9)
Amman	%	53	75	88	(78)	67	73	100	(81)	88	90	100	(94)	100	92	100	(96)	100	100	100	(100)
	N	17	61	51	(129)	9	55	30	(94)	8	21	22	(51)	6	12	7	(25)	2	7	7	(16)
Damascus	%	100	96	100	(96)	100	100	100	(100)	88	97	100	(96)	100	96	100	(96)	100	94	100	(95)
	N	3	46	6	(55)	4	55	4	(63)	8	32	8	(48)	1	23	3	(27)	1	17	4	(22)
Tripoli	%	100	98	98	(98)	95	98	99	(98)	100	100	100	(100)	100	100	100	(100)	100	100	100	(100)
	N	19	95	64	(178)	19	83	84	(186)	5	39	37	(81)	3	16	10	(29)	1	9	7	(17)
Beirut	%	100	100	100	(100)	96	100	100	(99)	100	98	100	(99)	100	100	–	(100)	100	100	–	(100)
	N	29	43	18	(90)	25	81	7	(113)	18	44	5	(67)	15	16	0	(31)	8	10	0	(18)

*The Fast of Ramadan

TABLE VI-7

Per Cent of Wives whose Mothers Completed at least Primary Schooling

Year of Marriage Social Class	1960's				1950's				1940's				1930's				Before 1930			
	U	M	L	(T)	U	M	L	(T)	U	M	L	(T)	U	M	L	(T)	U	M	L	(T)
Artas				(2)				(00)				(00)				(00)				(00)
Buarij				(00)				(00)				(00)				(00)				(00)
Amman	87	72	37	(60)	89	71	30	(60)	75	71	23	(51)	17	42	00	(24)	++	71	14	(44)
Damascus	++	43	00	(39)	80	30	++	(31)	50	36	00	(33)	++	9	++	(7)	++	6	++	(5)
Tripoli	46	8	00	(10)	30	4	00	(5)	20	00	00	(1)	++	00	00	(00)	++	00	00	(00)
Beirut	100	77	00	(72)	100	69	00	(73)	85	62	00	(65)	79	31	–	(86)	75	30	–	(50)

TABLE VI-8

Per Cent of Wives whose Fathers Completed at Least Primary Schooling

Year of Marriage	1960's				1950's				1940's				1930's				Before 1930			
Social Class	U	M	L	(T)	U	M	L	(T)	U	M	L	(T)	U	M	L	(T)	U	M	L	(T)
Artas				(2)				(3)				(2)				(4)				(00)
Buarij				(19)				(14)				(20)				(20)				(00)
Amman	100	89	71	(83)	100	85	53	(77)	87	86	59	(75)	50	67	14	(48)	++	100	57	(75)
Damascus	++	69	14	(63)	80	72	++	(70)	88	79	00	(67)	++	61	++	(52)	++	65	++	(50)
Tripoli	63	16	2	(17)	75	7	00	(11)	40	5	00	(5)	++	6	00	(7)	++	40	00	(22)
Beirut	100	80	00	(74)	100	79	00	(80)	100	79	00	(81)	89	31	–	(63)	87	50	–	(67)

TABLE VI-9

Per Cent of Husbands whose Mothers Completed at Least Primary Schooling

Year of Marriage / Social Class	1960's				1950's				1940's				1930's				Before 1930			
	U	M	L	(T)	U	M	L	(T)	U	M	L	(T)	U	M	L	(T)	U	M	L	(T)
Artas				(00)				(2)				(00)				(00)				(00)
Buarij				(00)				(5)				(00)				(00)				(00)
Amman	88	67	24	(50)	78	56	13	(45)	50	48	27	(39)	33	42	00	(28)	++	14	14	(19)
Damascus	++	13	00	(13)	20	10	++	(10)	25	16	00	(15)	++	00	++	(00)	++	6	++	(5)
Tripoli	21	5	00	(5)	25	1	0	(3)	00	00	00	(00)	++	00	00	(00)	++	00	00	(00)
Beirut	86	73	00	(66)	88	49	00	(56)	88	49	00	(41)	79	31	–	(57)	50	40	–	(44)

TABLE VI–10

Per Cent of Husbands whose Fathers Completed at Least Primary Schooling

Year of Marriage Social Class	1960's				1950's				1940's				1930's				Before 1930			
	U	M	L	(T)	U	M	L	(T)	U	M	L	(T)	U	M	L	(T)	U	M	L	(T)
Artas				(12)				(2)				(5)				(00)				(00)
Buarij				(31)				(24)				(40)				(30)				(00)
Amman	100	82	45	(70)	89	73	40	(64)	87	76	45	(65)	33	67	00	(40)	++	71	43	(56)
Damascus	++	66	00	(60)	60	54	++	(52)	100	72	00	(64)	++	64	++	(58)	++	53	++	(41)
Tripoli	54	12	00	(13)	55	6	1	(9)	40	00	00	(2)	++	6	10	(10)	++	40	00	(28)
Beirut	97	70	00	(67)	100	71	00	(74)	96	72	00	(76)	95	37	–	(69)	88	70	–	(78)

TABLE VI–11

Wives who Approve Daughters Attending College

Year of Marriage / Social Class	1960's U	M	L	(T)	1950's U	M	L	(T)	1940's U	M	L	(T)	1930's U	M	L	(T)	Before 1930 U	M	L	(T)
Artas %W				(43)				(14)				(14)				(12)				(10)
%C				(0)				(0)				(0)				(0)				(0)
N				(42)				(65)				(44)				(24)				(31)
Buarij %W				(79)				(53)				(77)				(67)				(33)
%C				(29)				(20)				(15)				(22)				(0)
N				(14)				(20)				(13)				(9)				(9)
Amman %W	100	97	88	(94)	100	95	80	(92)	100	100	91	(98)	100	83	86	(88)	100	86	86	(87)
%C	100	89	76	(85)	78	89	40	(71)	100	86	59	(78)	83	83	43	(72)	100	43	29	(44)
N	17	61	51	(129)	9	55	30	(94)	8	21	22	(51)	6	12	7	(25)	2	7	7	(16)
Damascus %W	67	91	100	(91)	100	83	75	(84)	75	88	25	(75)	100	96	100	(96)	100	93	75	(90)
%C	100	98	86	(97)	100	92	50	(90)	100	91	50	(76)	100	87	0	(82)	100	60	50	(60)
N	3	56	7	(66)	5	60	4	(69)	8	33	8	(49)	1	23	3	(27)	1	15	4	(20)
Tripoli %W	96	95	91	(94)	95	97	93	(95)	80	85	84	(84)	100	88	60	(79)	0	70	43	(56)
%C	100	93	87	(92)	100	96	87	(92)	80	85	81	(83)	100	75	60	(72)	0	60	57	(50)
N	24	101	64	(189)	20	90	85	(195)	5	40	37	(82)	3	16	10	(29)	1	10	7	(18)
Beirut %W	86	100	100	(96)	97	97	100	(97)	96	98	100	(97)	95	94	—	(94)	100	100	—	(100)
%C	100	97	100	(98)	97	88	100	(91)	88	87	100	(88)	95	75	—	(86)	87	80	—	(83)
N	36	60	18	(114)	34	90	7	(131)	26	47	5	(78)	19	16	0	(31)	8	10	0	(18)

N is number of women replying to the question

% W is percent of those replying who would approve or strongly approve daughters attending a women's college

% C is percent of those replying who would approve or strongly approve daughters attending a coeducational college

TABLE VI-12

RESPONDENTS WHO WORKED FULL-TIME OUTSIDE THE HOME

Year of Marriage		1960's				1950's				1940's				1930's				Before 1930			
Social Class		U	M	L	(T)	U	M	L	(T)	U	M	L	(T)	U	M	L	(T)	U	M	L	(T)
Artas	% B				(0)				(0)				(2)				(9)				(0)
	% A				(0)				(0)				(0)				(2)				(0)
	N				(42)				(64)				(44)				(25)				(31)
Buarij	% B				(19)				(0)				(0)				(0)				(11)
	% A				(6)				(0)				(0)				(0)				(0)
	N				(16)				(21)				(15)				(10)				(9)
Amman	% B	53	57	33	(47)	33	38	7	(28)	50	14	23	(24)	0	8	14	(8)	0	0	0	(0)
	% A	29	43	20	(32)	0	18	0	(11)	0	10	5	(6)	0	0	14	(4)	0	0	0	(0)
	N	17	61	51	(129)	9	55	30	(94)	8	21	22	(51)	6	12	7	(25)	2	7	7	(16)
Damascus	% B	33	46	57	(47)	20	15	25	(16)	50	12	25	(20)	100	14	0	(15)	0	0	0	(0)
	% A	33	45	57	(46)	40	32	25	(32)	12	24	50	(32)	0	14	0	(12)	0	0	25	(5)
	N	3	56	7	(66)	5	60	4	(69)	8	33	8	(49)	1	22	3	(26)	1	17	4	(22)
Tripoli	% B	29	30	12	(24)	15	22	19	(20)	20	7	14	(11)	0	6	20	(10)	0	10	29	(17)
	% A	17	26	6	(18)	20	20	9	(15)	0	20	14	(16)	0	12	10	(10)	0	20	29	(22)
	N	24	101	64	(189)	20	90	84	(194)	5	40	37	(82)	3	16	10	(29)	1	10	7	(18)
Beirut	% B	14	30	39	(26)	6	9	29	(9)	0	9	40	(8)	0	12	—	(6)	0	0	—	(0)
	% A	3	25	17	(16)	3	8	14	(7)	0	6	40	(6)	0	6	—	(3)	0	0	—	(0)
	N	36	60	18	(114)	34	90	7	(131)	26	47	5	(78)	19	16	0	(35)	8	10	0	(18)

N is number of wives replying to this question

% B is percent of wives responding who had worked full-time outside the home before marriage

% A is percent of wives responding who had worked full-time outside the home after marriage

TABLE VI–13

NON-WORKING WIVES WHO DISAPPROVE OF WOMEN WORKING OUTSIDE THE HOME

Year of Marriage		1960's				1950's				1940's				1930's				Before 1930			
Social Class		U	M	L	(T)	U	M	L	(T)	U	M	L	(T)	U	M	L	(T)	U	M	L	(T)
Artas	%				(95)				(95)				(86)				(83)				(93)
	N				(42)				(65)				(42)				(23)				(30)
Buarij	%				(0)				(11)				(0)				(10)				(0)
	N				(15)				(19)				(14)				(10)				(8)
Amman	%	33	43	60	(49)	78	51	73	(62)	50	45	68	(55)	50	42	50	(46)	100	57	43	(56)
	N	15	37	42	(94)	9	45	30	(84)	8	20	19	(47)	6	12	6	(24)	2	7	7	(16)
Damascus	%	0	7	0	(6)	0	19	67	(20)	00	15	75	(19)	0	6	33	(9)	0	29	33	(29)
	N	2	30	3	(35)	3	43	3	(49)	7	26	4	(37)	1	18	3	(22)	1	17	3	(21)
Tripoli	%	18	22	36	(27)	33	15	31	(24)	25	22	21	(22)	0	31	38	(29)	100	62	60	(64)
	N	17	64	53	(134)	15	66	67	(148)	4	32	29	(65)	3	13	8	(24)	1	8	5	(14)
Beirut	%	0	16	60	(15)	6	14	80	(15)	8	18	33	(15)	21	40	–	(29)	12	30	–	(22)
	N	33	44	10	(87)	31	83	5	(119)	26	44	3	(73)	19	15	0	(34)	8	10	0	(18)

% – per cent of these wives who disapprove of women working outside the home, either before or after marriage.
N – number of wives, none of whom had worked (full-time or part-time) outside the home after marriage, who replied.

TABLE VI-14

Non-Working Wives who Say their Husbands Disapprove of Women Working outside the Home

Year of Marriage →		1960's				1950's				1940's				1930's				Before 1930			
Social Class		U	M	L	(T)	U	M	L	(T)	U	M	L	(T)	U	M	L	(T)	U	M	L	(T)
Artas	%				(95)				(97)				(97)				(100)				(97)
	N				(42)				(64)				(64)				(23)				(30)
Buarij	%				(73)				(55)				(36)				(60)				(38)
	N				(15)				(20)				(14)				(10)				(8)
Amman	%	71	73	90	(81)	78	71	80	(75)	88	60	100	(81)	100	83	100	(92)	100	100	71	(87)
	N	14	37	42	(93)	9	45	30	(84)	8	20	19	(47)	6	12	6	(24)	2	7	7	(16)
Damascus	%	0	63	100	(62)	67	80	100	(81)	43	65	75	(62)	100	44	67	(50)	0	88	100	(85)
	N	2	30	2	(34)	3	41	3	(47)	7	26	4	(41)	1	18	3	(22)	1	17	2	(20)
Tripoli	%	59	53	74	(62)	67	59	69	(64)	75	68	62	(66)	100	67	71	(73)	100	62	80	(71)
	N	17	62	54	(133)	15	66	67	(148)	4	31	29	(64)	3	12	7	(22)	1	8	5	(14)
Beirut	%	15	45	60	(36)	16	49	100	(43)	12	48	67	(36)	39	73	–	(55)	25	60	–	(44)
	N	33	44	10	(87)	31	83	5	(119)	26	44	3	(73)	18	15	0	(33)	8	10	0	(18)

% – per cent of these wives who said their husbands disapprove of women working outside the home, either before or after marriage.

N – number of wives, none of whom had worked (full-time or part-time) outside the home after marriage, who replied.

TABLE VI-15

Wives who Went to Cinema alone or with Other Women before Marriage

Year of Marriage	1960's				1950's				1940's				1930's				Before 1930			
Social Class	U	M	L	(T)	U	M	L	(T)	U	M	L	(T)	U	M	L	(T)	U	M	L	(T)
Artas				(00)				(00)				(00)				(00)				(00)
Buarij				(6)				(6)				(00)				(00)				(00)
Amman	100	97	75	(88)	89	87	53	(77)	87	33	14	(33)	50	17	29	(28)	++	00	00	(00)
Damascus	++	82	43	(79)	100	67	++	(67)	87	58	25	(57)	++	00	++	(4)	++	18	++	(14)
Tripoli	87	84	72	(80)	95	77	68	(75)	100	62	70	(68)	++	37	60	(52)	++	10	14	(11)
Beirut	100	88	100	(94)	94	82	57	(84)	88	72	40	(76)	68	87	–	(77)	62	20	–	(39)

TABLE VI-16

Per Cent of Wives who Went to Cinema Alone or with Other Women after Marriage

Year of Marriage	1960's				1950's				1940's				1930's				Before 1930			
Social Class	U	M	L	(T)	U	M	L	(T)	U	M	L	(T)	U	M	L	(T)	U	M	L	(T)
Artas				(00)				(00)				(00)				(00)				(00)
Buarij				(6)				(00)				(00)				(00)				(00)
Amman	94	100	82	(92)	100	100	93	(98)	100	100	45	(76)	100	100	71	(92)	++	14	14	(12)
Damascus	++	41	14	(39)	80	46	++	(46)	62	42	37	(45)	++	74	++	(70)	++	12	++	(9)
Tripoli	83	81	64	(75)	95	67	60	(67)	100	52	68	(62)	++	56	50	(59)	++	40	14	(33)
Beirut	100	93	100	(96)	100	94	86	(95)	100	91	80	(94)	100	100	–	(100)	100	80	–	(89)

TABLE VI–17

Per Cent of Wives who Approve of Daughters Going to Cinema Chaperoned

Year of Marriage	1960's				1950's				1940's				1930's				Before 1930			
Social Class	U	M	L	(T)	U	M	L	(T)	U	M	L	(T)	U	M	L	(T)	U	M	L	(T)
Artas				(90)				(75)				(73)				(64)				(29)
Buarij				(40)				(00)				(8)				(20)				(00)
Amman	100	98	96	(98)	100	98	97	(98)	100	100	95	(98)	100	100	100	(100)	++	86	100	(94)
Damascus	++	100	71	(97)	100	83	++	(80)	100	91	37	(84)	++	96	++	(96)	++	60	++	(55)
Tripoli	100	89	69	(84)	100	77	62	(73)	100	50	51	(54)	++	37	40	(45)	++	30	29	(33)
Beirut	100	100	100	(100)	100	98	71	(97)	100	96	100	(97)	100	100	–	(100)	100	90	–	(94)

TABLE VI-18

Per Cent of Wives who Approve of Daughters Going to Cinema Unchaperoned

Year of Marriage	1960's				1950's				1940's				1930's				Before 1930			
Social Class	U	M	L	(T)	U	M	L	(T)	U	M	L	(T)	U	M	L	(T)	U	M	L	(T)
Artas				(2)				(00)				(2)				(00)				(00)
Buarij				(20)				(00)				(00)				(00)				(00)
Amman	24	2	00	(4)	00	2	00	(1)	25	00	00	(4)	00	00	00	(00)	++	00	00	(00)
Damascus	++	25	00	(25)	40	17	++	(17)	37	18	00	(18)	++	9	++	(7)	++	7	++	(5)
Tripoli	50	32	9	(26)	50	13	1	(12)	20	2	3	(4)	++	00	20	(10)	++	00	00	(00)
Beirut	100	67	11	(68)	88	61	00	(65)	92	51	00	(62)	79	44	–	(63)	87	20	–	(50)

TABLE VI-19

PER CENT OF WIVES WHO SMOKED AFTER MARRIAGE

Year of Marriage	1960's				1950's				1940's				1930's				Before 1930			
Social Class	U	M	L	(T)	U	M	L	(T)	U	M	L	(T)	U	M	L	(T)	U	M	L	(T)
Artas				(00)				(00)				(00)				(00)				(3)
Buarij				(6)				(6)				(15)				(10)				(11)
Amman	82	67	33	(56)	89	82	33	(67)	100	86	55	(75)	83	92	71	(84)	++	71	57	(69)
Damascus	++	39	29	(39)	40	33	++	(33)	37	36	25	(35)	++	17	++	(22)	++	24	++	(27)
Tripoli	71	41	30	(41)	65	56	22	(42)	80	42	43	(45)	++	44	30	(45)	++	70	00	(44)
Beirut	78	78	28	(70)	91	77	29	(78)	100	81	100	(88)	84	69	–	(77)	87	60	–	(72)

TABLE VI–20

PER CENT OF WIVES WHO SMOKED BEFORE MARRIAGE

Year of Marriage / Social Class	1960's				1950's				1940's				1930's				Before 1930			
	U	M	L	(T)	U	M	L	(T)	U	M	L	(T)	U	M	L	(T)	U	M	L	(T)
Artas				(00)				(00)				(00)				(00)				(00)
Buarij				(6)				(6)				(00)				(00)				(00)
Amman	82	59	25	(49)	56	49	20	(40)	50	14	9	(18)	17	33	14	(24)	++	00	00	(00)
Damascus	++	30	00	(27)	20	13	++	(14)	00	6	12	(6)	++	00	++	(00)	++	6	++	(5)
Tripoli	42	17	8	(17)	30	18	8	(15)	20	12	16	(15)	++	6	20	(10)	++	20	14	(17)
Beirut	61	62	17	(54)	50	29	14	(34)	31	00	40	(23)	00	12	–	(6)	00	10	–	(6)

TABLE VI-21

PER CENT OF WIVES WHO APPROVE OF A DAUGHTER SMOKING

Year of Marriage	1960's				1950's				1940's				1930's				Before 1930			
Social Class	U	M	L	(T)	U	M	L	(T)	U	M	L	(T)	U	M	L	(T)	U	M	L	(T)
Artas				(00)				(00)				(2)				(00)				(3)
Buarij				(00)				(00)				(00)				(00)				(00)
Amman	47	30	12	(25)	11	24	3	(16)	00	24	5	(12)	00	00	00	(00)	++	00	00	(00)
Damascus	++	43	14	(42)	40	20	++	(20)	37	24	00	(22)	++	13	++	(15)	++	18	++	(18)
Tripoli	58	42	11	(33)	50	14	5	(14)	20	2	00	(2)	++	6	20	(21)	++	20	29	(28)
Beirut	72	47	6	(48)	47	29	00	(32)	65	17	00	(32)	42	19	–	(31)	62	10	–	(33)

TABLE VI-22

Per Cent of Wives who Engaged in Mixed Dancing before Marriage

Year of Marriage	1960's				1950's				1940's				1930's				Before 1930			
Social Class	U	M	L	(T)	U	M	L	(T)	U	M	L	(T)	U	M	L	(T)	U	M	L	(T)
Artas				(00)				(00)				(00)				(00)				(00)
Buarij				(00)				(00)				(00)				(00)				(00)
Amman	65	13	2	(15)	22	13	00	(10)	00	00	00	(00)	00	00	00	(00)	++	00	00	(00)
Damascus	++	25	00	(24)	80	10	++	(14)	12	3	00	(4)	++	00	++	(00)	++	00	++	(00)
Tripoli	21	9	00	(7)	40	3	00	(6)	00	00	00	(00)	++	00	00	(00)	++	00	00	(00)
Beirut	78	45	00	(48)	71	19	00	(31)	46	13	00	(23)	26	6	–	(17)	12	00	–	(6)

TABLE VI–23

PER CENT OF WIVES WHO ENGAGED IN MIXED DANCING AFTER MARRIAGE

Year of Marriage	1960's				1950's				1940's				1930's				Before 1930			
Social Class	U	M	L	(T)	U	M	L	(T)	U	M	L	(T)	U	M	L	(T)	U	M	L	(T)
Artas				(00)				(00)				(00)				(00)				(00)
Buarij				(00)				(00)				(00)				(00)				(00)
Amman	29	8	2	(9)	33	16	00	(13)	12	00	00	(2)	00	8	00	(00)	++	00	00	(00)
Damascus	++	32	00	(30)	60	25	++	(25)	50	9	00	(14)	++	4	++	(4)	++	00	++	(00)
Tripoli	67	17	00	(17)	60	8	00	(10)	00	00	00	(00)	++	00	00	(00)	++	00	00	(00)
Beirut	97	62	00	(63)	91	39	00	(50)	73	36	00	(46)	37	19	–	(29)	12	10	–	(11)

TABLE VI-24

PER CENT OF WIVES WHO APPROVE OF DAUGHTERS GOING TO DANCING PARTIES UNCHAPERONED

Year of Marriage	1960's				1950's				1940's				1930's				Before 1930			
Social Class	U	M	L	(T)	U	M	L	(T)	U	M	L	(T)	U	M	L	(T)	U	M	L	(T)
Artas				(00)				(00)				(00)				(00)				(00)
Buarij				(00)				(00)				(00)				(00)				(00)
Amman	++	6	00	(1)	00	00	00	(00)	00	00	00	(00)	00	00	00	(00)	++	00	00	(00)
Damascus	++	11	00	(11)	00	7	++	(6)	12	6	00	(6)	++	00	++	(00)	++	00	++	(00)
Tripoli	12	8	3	(7)	15	1	00	(2)	00	00	00	(00)	++	00	00	(00)	++	00	00	(00)
Beirut	58	25	00	(32)	29	23	00	(24)	62	17	00	(31)	21	6	–	(14)	37	10	–	(22)

TABLE VI-25

PER CENT OF WIVES WHO APPROVE OF DAUGHTERS GOING TO DANCING PARTIES CHAPERONED

Year of Marriage	1960's				1950's				1940's				1930's				Before 1930			
Social Class	U	M	L	(T)	U	M	L	(T)	U	M	L	(T)	U	M	L	(T)	U	M	L	(T)
Artas				(00)				(00)				(00)				(00)				(00)
Buarij				(6)				(5)				(00)				(00)				(00)
Amman	88	46	18	(41)	22	36	13	(29)	62	14	5	(7)	17	17	14	(4)	++	00	00	(00)
Damascus	++	62	29	(61)	80	41	++	(43)	87	33	00	(47)	++	39	++	(37)	++	00	++	(5)
Tripoli	83	33	6	(30)	60	16	00	(13)	20	2	3	(4)	++	6	00	(10)	++	00	00	(00)
Beirut	100	75	00	(71)	88	59	00	(63)	92	49	00	(60)	79	19	–	(51)	75	20	–	(44)

TABLE VI-26

Per Cent of Wives who Approve of Daughters Swimming at a Public Beach Chaperoned

Year of Marriage Social Class	1960's				1950's				1940's				1930's				Before 1930			
	U	M	L	(T)	U	M	L	(T)	U	M	L	(T)	U	M	L	(T)	U	M	L	(T)
Artas				(00)				(2)				(3)				(00)				(00)
Buarij				(00)				(00)				(00)				(00)				(00)
Amman	76	51	12	(39)	44	36	20	(33)	50	10	5	(18)	17	17	14	(16)	++	00	00	(12)
Damascus	++	66	14	(62)	100	49	++	(50)	75	33	00	(35)	++	30	++	(30)	++	00	++	(5)
Tripoli	79	33	10	(31)	85	20	00	(18)	20	00	00	(1)	++	00	00	(7)	++	00	00	(00)
Beirut	97	73	00	(69)	97	51	00	(60)	96	45	00	(59)	84	62	–	(74)	75	10	–	(39)

TABLE VI-27

PER CENT OF WIVES WHO HAD GONE SWIMMING BEFORE MARRIAGE

Year of Marriage	1960's				1950's				1940's				1930's				Before 1930			
Social Class	U	M	L	(T)	U	M	L	(T)	U	M	L	(T)	U	M	L	(T)	U	M	L	(T)
Artas				(00)				(00)				(00)				(00)				(00)
Buarij				(00)				(00)				(00)				(00)				(00)
Amman	35	3	2	(7)	11	4	00	(3)	00	00	00	(00)	00	00	00	(00)	++	00	00	(00)
Damascus	++	14	00	(15)	60	8	++	(13)	00	00	00	(00)	++	57	++	(48)	++	00	++	(00)
Tripoli	29	4	3	(7)	30	2	1	(5)	00	00	00	(00)	++	00	00	(00)	++	00	00	(00)
Beirut	92	47	00	(54)	82	18	00	(34)	73	9	00	(29)	26	6	–	(17)	25	10	–	(17)

TABLE VI–28

PER CENT OF WIVES WHO HAD GONE SWIMMING AFTER MARRIAGE

Year of Marriage Social Class	1960's				1950's				1940's				1930's				Before 1930			
	U	M	L	(T)	U	M	L	(T)	U	M	L	(T)	U	M	L	(T)	U	M	L	(T)
Artas				(00)				(00)				(00)				(00)				(00)
Buarij				(00)				(00)				(00)				(00)				(00)
Amman	12	00	00	(2)	00	00	00	(00)	00	00	00	(00)	00	00	14	(4)	++	00	00	(00)
Damascus	++	18	00	(18)	60	11	++	(14)	62	6	00	(14)	++	4	++	(4)	++	00	++	(00)
Tripoli	54	12	5	(15)	55	8	00	(9)	00	00	00	(00)	++	00	00	(00)	++	00	00	(00)
Beirut	92	50	00	(55)	91	24	00	(40)	69	15	00	(32)	00	12	–	(23)	25	00	–	(11)

TABLE VI–29

Per Cent of Wives who Drank Alcohol after Marriage

Year of Marriage Social Class	1960's				1950's				1940's				1930's				Before 1930			
	U	M	L	(T)	U	M	L	(T)	U	M	L	(T)	U	M	L	(T)	U	M	L	(T)
Artas				(00)				(00)				(00)				(00)				(00)
Buarij				(00)				(00)				(00)				(00)				(00)
Amman	35	5	2	(8)	78	24	3	(22)	75	14	00	(18)	17	25	14	(20)	++	00	00	(00)
Damascus	++	14	00	(12)	40	10	++	(11)	12	12	00	(10)	++	4	++	(4)	++	00	++	(00)
Tripoli	41	10	00	(9)	25	6	00	(5)	00	00	00	(00)	++	00	00	(00)	++	00	00	(00)
Beirut	44	25	00	(27)	59	17	00	(27)	73	23	00	(38)	37	00	–	(20)	25	10	–	(17)

TABLE VI–30

Per Cent of Wives who Cooperate with their Husbands on the Final Decision on Place of Residence

Year of Marriage	1960's				1950's				1940's				1930's				Before 1930			
Social Class	U	M	L	(T)	U	M	L	(T)	U	M	L	(T)	U	M	L	(T)	U	M	L	(T)
Artas				(21)				(18)				(23)				(29)				(6)
Buarij				(19)				(15)				(57)				(30)				(22)
Amman	71	57	43	(53)	67	64	43	(59)	62	67	41	(56)	33	33	59	(32)	++	29	43	(31)
Damascus	++	55	71	(58)	80	62	++	(61)	37	48	25	(43)	++	48	++	(50)	++	35	++	(32)
Tripoli	67	40	16	(35)	55	22	18	(24)	60	25	16	(23)	++	31	20	(34)	++	40	14	(28)
Beirut	72	58	17	(56)	65	38	00	(50)	62	30	00	(38)	53	47	–	(50)	50	00	–	(22)

TABLE VI-31

PER CENT OF WIVES WHO ARE INVOLVED IN THE FINAL DECISION ON THEIR CHILDREN'S MARRIAGES

Year of Marriage / Social Class	1960's				1950's				1940's				1930's				Before 1930			
	U	M	L	(T)	U	M	L	(T)	U	M	L	(T)	U	M	L	(T)	U	M	L	(T)
Artas				(47)				(58)				(48)				(76)				(58)
Buarij				(31)				(37)				(33)				(30)				(33)
Amman	100	100	98	(99)	89	100	93	(99)	87	100	100	(99)	83	91	85	(88)	++	86	100	(87)
Damascus	++	64	+-	(60)	+-	50	++	(43)	+-	58	33	(55)	++	75	++	(70)	++	43	++	(53)
Tripoli	52	31	47	(39)	50	56	44	(49)	80	51	57	(56)	++	73	50	(68)	++	49	57	(53)
Beirut	+-	100	72	(86)	+-	75	29	(61)	100	93	40	(85)	100	93	–	(97)	100	100	–	(100)

TABLE VI–32

PER CENT OF WIVES WHO COOPERATE WITH THEIR HUSBANDS ON THE FINAL DECISION ON WHOM TO VISIT

Year of Marriage	1960's				1950's				1940's				1930's				Before 1930			
Social Class	U	M	L	(T)	U	M	L	(T)	U	M	L	(T)	U	M	L	(T)	U	M	L	(T)
Artas				(19)				(9)				(27)				(24)				(10)
Buarij				(60)				(53)				(53)				(60)				(33)
Amman	29	28	24	(27)	44	18	10	(19)	12	33	18	(24)	17	17	14	(16)	++	00	00	(00)
Damascus	++	64	43	(61)	80	64	++	(61)	62	52	71	(56)	++	35	++	(30)	++	31	++	(29)
Tripoli	17	3	2	(4)	00	4	00	(2)	00	00	00	(00)	++	6	00	(3)	++	00	14	(6)
Beirut	72	48	00	(48)	50	28	00	(32)	54	23	00	(32)	63	19	–	(43)	62	70	–	(67)

TABLE VI–33

PER CENT OF WIVES WHO REPORT HUSBANDS MAKE THE FINAL DECISION ON HOW THE WIFE DRESSES

Year of Marriage	1960's				1950's				1940's				1930's				Before 1930			
Social Class	U	M	L	(T)	U	M	L	(T)	U	M	L	(T)	U	M	L	(T)	U	M	L	(T)
Artas				(38)				(45)				(39)				(60)				(58)
Buarij				(6)				(20)				(20)				(30)				(22)
Amman	00	8	12	(7)	00	9	13	(10)	12	5	9	(8)	17	8	00	(8)	++	14	43	(25)
Damascus	++	14	29	(15)	00	13	++	(14)	12	9	25	(12)	++	00	++	(7)	++	12	++	(14)
Tripoli	12	23	23	(22)	10	17	21	(18)	00	7	8	(7)	++	19	20	(17)	++	00	00	(00)
Beirut	00	2	00	(1)	3	1	00	(2)	00	00	00	(00)	00	00	–	(00)	00	00	–	(00)

TABLE VI–34

Aspect of the Role and Status of Women in Two Villages

Village	Buarij		Artas	
Year of Marriage	After 1940	Before 1940	After 1940	Before 1940
Number of Respondents	(N=16)	(N=14)	(N=54)	(N=17)
Wife was consulted regarding the arranging of her own marriage	–	–	33%	24%
Wife consulted with her daughter on the arranging of the daughter's marriage	75%	71%	*	27%
Wife addresses her husband by his first name rather than title or teknonym	81%	14%	59%	24%
Wife does not feel free to argue with her husband	–	–	45%	58%
Wife never walks in public with her husband	50%	93%	15%	18%
Wife walks with husband in public, but walks behind him	6%	7%	46%	70%
Physical contact between husband and wife in public is permissible within limits	6%	0%	0%	0%
Husband and wife dine together when there are no guests	94%	93%	93%	82%
When there are guests, wife joins them at dinner	56%	29%	9%	0%
Husband has seating priority at home or when visiting	12%	43%	48%	71%
Wife usually rises or stands when husband comes in	6%	14%	50%	65%

*46 of the 54 mothers had no married daughters.

169

CHAPTER SEVEN

Divorce and Polygyny

Prophet and believers, if you divorce your wives, divorce them at the end of their waiting period . . . . When their waiting period is ended, either keep them with kindness or part with them honorably.

SURA 65

Divorce may be pronounced twice, and then a woman must be retained in honor or allowed to go with kindness....If a man (finally) divorces his wife, he cannot remarry her until she has wedded another man and been divorced by him.

SURA 2

I T IS EVIDENT from references in the Quran that divorce was common in pre-Islamic times, and was available to the husband upon the pronouncement of a formula of dismissal and payment of a fee to the wife's father or guardian. The Quran emphasized fairness and kindness in divorce proceedings, and spelled out procedures which would insure such, but did not condemn divorce *per se*. There is, however, a widely quoted saying attributed to the Prophet, that of all permitted acts, divorce is most hateful in the sight of Allah.

A person unacquainted with Middle Eastern culture but aware of the tensions which the nuclear family may generate when husband and wife scarcely know each other before marriage, might assume that the divorce rate in Islamic societies is quite high. Indeed, this seems to have been true in that portion of nineteenth century Egyptian society known to Lane:

> ". . . there are certainly not many persons in Cairo who have not divorced one wife, if they have been long married." (p. 185) and "There are many men in this country who, in the course of ten years, have married as many as twenty, thirty, or more wives; and women not far advanced in age who have been wives to a dozen or more men successively " (p. 188).

The divorce rate has continued high in Egypt down to the present,

171

though not so high as Lane implies, and Egyptian statistics are sometimes cited as proof that divorce is frequent throughout the Middle East (e.g., Beck, 1957). Other Middle Eastern scholars of the twentieth century, however, have emphasized factors in Islamic society which militate against divorce. Marriage does not involve only man and wife, but a whole network of family relationships. If a man repudiates his wife, then he may find that his own sister is likewise repudiated, or that other family pressures are brought to bear on him. In many cases the late *mahr* payment required is a serious deterrent, especially in view of the additional early *mahr* required if he remarries. Then of course there are the disruptive effects, emotional and otherwise, in the breaking up of the conjugal family itself. To determine the weight of these considerations, let us turn to the available studies of divorce rates.

Frequency of Divorce

VILLAGES. Data are scarce on the rate of divorce in the Levant in the early twentieth century, but the little that is known points to a low divorce rate in the villages. Fuller said of Buarij (p. 68): "Divorce is uncommon in the village. It is economically impractical because a husband must forfeit the remaining one-third of the bride-price. ... Couples often quarrel noisily, and husbands beat their wives cruelly...but unless incompatibility is extreme, man and wife continue to live under one roof." Granqvist found in Artas that 11 wives out of 243 (4.5 per cent) had divorced and nine of these had remarried (1935, p. 269). She also noted that of 65 Artas women who had married outside the village, only two (3 per cent) had been divorced.

Several more recent studies of Arab villages also found the divorce rate to be quite low. In Rosenfeld's study in the fifties of marriage statistics of a Muslim Arab village, only 2.2 per cent of the village women had been divorced (Goode, p. 158). In Lutfiyya's description of life in Baytin in the sixties, he states that "divorce is rare" (1966, p. 162). In her study of a Muslim village in the Beqa'a Valley of Lebanon in the sixties, Williams found 283 intact marriages as opposed to three divorces and four separations-by-emigration (1968, pp. 96-97).

In spite of the agreement among anthropologists that divorce is rare in these Muslim villages, a number of writers have asserted the opposite. An oft-quoted survey of five Muslim villages, published by the government of Palestine in 1945, stated that 30.8 per cent of the women over 38 years of age had been married more than once. Patai (1969, p. 106) and others have deduced from this fact that the rate of divorce and subsequent remarriage must have been high in Middle Eastern villages. We do not believe this one datum compels such an interpretation. If we count mature women only (those over 38 years of age), it is reasonable to assume that a remarriage occurred after widowhood more often than after divorce. In Artas, for example, Granqvist counted 21 widows who had remarried, but only nine divorcees who had done so (1950, p. 90). In Jordan as a whole (cities and towns included) in the late fifties, official figures showed that, among women 40 and over, about as many widows as divorcees remarried. Remarriage of widows was facilitated in Palestinian villages by the tradition that a brother of the deceased marry the widow and thereby keep the patrilineal family and possessions together (cf. Goode, p. 161). In view of these considerations, we do not believe the findings of the 1945 survey refute the many observers who found divorce rates in Muslim villages to be quite low.

CITIES. Divorce rates in Arab cities are high, and contrast sharply with the low rates in the villages. Historical data on this matter are not available, but some official statistics on marriage and divorce (without regard for religious sect) in the districts of Beirut, Tripoli, Damascus and Amman from 1958 through 1967 are summarized in Table VII-1. In every case, the rate of divorce in the city is much higher than that in the country as a whole, and is fairly high by world standards.

Official Lebanese statistics do not provide specific data on divorce among Sunnis. In order to get such information, we had an assistant in Tripoli and one in Sidon obtain permission to study the records of the Sunni religious court in each city. The number of marriages and divorces over a period of more than forty years is summarized in Table VII-2. The divorce rate is even higher than that of Table VII-1. In Tripoli from 1921 to 1934, there were 40 per cent as many divorces as marriages! The rate has dropped since then, but it remains fairly high. There was no clear time trend in Sidon, but the divorce rate there since 1945 is fairly similar to that in Tripoli—between one and two hundred divorces per thousand marriages.

NATIONAL RATES. Goode says of the rate of divorce in Arabic Islam "there is no question but that it was high by Western standards" (p. 158). This was probably true of the Levant in the first half of the twentieth century, but it is less true today. A comparison of Jordan, Lebanon and Syria with three selected countries is shown in Table VII-3. Lebanon has the lowest

173

rate of the six, partly because a number of Lebanese Christians follow the Vatican on the subject of divorce. But note also that rates in Syria and Jordan are not inordinately high in comparison with France, Israel or the United States. Of course comparative judgements depend on the countries chosen for comparison. These Arab states would today be high in comparison with Italy or Spain, but they would be low in comparison with Eastern Europe, where rates run above 1.00, or the U.S.S.R., where rates are consistently above 2.50. To summarize, among Muslims of the Eastern Mediterranean, divorce is rare in peasant villages but frequent in the cities, so that overall divorce rates are at present only moderately high in comparison with those countries of Europe and North America where divorce is legal.[1]

Changing Divorce Rates

The ratio between the number of marriages and the number of divorces in a given country will fluctuate from year to year. Wars, insurrections, business recessions, and other factors affect decisions to marry and to divorce. As in stock market analyses, however, there are often long term trends behind the short term fluctuations. Goode (p. 158) believes that divorce rates in the West are rising as the social pressures against divorce weaken, but declining in Arabic Islam as the status of women improves. The data in Table VII-4 provide a test for his expectations so far as the Levant is concerned. In Syria the divorce rate has indeed declined since 1944. In Jordan too it seems to have declined somewhat since the early fifties. Counting Muslims only, the rate was 177 divorces per thousand marriages in 1952 and 160 in 1953, according to official statistics. Beginning with 1954, it has stayed below 150.

In Lebanon the divorce rate declined between 1944 and 1957 from 75 to 53, as Goode noticed (p. 159), but it has been climbing since then (Table VII-4). In 1969 there were 71 divorces per thousand marriages and in 1970 there were 75. An unofficial count of the first half of 1971 showed the ratio to have reached 85 (Hajjaj, 1971, p. 9). Has Lebanon reached a state of modernization which produces an increase in divorce rate, as in Europe and North America? Our interest in this study is more on the divorce rate among Sunnis than

[1] Divorce statistics based on data from Muslim courts include cases of broken engagements and temporary separations which would not be counted as divorces in Western countries (see infra "Duration of Marriages").

the rate in Lebanon as a whole. Official statistics do not give this information by sect, so we must turn again to the data obtained from the Sunni religious courts in Tripoli and Sidon (Table VII-2). In Tripoli the long-term decline in frequency of divorce is clear. Before 1935 the rate was around 400 divorces per thousand marriages. From 1935 to 1944, it was a little over 250. Since 1945 there has not been a year when the rate reached the 200 mark. Tripoli shows the same trend as Jordan and Syria—a declining divorce rate from one decade to the next.

It is difficult to discern a trend in the data from the Sidon court. On the whole, the divorce-marriage ratio in Sidon was similar to that in Tripoli, except for the period 1927 through 1931, when it was exceptionally low. It is possible that the divorce records were incomplete in those years. This possibility is strengthened by the fact that divorce records were missing altogether for the period 1923 through 1926.

Generally speaking, the data seem to bear out Goode's belief that the divorce rate is declining among the Muslims of this area.

Kinds of Divorce

Muslim marriages may be terminated in one of three ways, and official statistics report all of these as "divorce."[1] The first of these we might call a repudiation or traditional divorce. The husband pronounces the divorce formula and has his action recorded by the religious court. The divorce terms of the marriage contract go into effect.[2] The Arabic term for this type is *talaq*, which is the term for divorce found in the Quran. In the second type, the wife agrees to give up all or a part of the dowry payment due on divorce (the late *mahr*), presumably to encourage the husband to divorce her, and the agreement to divorce is recorded in the court. The Arabs call this type *mukhala'at*, which can be translated as "mutual dissolving" or "joint divestiture." The third way of ending a marriage is called *tafreeq*, which means disuniting, separating, parting or dividing. This kind of "separation" is equivalent to divorce, for either party can remarry (Mahmassani, 1962, pp. 453-456). Either husband or wife can sue for a "disuniting" on grounds of prolonged absence (including, for example, a prison term of more than three years), serious physical or mental

[1] Cf. Gardet, 1954, p. 251.

[2] Under Islamic law a woman can obtain the right to divorce at will by placing a clause to that effect in the marriage contract, but few women do so (Mahmassani 1962, p. 453;Hamamsy 1970, p. 593).

175

illness, failure of husband to provide financial support, or even prolonged disputing which family arbitration fails to relieve. The court verdict, rather than the provision in the marriage contract, determines the financial and other terms of the settlement.

If a husband pronounces divorce in the traditional fashion, he may do so without the definite, firm intent that it be a divorce. Such a revocable pronoucement is called *raj'i*. In such a case the husband is free to bring back his wife without a new contract, with or without her consent, within a period of three months or, if she is pregnant, before she delivers. During the waiting period, he must provide for his wife. If he does not bring her back, the divorce becomes definite and the divorce payments stipulated in the marriage contract fall due at the end of the waiting period.

The vast majority of divorces recorded in the courts are not of the revocable type. Definite divorces without a waiting period are called *ba'in*, which is translated as "explicit" or "overt." It might also be noted that *ba'inat* can mean the late payment due upon divorce. In such explicit, definite divorces, the late payment becomes due at the time the divorce is recorded. Moreover, the husband cannot bring back his ex-wife without a new marriage contract, which involves her consent.

A husband may divorce his wife once or twice and remarry her with a new contract. But if he divorces her a third time, or if he divorces her triply on one occasion by pronouncing three times "I divorce you" before witnesses, and records this in the religious court, then he cannot remarry her unless she has in the meantime married and divorced someone else. Such a provision evidently gives some protection to the wife, for a man who divorces triply in haste cannot change his mind overnight. As might be expected, the number of "triple" divorces is not large.

The court records in Sidon and Tripoli specify the type of divorce (*talaq*, *mukhala'at*, or *tafreeq*) and data from these records are summarized in Tables VII-5 and VII-6. The most striking fact emerging from an examination of these tables is that the standard form of divorce, in which the husband simply pronounces the wife divorced and records it in the courts, is not the most usual form. In Tripoli since 1920 and in Sidon since 1930, the most common form of divorce is one on which there is a *mutual* decision to dissolve the marriage, and the wife agrees to forgo at least part of the late payment specified in the marriage contract.

The least common type of divorce is the disuniting or separation. It has not been recorded in Sidon as yet. In Tripoli there have been a few cases since 1940, and the number has been increasing slightly from decade to decade.

176

The court records also show the degree of divorce—whether it is merely a revocable statement of intent and, if not, whether the definite and explicit divorce is a first, second, or third divorce. Data from these records are shown in Tables VII-7 and VII-8. In both courts and in all decades, the definite (*ba'in*) first divorce is the most common. Such divorces are similar to the Western concept of divorce. They are definite, and allow either party to enter into a new marriage—even a remarriage. The revocable divorce (*raj'i*) is rarely recorded, and such recording seems to serve only as a threat. Recording such revocable decisions of the husband has little legal significance. If such divorces become definite, they can be recorded as such on that occasion. If the husband takes the wife back during the waiting period, there is no need for a legal record.

From this examination of kinds of divorce, it is evident that wife is by no means as helpless and victimized in divorce courts as she is sometimes depicted, by Eastern feminists as well as Western observers. In a majority of all divorces examined in Sidon and Tripoli the wife reached an agreement with the husband on the modification of the terms of the late payment, the divorce payment. Moreover, she in some cases *initiated* a petition of "disuniting" which effectively dissolved the marriage.

Duration of Marriages

If husband and wife have hardly seen each other before their engagement, and have never been alone together before their marriage, it is evident that there is a heavy burden of adjustment during the early years of marriage. Even in the West, where couples have far better opportunity to get acquainted before marriage, most divorces come in the first few years of marriage. It is hardly surprising, then, that Arab couples who divorce are likely to do so rather soon.

Once a marriage contract has been written, the engaged couple cannot break it except by divorce. As is evident from Table VII-9, a number of couples do decide upon getting better acquainted that they will not go through with the marriage. Growing independence of youth is shown by the fact that the number of such "divorces" is on the increase. In Sidon and Tripoli alike, about a third of all recorded divorces in recent years were divorces prior to the marriage.

In comparing divorce rates in Muslim countries with those of non-Muslim countries it should be kept in mind that many Muslim "divorces" would not be considered divorces elsewhere. About a third of the "di-

177

vorces" in Sidon and Tripoli since 1955 might be called "broken engagements" in other places. Also, the revocable divorces would probably be classified elsewhere as temporary legal separations.

If we consider only divorces occurring after marriage, again there is much evidence that they occur early. Goode (p. 160) cites official statistics from Jordan and Syria indicating that about forty per cent of divorces in 1960 were in the first two years of marriage, and more recent *Statistical Yearbooks* (Jordan) and *Statistical Abstracts* (Syria) report similar figures. Data on duration of marriage were also recorded in a number of instances of divorce by the Sunni court in Sidon. These are presented in Table VII-10. Even if we make allowance for the fact that any divorces occurring after we gathered the data in 1967 would be added to the "After Second Year" group, it is still evident that most divorces in Sidon had occurred early after marriage. More than half were in the first two years. This was as true for the divorces of the 1920's as for those in the late fifties or sixties.

When we consider the number of "divorces" which occur before marriage, and the number occurring within a year or so after, we can surmise that a major factor in Middle Eastern divorce is the problem of adjusting to life with a stranger (even though perhaps a relative). Although most Western divorces also occur early in marriage, it is interesting to note by way of contrast that fewer occur in the first year than in the second, third or fourth (Berelson & Steiner, 1964, p. 312). In Britain divorce rates do not reach their peak until after about three years of marriage (Lowe, 1972, p. 213).

Who Seeks a Divorce and Why

"Divorce in the East is a masculine prerogative" say some writers, but our analysis of kinds of divorce has shown this to be an oversimplification. The myth of the Arab male divorcing casually and callously on his slightest whim is hardly compatible with what we know of marriage courts. Indeed, there is some evidence which suggests that women may instigate divorce as often as do men.

The divorce court records include information on the party asking for the divorce. Obviously a couple could arrange not to give a true answer to this question, and indeed they might not know the true answer. Consequently, replies can hardly be taken at face value. On the other hand, if divorce were accepted as a masculine prerogative, the answers should reflect this norm. The data from the courts of Sidon and Tripoli are shown in Table VII-11. In Sidon before 1930, the husbamd was recorded as asking for the divorce in a majority of cases. Since 1930 it is usually the wife who is listed as requesting it. In Tripoli before 1930 as well as after most divorces were requested by the wife. When divorces are of the "mutual dissolving" (*mukhala'at*) type, it is usually the wife who is listed as instigator.

The situation in Lebanon may not hold elsewhere, especially as regarding divorce by mutual agreement being recorded as requested by the wife. One report on 3046 divorces in Damascus in 1969 found that the wife had asked for the divorce in nine per cent of the cases and the husband in 30 per cent, with the other 61 per cent presumably being by agreement (Anon., 1970, p. 14).

Of the divorced women we interviewed in Tripoli, 84 were asked who had really wanted the divorce. Of these women, 54 per cent said they had and 36 per cent said the husband had. Two of the women blamed the in-laws and the remainder said it was by mutual agreement. Here again what evidence we have points to divorce being at least as often (if not more often) the wife's idea as it is the husband's.

Unhappiness in marriage is obviously difficult to assess with any accuracy. Nevertheless, at least one survey, in Iraq, concluded that the proportion of men who were unhappily married was as great as the proportion of women—among persons not suing for divorce (Nahas, 1956). For both sexes, the proportion stating they were unhappily married was about one-half. If this small sample of 924 literate adults is at all typical, then divorce is *not* readily available to any and every dissatisfied husband.

A number of religious courts ask that the cause of a divorce be a part of the record. The recorded replies proved of little use for our investigation, for most of them cite "incompatibility" as the cause. We also asked the 88 Tripoli divorcees the causes of their divorces, and here the answers were somewhat more revealing. The three most common replies were: incompatibility, including lack of understanding, lack of feeling, etc.; other women, real or potential; and interference of relatives, especially the in-laws. Among the women divorced during the first year, impotence and other sex problems ranked highest, but it was not significant thereafter. Among those divorced after ten years or more, the problem of "other women" played the most important role.

Failure of a wife to bear children is frequently mentioned by Middle East scholars as a reason impelling a husband to seek a divorce. It is true

179

that a majority of divorces in the Middle East take place between childless couples. Both the *Statistical Abstracts* of Syria and the *Statistical Yearbook* of Jordan reported regularly in the period 1961-1970 that 60 per cent or more of all divorces were childless. This figure is somewhat higher than in the West (cf. Goode, p. 85), but this may be due in part to the fact that divorces in the Levant occur more quickly after marriage than they do in the West.

Official figures for Jordan also show the number of children in marriages terminated after specified periods of time. Of those marriages ending after ten years or more, more than a fourth were childless. In 1964, for example, there were in Jordan 269 couples who divorced after ten years or more of marriage, and 107 of these (40 per cent) were childless. The number of Jordanians married ten years or more without children is quite small, less than five per cent, so there is a clear association between childlessness and divorce.

Of the divorced women we interviewed in Tripoli, 72 had been married at least one year and answered our query on reasons for the divorce. Of the 72, only seven mentioned lack of children or lack of desire for children as the chief reason for divorce.

The evidence as a whole seems to indicate that there is in the Levant, as in the West, some correlation between childlessness and divorce. On the other hand, failure to have children is apparently not the chief reason for most divorces. We would guess that it is an important factor, however, for that minority who have not had children after ten years or more of marriage.

Remarriage after Divorce

Remarriage after divorce is permitted by the Quran. A man can remarry immediately, but a woman must wait three menstrual periods or, if she is pregnant, until the child is weaned. Remarriage is in fact quite common in Islamic countries, and this seems generally to have been true throughout Islamic history.

It was mentioned earlier in the chapter that nine of the eleven divorced women in Artas had remarried, and that more than 30 per cent of the women 38 years of age or over in five Muslim villages of Palestine had married more than once. More recent census data show that these villages were not exceptional. Remarriage is definitely the norm in the Levant.

In the 1960 Syrian census and in the 1961 Jordanian census, fewer than one per cent of females over 16 years of age and fewer than one-half of one percent of males over 18 years of age were classified as divorced.[1] For the majority who get divorced, particularly at the younger ages, the status "divorced" is temporary. Consequently, in any given census, the number tabulated as "divorced" is quite small.

The number of marriages and divorces in Jordan over an eight year period are shown in Table VII-12. Each year from 7.3 to 8.8 per cent of all women who married were divorcees. The number of women leaving the category "divorced" was each year about 60 per cent as great as the number entering that category. Indeed, the number of younger divorced women who remarry each year is probably about as large as the number of younger women who divorce. In the Jordanian census of 1961, 0.9 per cent of the women in the age group 20 through 24 were divorced, and the per cent did not exceed 0.9 for any age group up through 40 through 44. Somewhat similar results were found in the 1960 census of Syria. For Muslim Arab women in the 20 through 24 age category, 0.7 per cent were divorced. For the 25 through 29 age group, the percentage was the same. Of women 30 through 39, 0.8 per cent were divorced. When we consider the fact that divorce rates are declining, so that the rate of divorce among older women is expected to be somewhat higher than the rate among younger women, then the fact that the per cent of women who *are* *currently* divorced increases so little with increasing age suggests that remarriage is indeed frequent. Goode's guess (p. 161) that over 95 per cent of those who divorce early will eventually remarry is probably correct.

Both in Jordan and in Syria, the census reported less than half as many males as females in the "divorced" category. In no age group in Syria or Jordan were as many as one per cent of the males divorced. Impressive evidence that remarriage is the rule for men is found in the fact that in Jordan more men were divorced during the year 1961 (1,901) than were listed as divorced in the census conducted in September, 1961 (1,856)! The only puzzling fact about remarriage of males is that, of persons marrying, there are each year in Jordan fewer divorced men than divorced women (Table VII-12). That this should happen occasionally is plausible, but its happening each year calls for some explanation. If more divorced women than divorced men remarry, why are there far more divorced women counted in the census? One possibility is that a number of males divorcing each year are divorcing a second wife, so that they remain in the married category. Another possibility, closely related, is that a number

---

[1] Corresponding figures for the United States are around two per cent.

of those marrying each year quite properly list their marital status as married even though they had previously divorced a second or third wife. Finally, it should be noted that it would not be as serious for males as for females to write on a marriage contract that they were single when they were in reality divorced. Whatever the correct explanation, the fundamental fact which must remain is that remarriage by men is higher than it is by women, so that at any given time few men are in the divorced state.

Polygyny

It has been suggested by several writers (cf. Baer, 1964, p. 38n) that there may be in the Middle East an inverse relationship between frequency of divorce and frequency of polygyny. Others, including Goode (p. 101), have noted that "educated opinion" in the Arab world sees limitations on divorce and polygyny as a part of one trend toward a redefinition of the role of women. We believe the evidence points toward a decline in polygyny as well as in divorce among Muslims of the Levant in the twentieth century.

In spite of the degree to which polygyny has captured the interest of Western writers, rather little information has been published on its frequency and distribution in various elements of the population in the Levant. In the early nineteenth century, Lane (p. 188) estimated that only one Egyptian husband in 20 had two wives, and his estimate has been echoed fairly often through the years. Most Middle Eastern scholars since then have agreed that polygyny is rare, and have emphasized the economic, emotional and other obstacles to polygyny.

To judge from their observations, only the stout of heart and strong of purse would venture to take a second wife and face the jealousy, bickerings and hostility thus engendered. The prospective polygynist would not only be required to make a new bridal payment (*mahr*), but would in all probability need to give his first wife a sizable placating gift. Then he would have to face the probability that the wives—and their offspring— would work against each other, and also that he would have to deal with two sets of suspicious in-laws. Perhaps it is because of these many problems that Middle Easterners enjoy the joke of the man with two wives who became bald because one night his young wife would pluck out his grey hairs and the next his older wife would pluck out the black ones. Small wonder that polygyny, though legal, is rare.

In 1934 Chatila, writing of the Muslims of Syria, estimated that about

182

five per cent of all married men had more than one wife. He asserted that the practice was more common in rural areas than in the cities, virtually absent among the educated upper class, and—in the cities—more common among artisans and small businessmen than among others (pp. 239-245). Goode (p. 102) cites several observers who agree that the practice is declining in the cities and in rural areas is limited to the well-to-do.

In the 1920's Granqvist found that 11 per cent of the married men of Artas had more than one wife, and noted that the per cent had been higher in earlier generations (1935, p. 205). By the time of our 1967 survey, the percentage was down to 8.7, so polygyny in Artas is apparently declining, but slowly. In Tur'an, an Arab village in Israel, Rosenfeld (1957 p. 53) found in a five-generation study in the fifties that 11 per cent of the married men who had died had been polygynous, but only 5.5 per cent of the married men alive. His findings probably indicate some decline in the practice, but it must be kept in mind that the per cent of married men with more than one wife increases with age (Table VII-13), so that comparisons between all married men living, including young men newly married, and records of married men who had died, would show differences even if there were no change at all in incidence of polygyny from one generation to the next.

In a village of northern Jordan in the 1960's, Antoun (1972, p. 52) found that slightly more than 10 per cent of the households were polygynous.[1] Data on previous generations in that village are not available, but a survey in 1949 of Arab refugees from an agricultural area near there found that 16 per cent of heads of household were polygynous (Patai, 1969, p. 93), so here again there is at least a suggestion of a decrease over time.

Around mid-century, it was estimated that in Jordan as a whole, about 10 per cent of all married men were polygynous (Harris, 1958, p. 190). There is fairly reliable evidence that the percentage has declined since then. For some years the *Statistical Yearbook* issued annually by the Jordanian government has included data on previous marital status of bridegrooms. Table VII-14 summarizes the data on polygynous grooms from 1952 through 1969. There are fluctuations from year to year, but there is nevertheless a discernible trend away from polygyny. During the 1950's

---

[1] Antoun noted in his village that *de facto* polygyny was much rarer than legal polygyny (quite the opposite of the situation in the West). In about three-fourths of polygynous marriages, only one wife was living with the husband, and the other wives lived with their respective sons. This distinction between legal and *de facto* polygyny is an important one which has been given rather little attention in studies of the Levant.

nearly seven per cent of all marriages taking place were polygynous. In the late 1960's the number had dropped to around six per cent. The census of 1961 showed that married women outnumbered married men by 8 per cent. While this is only a crude way to estimate amount of polygyny, it does yield a figure that fits reasonably well with other available information. In any case, we can safely conclude from the annual statistics that polygyny in Jordan is declining, though slowly.

In Lebanon polygyny seems almost to have disappeared, among Sunnis, by the 1950's. Fuller had found one polygynous male in Buarij in the 1930's, but we found none. In the 1960's Williams found only two polygynous households out of 107 in her study of a village in the Beqa'a Valley (1968, pp. 137-143). Gulick's informant estimated in the early sixties that two per cent of the Muslims of Tripoli had more than one wife (1967, p. 130). The survey of Beirut conducted in the 1950's found only two polygynous men in a sample of 1900 households, of which perhaps half were Muslim. Evidently, polygyny is rare among the Sunnis of Lebanon.

According to the 1960 census of Syria, 4.29 per cent of all Muslim married men have more than one wife. As can be seen in Table VII-15, most of the polygynists are from rural areas. More than five per cent of rural married men are polygynous, but less than three per cent of married men living in cities. There is a clear relationship between education and polygyny, with those who are illiterate or just able to read and write having the highest incidence. University graduates, however, are polygynous as often as are those who complete only elementary, primary or secondary school.

There is in Syria a correlation between occupation and polygyny, as there was in Antoun's Jordanian village (1972, p. 53), with a majority of polygynous males being persons who cultivate the land. As is shown in Table VII-16, nearly six per cent of farmers and farm workers had more than one wife. After farmers, it is men classified as having "no occupation" who show the highest rate of polygyny. This is a somewhat puzzling datum, and conjures up images of idle husbands living off the toil of multiple wives until we note elsewhere in the report that about half of these are over sixty years of age and presumably retired. Given the association between age and number of wives (Table VII-15), this datum is less puzzling. The only other occupational category with a rate above the national average was "administrative and managerial," which included government executives, business managers and proprietors of large business. It should be noted that craftsmen, artisans and workers in manufacturing plants, the second largest occupational category in terms of numbers, had a polygyny rate less than half the national average. It is farmers and executives who practice polygyny most, not the workers. In the cities married women are rarely employed (see Chapter VI), and are thus an economic burden which the working class cannot afford. On farms however wives may be an economic asset.

What can we conclude about the practice of polygyny among Muslims of Lebanon, Syria and Jordan? We believe the evidence presented here points toward several conclusions. First, polygyny has been uncommon for at least half a century, and probably for many centuries. Second, there has been in the twentieth century a general trend away from polygyny. Lebanon, and especially Beirut, has led the way. Today the proportion of married men with more than one wife is probably under two per cent in Lebanon, a little over four per cent in Syria and around eight per cent in Jordan. The practice is less common in urban than in rural areas, and among persons with some schooling than among illiterates or those who can only read and write. Peasants and others who do farming for a living are more likely to be polygynous than are those of any other occupational group. The trend away from polygyny seems to be led by those groups which are most "modern" in other respects. There is, however, one exception. In the cities it is the executive and managerial class which has the highest proportion of polygynists, while factory workers, artisans and miners have a lower proportion than any other occupational group.

It has already been suggested that economic factors seem to be important in the maintaining of polygyny. Extra wives may be an asset for the farmer who is moderately well off, with housing space and cultivable land—and who can afford the capital investments required by the marriages. In the cities extra wives would not ordinarily be an asset, especially among workers. In addition to the economic factor, there were others mentioned by some of the women interviewed. Muslims are well aware that non-Muslims think of polygyny in terms of sensuality and look upon it as a sign of "backwardness." The educated often say that it is only the poor and uneducated who practice it (cf. Gulick, 1967, pp. 129-130). Educated parents are reluctant to give their daughters to a man already married and of course educated young women are reluctant to become "second" wives.

Some of our uneducated, lower class informants offered additional explanations. Today, they said, sons play more of a role in the choice of a mate,

185

so there are fewer occasions where these is a first marriage arranged by the parents and a second marriage in which the son's preferences play a major part. Others argue, as did Qasim Amin in the nineteenth century, that the Quranic stipulation that a husband must treat all wives equally or not marry more than one, implies that a man should have only one. Evidently a number of factors are converging against the practice of polygyny, which has always been rare, so that its continued decline can be predicted with assurance.

Summary

To the Western mind, nothing (except, perhaps, polygyny and the harem) so epitomizes the low status of women in Islam as does the easy divorce, readily available to men only. Women are seen as living in state of submission enforced by the threat of divorce. Like Scheherazade of old, they live in suspense from day to day, and night to night. Goode (p. 155) has identified this picture as one of the "fantasies of the Western male." As so many fantasies, it fades on contact with reality.

In the Arab Levant divorce is rare among peasants, and has probably been so in most villages of the area during much of this century. The rate of divorce is much higher in cities, so that national rates are similar to those of Western countries, such as France, where divorce is allowed. Muslim divorce rates are inflated, moreover, by the fact that the religious courts, which handle all divorces, include in their statistics cases of "broken engagements" which occur after the signing of the marriage agreement as well as a number of cases of revocable divorces which are really temporary separations. Even so, divorce rates are lower than in the United States or the Soviet Union.

Generally speaking, the divorce rate among Muslims of the Levant has been decreasing since 1940, and perhaps the decline began as early as 1920. The assertion that this decrease testifies to an improvement in the status of women is strengthened by the fact that polygyny has decreased over the same period.

In Lebanon at least the classical divorce (*talaq*) in which the husband pronounces the wife divorced, and records this fact in the courts, is on the decline. The divorce by mutual agreement (*mukhala'at*) is the dominant type. A few marriages are terminated by a legal disuniting (*tafreeq*), which can be initiated by the wife.

Marriages are still under control of the elders in most cases, and couples usually have little opportunity for close acquaintance before marriage. It is hardly surprising, then, that divorces occur early. Many take place after engagement and before marriage. Of those occurring after marriage, nearly half are in the first two years.

Perhaps most damaging to the myth of easy divorce for males is the fact that the wife initiates, or at least agrees to, the divorce much of the time. Indeed, in some courts, the wife is recorded as requesting the divorce in a *majority* of cases. In interviews with 88 divorced women in Tripoli, a majority said the divorce had been their own idea.

The stated cause for most divorces was simply "incompatibility." The divorced women we interviewed also mentioned "other women" and "relatives" fairly often. In most divorces, the couple had no children, partly because divorce occurred soon. Failure to have children may have been a major factor in the divorces of that minority of couples who remained childless for a number of years.

The great majority of those who divorce later remarry. Consequently, in both Syria and Jordan, fewer than one per cent of females over 16 and fewer than one-half of one per cent of males over 18 were divorced (and not remarried) at the time of the census in the early 1960's.

Polygyny was found to be rare and becoming rarer. Lebanon, and especially Beirut, is in the vanguard of this trend. The practice survives chiefly among the uneducated rural people and, to a lesser degree, among the executive and managerial class of the cities of Syria and Jordan. Among urban workers frequency of polygyny is only half the national average. A combination of economic, ideological and other factors are against the practice, and lead us to predict with confidence its continued decline.

TABLE VII-1

NUMBER OF DIVORCES PER THOUSAND MARRIAGES IN THREE COUNTRIES
AND FOUR CITIES, 1958–1967

	Lebanon	Beirut District	Tripoli District	Syria	Damascus District	Jordan*	Amman District
1958	–	–	–	66	190	133	204
1959	61	104	82	64	170	133	210
1960	61	105	96	82	–	147	230
1961	67	118	101	104	195	149	236
1962	64	114	105	104	–	139	219
1963	70	121	109	105	201	131	221
1964	65	116	112	94	190	119	166
1965	65	116	114	92	179	139	192
1966	74	129	141	90	199	134	–
1967	65	103	118	98	–	130	–

Source: *Bulletin Statistique Trimestriel*, Republique Libanaise, Ministere de L'Economie Nationale, Service de Statistique Generale; *Statistical Abstract of Syria*, Syria, Directorate of Statistic; *Statistical Yearbook*, H.K. of Jordan, Ministry of National Economy, Department of Statistics.

*Data in this column are for Moslems only; in all other columns, all sects are represented.

TABLE VII–2

NUMBER OF MARRIAGES AND DIVORCES REGISTERED IN TWO SUNNI RELIGIOUS
COURTS, BY FIVE-YEAR INTERVALS

Years*	Sidon			Tripoli		
	Marriages	Divorces	Divorce-Marriage Ratio	Marriages	Divorces	Divorce-Marriage Ratio
1920–1924	41	19	.463	560	250	.385
1925–1929	208	14	.067	655	262	.400
1930–1934	371	64	.173	614	247	.402
1935–1939	480	100	.245	961	264	.275
1940–1944	431	78	.181	1169	315	.269
1945–1949	532	76	.143	1311	221	.169
1950–1954	679	86	.127	1478	220	.149
1955–1959	829	98	.118	1997	215	.108
1960–1964	894	152	.170	2113	286	.135

*Only years in which number of marriages *and* divorces were known are included. Consequently, data from the Sidon court cover the years 1922 and 1927-1964 and data from Tripoli court cover the period 1921-1964.

TABLE VII–3

Number of Divorces per one Thousand Population in Selected Countries

Country	1966	1967	1968	1969	1970
Jordan*	1.08	–	–	–	–
Lebanon	0.48	0.39	0.40	0.41	0.45
Syria**	0.59	0.60	0.54	0.61	–
France	0.74	0.75	0.72	–	–
Israel	0.85	0.80	0.87	0.83	0.80
U.S.A.	2.55	2.64	2.92	3.16	3.50

Source: U.N. *Demographic Yearbook* 1970, p. 745.
*Data not available on Jordanians living west of Jordan River after June 1967.
**Nomads included in population, but their divorces not included.

TABLE VII–4

Changing Divorce Ratios in Selected Countries

Country	Number of Divorces Per Thousand Marriages							
Jordan	169	(1951) +	133	(1958)*	134	(1966)	138	(1969)**
Lebanon	75	(1944–45)	53	(1957)	67	(1968)	75	(1970)
Syria	156	(1944)	80	(1957)	76	(1968)	63	(1969)
U.S.A.	165	(1940)	246	(1956)	269	(1966)	336	(1969)
France	80	(1940)	100	(1956)	107	(1966)	101	(1968)

Source: Goode, p. 159 and U.N. *Demographic Yearbook 1970*, pp. 732 and 745.
+ Data not available for 1944. In Palestine in 1944, there were among Muslims 177 divorces per thousand marriages (Office of Statistics, Government of Palestine, 1948. p. 5).
*Goode cites 1957, when the number was 104, but that was an unusual year. Indeed, according to official statistics of Ministry of National Economy, in no other year from 1952 to 1963 was the number below 120.
**After 1966 data are from East side of Jordan River only.

TABLE VII–5

KINDS OF DIVORCE CASES REGISTERED IN THE SIDON SUNNI COURT
FROM 1920 THROUGH 1965

| Years | No. of Divorces | Kinds of Divorce | | | |
| | | Traditional (talaq) | | Mutual (mukhala'at) | |
		No.	%	No.	%
1920–24	42	(29)	69	(13)	31
1925–29	14	(8)	57	(6)	43
1930–34	64	(22)	34	(42)	66
1935–39	100	(31)	31	(69)	69
1940–44	78	(23)	29	(55)	71
1945–49	76	(32)	42	(44)	58
1950–54	86	(33)	38	(53)	62
1955–59	98	(25)	26	(73)	74
1960–64	152	(35)	23	(117)	77
1965	35	(14)	40	(21)	60

TABLE VII–6

KINDS OF DIVORCE CASES REGISTERED IN THE TRIPOLI SUNNI COURT
FROM 1920 THROUGH 1965

Years	No. of Divorces	Kinds of Divorce					
		Traditional (talaq)		Mutual (mukhala'at)		Disuniting (tafreeq)	
		No.	%	No.	%	No.	%
1920–24	250	(74)	30	(176)	70		
1925–29	262	(24)	9	(238)	91		
1930–34	247	(35)	14	(212)	86		
1935–39	264	(40)	15	(224)	85		
1940–44	315	(47)	15	(262)	83	(6)	2
1945–49	221	(51)	23	(155)	70	(15)	7
1950–54	220	(55)	25	(147)	67	(18)	8
1955–59	215	(48)	22	(141)	66	(26)	12
1960–64	286	(45)	16	(205)	72	(36)	12
1965	116	(24)	21	(75)	65	(17)	14

192

TABLE VII–7

DEGREE OF DIVORCES REGISTERED IN THE SIDON SUNNI COURT
FROM 1920 THROUGH 1965

Years	No. of Divorces	Degree of Divorce							
		First		Second		Third		Revocable	
		N	%	N	%	N	%	N	%
1920–24	42	(38)	91	(0)	0	(2)	5	(2)	5
1925–29	14	(12)	86	(0)	0	(1)	7	(1)	7
1930–34	64	(56)	87	(1)	2	(3)	5	(4)	6
1935–39	100	(86)	86	(6)	6	(8)	8	(0)	0
1940–44	78	(66)	85	(10)	13	(0)	0	(2)	2
1945–49	76	(71)	94	(1)	1	(3)	4	(1)	1
1950–54	86	(75)	87	(7)	8	(3)	4	(1)	1
1955–59	98	(92)	94	(2)	2	(2)	2	(2)	2
1960–64	152	(143)	94	(7)	5	(2)	1	(0)	0
1965	35	(33)	94	(0)	0	(1)	3	(1)	3

TABLE VII–8

DEGREE OF DIVORCES REGISTERED IN THE TRIPOLI SUNNI COURT FROM 1920 THROUGH 1965

Years	No. of Divorces	Degree of Divorce							
		First		Second		Third		Revocable	
		N	%	N	%	N	%	N	%
1920–24	250	(194)	78	(19)	8	(37)	14	(0)	0
1925–29	262	(238)	91	(7)	3	(17)	6	(0)	0
1930–34	247	(218)	88	(6)	3	(23)	9	(0)	0
1935–39	264	(247)	94	(5)	2	(12)	4	(0)	0
1940–44	315	(280)	89	(8)	2	(27)	9	(0)	0
1945–49	221	(189)	86	(19)	9	(13)	5	(0)	0
1950–54	220	(190)	86	(22)	10	(8)	4	(0)	0
1955–59	215	(172)	80	(33)	15	(10)	5	(0)	0
1960–64	286	(243)	85	(33)	12	(10)	3	(0)	0
1965	116	(105)	91	(8)	7	(3)	2	(0)	0

TABLE VII–9

PROPORTION OF "DIVORCES" BEFORE MARRIAGE, AS REGISTERED IN TWO
SUNNI RELIGIOUS COURTS FROM 1920 THROUGH 1965

Years	Sidon			Tripoli		
	No. of Divorces	Per cent Before Marriage	Per cent After Marriage	No. of Divorces	Per cent Before Marriage	Per cent After Marriage
1920–24	42	12	88	250	8	92
1925–29	14	7	93	262	8	92
1930–34	64	2	98	247	6	94
1935–39	100	11	89	264	11	89
1940–44	78	15	85	315	14	86
1945–49	76	18	82	221	18	82
1950–54	86	28	72	220	20	80
1955–59	98	44	56	215	23	77
1960–64	152	37	63	286	32	68
1965	35	29	71	116	29	71ⁱ

TABLE VII–10

DURATION OF MARRIAGE IN DIVORCE CASES REGISTERED IN THE SIDON SUNNI COURT FROM 1920 THROUGH 1964

Years	Number of Divorces*	Per Cent During First Year	Per Cent During Second Year	Per Cent After Second Year
1920–24	20	55	15	30
1935–39	38	34	11	55
1940–44	17	36	29	35
1945–49	61	37	18	45
1950–54	62	40	21	39
1955–59	42	64	12	24
1960–64	42	45	19	36

*Divorce after marriage where court record showed duration of marriage. Data not available for years 1925 through 1934.

TABLE VII–11

SPOUSE REQUESTING DIVORCE, AS REGISTERED IN TWO SUNNI RELIGIOUS COURTS FROM 1920 THROUGH 1965

Years	Sidon			Tripoli		
	N	Husband %	Wife %	N	Husband %	Wife %
1920–24	(42)	79	21	(250)	30	70
1925–29	(13)	54	46	(262)	10	90
1930–34	(64)	5	95	(247)	15	85
1935–39	(99)	15	85	(264)	17	83
1940–44	(78)	22	78	(315)	15	85
1945–49	(76)	16	84	(221)	25	75
1950–54	(86)	7	93	(220)	29	71
1955–59	(98)	16	84	(215)	30	70
1960–64	(152)	28	72	(286)	19	81
1965	(35)	34	66	(116)	22	78

TABLE VII–12

MARITAL STATUS OF BRIDES AND GROOMS IN JORDAN, 1958 THROUGH 1965

Year	Sex	Marital Status				Number of Marriages	Number of Divorces each year
		Divorced	Widowed	Married	Single		
1965	M	673	553	948	12,482	14,656	2,023
	F	1,217	296		13,143		
1964	M	630	519	929	13,806	15,884	1,873
	F	1,178	284		14,442		
1963	M	721	517	944	11,707	13,889	1,787
	F	1,222	294		12,373		
1962	M	692	558	914	12,449	14,643	1,980
	F	1,251	349		13,013		
1961	M	674	491	920	11,102	13,160	1,901
	F	1,094	328		11,738		
1960	M	610	523	895	10,821	12,849	1,823
	F	1,012	342		11,495		
1959	M	619	567	1,024	12,036	14,246	1,823
	F	1,121	360		12,765		
1958	M	571	562	920	12,395	14,448	1,860
	F	1,055	419		12,974		

Source: Statistical Yearbooks of the Hashimite Kingdom of Jordan

TABLE VII–13

Relation between Polygyny and Age
as Shown in the 1960 Census of the Syrian Arab Republic

Age Husband	Number of Husbands	Per Cent Polygynous	Per Cent of Husbands with			
			1 wife	2 wives	3 wives	4 wives
Below 20	10,005	0.18	99.82	0.18	0.01	0.01
20–14	42,360	0.50	99.50	0.49	0.01	0.01
25–29	92,178	0.85	99.15	0.82	0.02	0.01
30–34	106,838	1.99	98.01	1.93	0.06	0.01
35–39	95,093	3.25	96.75	3.10	0.14	0.01
40–44	70,333	5.04	94.96	4.79	0.23	0.02
45–49	61,863	5.99	94.01	5.59	0.36	0.04
50–54	49,049	6.98	93.02	6.51	0.42	0.05
55–59	37,814	7.59	92.41	6.97	0.54	0.08
60–64	41,823	7.94	92.06	7.30	0.58	0.07
65–69	27,243	8.04	91.95	7.33	0.63	0.10
70–74	23,655	7.72	92.28	7.00	0.60	0.11
75 and above	29,099	8.11	91.99	7.09	0.78	0.15
Unknown	451	5.32	94.68	4.66	0.44	0.22
Total	687,804	4.29	95.71	3.99	0.26	0.04

TABLE VII–14

Polygynous Marriages in Jordan – 1952 to 1969

Year*	No. Moslem Males Married	No. Grooms Already Married	Per Cent of Marriages Polygynous	
			Annually	Five Year Intervals
1969	12,365	741	5.99	
1968	11,908	734	6.16	
1967	10,703	642	6.00	6.12
1966	15,388	901	5.86	
1965	14,493	948	6.54	
1964	15,691	929	5.92	
1963	13,567	944	6.96	
1962	14,265	914	6.41	6.67
1961	12,759	920	7.21	
1960	12,755	895	7.02	
1959	13,715	1024	7.47	
1958	13,952	920	6.59	
1957	16,993	1116	6.57	6.86
1956	12,216	838	6.86	
1955	13,261	911	6.87	
1954	12,658	852	6.73	
1953	9,808	657	6.70	7.06
1952	7,946	639	8.04	

*For 1967, 1968 and 1969 data are from East Bank only
Source: Statistical Yearbooks, Hashimite Kingdom of Jordan

TABLE VII–15

POLYGYNY, PLACE OF RESIDENCE AND EDUCATION OF HUSBAND
AS REPORTED IN THE 1960 CENSUS OF THE SYRIAN ARAB REPUBLIC

	Number of Married Men	Per Cent of Group Reporting			
		1 wife	2 wives	3 wives	4 wives
Residence					
Rural	437,325	94.92	4.71	0.33	0.04
Urban	250,479	97.10	2.73	0.15	0.02
Educational Level					
Illiterate	379,779	95.21	4.45	0.29	0.04
Read or Read & Write	254,191	95.88	3.83	0.22	0.03
Elementary, Primary or Secondary Certificate	47,160	98.56	1.38	0.05	0.01
University Degree	5,089	98.37	1.59	0.01	0.01
*Total**	687,804	95.71	3.99	0.26	0.04

*Total includes 1,585 men whose educational level was not ascertained.

TABLE VII–16

POLYGYNY AND OCCUPATION OF HUSBAND
AS REPORTED IN THE 1960 CENSUS OF THE SYRIAN ARAB REPUBLIC

Occupational Classification	Number of Married Men	Per Cent Polygynous
Professional & Technical	9,964	2.47
Administrative & Managerial	4,571	4.70
Clerical	16,632	2.05
Salesmen	59,363	3.99
Farmers and Farm workers*	326,729	5.65
Miners and Quarrymen	2,383	1.34
Transport & Communication	22,496	3.01
Craftsmen & Factory Workers	123,206	1.99
Service and Recreation	28,283	2.68
Not Classifiable	1,902	0.95
Not Stated	24,305	1.95
No occupation	67,970	5.23
Total	687,804	4.29

*Of 687,804 men, only 249 had four wives, and 175 of these were classified as farmers or farm workers.

CHAPTER EIGHT

Summary and Conclusions

A S STATED IN THE FIRST CHAPTER, the aim of this investigation was to assemble data on some of the changes occurring during this century in Sunni Muslim family life in the Eastern Mediterranean, a region which lies in the heart of a vast "cultural continent" extending from Morocco on the Atlantic Ocean to Afghanistan in Central Asia. Changes relating to the role and status of women were given particular attention. The evidence of the preceding pages is clear. In the region studied, important changes are occurring in patterns of family life and in the role of women. That these changes are occurring without large scale industrialization, and are being initiated by the upper and middle classes, has implication for theories of modernization and social change.

Early Twentieth Century

In the early twentieth century the Arab family of the Levant was usually described as a typical patriarchy, and Westerners frequently noted the similarities between such families and those of Biblical patriarchs. From all evidence, the family was indeed extended and patrilineal, and married sons, with their wives and children, usually lived for some years at least with their fathers before establishing a separate residence nearby. The extended family was not only a residential unit, but an economic, social and psychological unit as well. Even when the extended family did not exist in fact, it was nonetheless the ideal.

The sexuality of both men and women was recognized and its lawful expression encouraged. The danger of improper expression was guarded against by patterns of avoidance and segregation of the sexes. Woman's place was the home and her status was generally low. If she went out she was not only properly chaperoned or accompanied, but also properly

202

cloaked and veiled, to avoid any hint of tempting or being tempted. The honor of a family required modesty of its female members, so that improper behavior, even by a married woman, was primarily the responsibility of the male members of her family of orientation.

Marriages were arranged by families, usually without consulting the girl. Often agreement was reached before either the boy or the girl had reached puberty. Early marriages were the rule, especially for girls, who frequently married before age 15. Marriage between relatives was preferred. Indeed, the ideal marriage was considered to be one between a boy and a girl whose fathers were brothers. The marriage ceremony was the occasion for celebrations lasting several days. The family of the groom bore most of the expenses of the wedding and the celebrations. In addition the marriage contract called for a substantial payment to the bride and an agreement to pay another sum in case of divorce. Consequently, any prospective groom was heavily dependent on the financial assistance of his family.

Large families of seven or more children (preferably with a predominance of males) were considered ideal, but health conditions were such that the ideal was infrequently realized.

Divorce was legally simple for males, although it carried financial and other disadvantages. The divorce rate in cities was probably fairly high but in villages fairly low. Even though a man could legally take as many as four wives, not more than one married man in ten or twenty had more than one wife.

The preceding description of family life in the Levant in the early twentieth century is of necessity generalized and stereotyped. An occasional woman exercised genuine power and authority in her family and clan, an occasional son revolted successfully against paternal authority, and an occasional couple eloped without first securing full approval of all concerned. The picture was by no means as static as our normalized and normative descriptions might imply. More important, a desire for change was by the 1920's openly expressed by some Muslim intellectuals—male as well as female. In the late nineteenth century a number of Egyptian writers had begun to call for changes in family life and in the status of women. By the end of World War I this movement had made itself felt in the Levant, in talk and exhortation if not in action.

The period between the two World Wars, when the Eastern Mediterranean was under French and British mandates, was the period when change became noticeable. Several observers of the 1930's wrote of such changes as the discarding of the veil. Our own data show fairly frequently that women married before 1940 had different experiences and attitudes from those married after that date.

After Mid-Century

What are some of the changes which have occurred in this century? The preceding chapters, and especially their tables of data, spell out in detail a number of evident and often interlocking changes. On the other hand, the picture is not simply one of generalized change, for there are some aspects of the traditional picture which have survived and others which have survived in some segments of society.

Marriages are still arranged by elders, but today daughters as well as sons are usually consulted in advance, and in the cities at least the couple have met (in a group situation, not alone) before the engagement. The young man's search for a bride is still through family contacts, though he undoubtedly plays a more important role than formerly in deciding whom to approach. Age at marriage for men continues to be rather late, particularly for a nonindustrial society, but age at marriage for women is increasing. Women now feel that marriage before age 17 is too early. Marriages are still expensive, but the celebrations are growing shorter and the early bride payment is growing less rapidly than the late payment, and neither as rapidly as the general cost of living, so the dependence by the groom on family financing may be lessening somewhat. At the same time, the comparative rise in the late payment offers greater protection for the bride.

The preference for marrying relatives is still noticeable, but in the cities it is on the decline. In the villages, however, this type of endogamy continues strong. The tradition that a newly married couple live in the home of the groom's parents for some time survives, but it is weakening in the cities. When village couples establish a separate home, they usually do so in a place near the parents of the husband. In the cities however only a minority settle near the husband's parents. Indeed, in recent decades, about as many live in the same neighborhood as the wife's parents as in that of the husband's parents. Even where there is no residential proximity, there remain many psychological family ties. Visiting parents is frequent in all classes and in city as well as village.

In the early twentieth century a large family was considered ideal, but in Artas at least health conditions were such that large families were the exception. To judge from our interviewees' reports of their families of orientation and procreation, however, an average of five children has been the norm in most of this century. There is indication that upper class city mothers, at least since mid-century, have had fewer children than lower class mothers (in Beirut, the trend began before 1950). Moreover, mothers of the upper and middle class, and younger mothers generally, describe the ideal family as smaller than do other mothers, and also more frequently report the practice of birth control.

Beliefs about the proper role of women are changing throughout the region, and there is evidently changing definition of behaviour that can be considered modest and compatible with family honor. Veiling of the face is everywhere disappearing. Education for girls is generally approved, and even coeducation is endorsed by city mothers. Employment for women is increasing, but is still less common than in industrialized countries, or even in Latin America. Modesty concerns are still shown in the type of employment accepted by women. For example, clerical (including secretarial) positions are rarely filled by Muslim women.

Older women still report that they observe the daily prayers, but younger women say they do not. On the other hand young and old alike say they observe the Fast of Ramadan and abstain from alcohol. Women now leave the house to visit, stroll or attend social gatherings. Cinema attendance by daughters, if chaperoned, is generally approved, except by the oldest group of women. Only the upper and middle class city women, however, would approve of a daughter going dancing or to a public beach, even with a chaperone. The modesty code is still much in evidence even if considerably altered.

When questioned about decision making in the home, the city mothers usually said that husband and wife cooperated on most important decisions, while village mothers said that most such decisions were made by the husband. Only in the village of Artas did the women report little authority and low status. These women rise when the husband enters the room, walk behind him in public, avoid any physical contact in public, refrain from disagreeing with him (because they deem it would be futile), and address him by a title or teknonym rather than by his first name. In most cases they had been married without being consulted. Evidently, these village women were in the late sixties the closest to the traditional role of all those interviewed.

Islam is thought of as a culture in which divorce is simple and easy for males and quite common. Whatever may have been the case in the past, this state of affairs is not found today. When we consider that divorce statistics include "broken engagements" and a few "temporary separations," we find the divorce rates in the Muslim cities studied no higher than the national rates in other countries where divorce is recognized, and indeed lower than in such countries as the U.S.A. and U.S.S.R. Divorce in Arab villages is uncommon, for there the counterpressures of financial and family considerations weigh most heavily. Throughout the Levant, the divorce rate among Muslims is declining. When divorce does occur it is usually early in the marriage (the first two years) and is usually by mutual consent rather than by the husband merely pronouncing the formula of repudiation. There is some evidence that divorce is about as often instigated by the wife as by the husband. Very few men or women remain in the divorced state, for remarriage is the rule.

Polygyny is declining throughout the region. Observers in the past have estimated the level of polygyny to be from five to ten per cent. Today the proportion of Sunni married men with even a second wife is probably less than two per cent in Lebanon, a little over four per cent in Syria and around eight per cent in Jordan. It is less common among city dwellers, the educated and workers than among others. It is more common among peasants and farmers, where an extra field hand is an economic asset, and among executive and managerial classes, where economic pressures are less severe. Among all groups, however, polygyny is rare and becoming rarer.

Reflections on Changing Family Patterns

The preceeding paragraphs provide abundant evidence that family patterns, and the role of women, are undergoing change in a number of areas. These changes have occurred gradually, and have usually spread from the upper and middle classes of the cities to the remainder of the population. Moreover, the changes are selective rather than general, and constitute modification rather than abandonment of established patterns. Women still marry within their religion, observe the Fast of Ramadan, abstain from alcohol, look to their brothers and fathers for assistance (even after marriage), depend on *mahr* rather than alimony or government aid, and in numerous other ways reflect traditional patterns of behavior. Consequently, it would probably be more accurate to describe the changes which have occurred this century in terms of "evolution" rather than "revolution."

In some instances traditional patterns have been strengthened, tempo-

206

rarily at least, by changes occurring in the society at large. The growth of family firms, based on the extended family, is an example. The extended family has made corporations possible even where legal institutions were inadequate. Such firms have strengthened family ties. As Lauer (1971) has argued, there is no necessary antithesis between tradition and modernity, for a variety of institutional forms are compatible with modernization. The extended family has in the Levant not only assisted in the beginnings of industrialization, it has also proved effective at helping cope with bureaucracy, introducing new ideas about agriculture and even paving the way for emigration. The changing patterns of family life do not constitute an abandoning or repudiation of the patterns of the past, but their continuous modification to fit (and bring about) changes in the larger society.

When we speak of evolution and modification of traditional patterns, there is danger of an implication that the traditional patterns were themselves unchanging over the centuries. In this study of the Levant, we have often used the term "traditional" to refer to the patterns which existed in the early twentieth century. In some cases we have emphasized similarities between these "traditional" patterns of the early twentieth century and patterns existing in the time of Abraham or in the early days of Islam. We do believe that there have been continuities over considerable periods of time in patterns of behavior relating to family life. At the same time, we recognize the obvious fact that changes did occur before this century. The traditional ways were by no means static. The historian who wished to emphasize changes between the time of Abraham and the early days of Islam, or between the seventh century A.D. and the nineteenth century A.D., could certainly find as many divergencies as parallels. Our comparison of "traditional" and "modern," then, can be described more accurately as a comparison of family patterns in the early part of this century with those of subsequent decades through the 1960's. It is a study of continuing changes, modifications and adaptations, and not of the collapse of a fixed tradition.

Changes in patterns of family living, and in the role of women, seem to have become noticeable to observers in the period immediately following World War I. The groundwork for such change had been laid in the late nineteenth century, as we have already seen. In 1920 the Treaty of San Remo established a French mandate over Lebanon and Syria and a British mandate over Palestine and Transjordan. Although neither the French nor the British made deliberate efforts to change family life in the area, their cultural influence was nevertheless considerable. It is no coincidence that "modernism" blossomed among middle and upper class Arabs during the mandate period. As Bendix (1967, p. 323) has pointed out, a colonial society is not truly traditional, for it is a dual society in which the cultural norms of the colonizing country present an alternative set of "traditions." Smelser too (1963, p. 106) has noted that the family, among other institutions, often changes under colonialism, even without industrialization.

The French and the British influenced the cultural life of the Arabs in a number of ways. They established schools for girls as well as for boys, and these schools presented European ideas.[1] They strengthened and encouraged those Arab intellectuals with European outlook.[2] European families presented an example of alternative patterns, especially to the urban upper class. The "demonstration effect" was enhanced by the high status of the foreigners. Those Arabs who interacted with the French and British may have felt some threat of what Hagen (1962, p. 185) has called "withdrawal of status respect" when they recognized that foreigners esteemed women with some education and some social skills in mixed gatherings (cf. Patai, 1973, p. 192).

The impact of colonialism, or the influence of the mandate powers, is hardly adequate as an explanation for the many changes that are continuing to occur in Muslim family life. We have already seen that industrialization is too slight to be looked upon as an important causative factor. Urbanization has long characterized the Middle East, and was for centuries quite compatible with traditional family ways, so urbanization, though on the increase, is an unlikely explanatory factor.

We would suggest two factors which contribute to the continuing evolution of the family in the post-mandate period. In the first place there has been since independence a continuing Western influence. To take an extreme case, the number of Westerners in Beirut more than doubled in the twelve years between 1952 and 1964, to reach nearly seven per cent. Western movies and television programs were shown in increasing numbers throughout the region, and tourism increased. Graduates of European

[1] A classical jest in this area, and elsewehere, describes dark-eyed and dark-skinned pupils reciting a lesson that begins "Our ancestors the Gauls were blue-eyed and fair-skinned."

[2] Christian minorities were particularly susceptible to such influence, for Europeans were often thought of as their "protectors" in a predominately Muslim society. These Arab minorities often played the role of cultural "brokers" or innovators in the Levant.

and American schools read foreign books and magazines. Even the challenge of Israel brought home to the Arabs the need for more effective use of womanpower in the pursuit of national goals.

A second important factor has been the spread of an egalitarian ideology in the pursuit of political objectives. Calls for freedom and equality have continued to resound throughout the area, from leaders of a wide variety of political persuasions. Communists denounced the imperialists' efforts to enslave men and women; devout Muslims called for a return to a true "brotherhood of believers." Arab political leaders[1] have adopted the views of the nineteenth and early twentieth century writers that improvement in the status of women is both necessary and compatible with Islam. They recognize that education of women and their increased freedom in family life will not only permit women to enter more productively into national life, but also permit them better to rear and educate their children and thereby enhance the nation's future.

Both the continuing influence of Western ideas, including Marxist ones, and the efforts of political leaders to encourage the ideology of egalitarianism, have been assisted by the increase in all forms of mass communications. It is not the increase in communications *per se* that has produced changes, though the increase has undoubtedly helped to speed up the process (cf. Rosenfeld, 1972, p. 56).

It can be inferred from the preceding remarks that the rate of change has varied and will vary from one group to another, and our data show that this has indeed been the case. The heterogeneous, cosmopolitan city of Beirut has evinced more change than has the more homogeneous city of Tripoli only fifty miles to the North, as well as more than Damascus and Amman. The lower class and especially the peasants in villages have had less stimulation and also less opportunity to adopt new patterns of behavior. The Muslims in the region we have studied have undoubtedly changed more rapidly than have those of the Arabian peninsula.

We believe that changes in patterns of family life in the direction of greater freedom and equality for women and for youth can be expected

---

[1] Of course, not all Arab leaders show concern for improving the status of women and not all declarations of equality are implemented in practice. In a speech to an important group of women in Cairo on July 5, 1973, Colonel Ghaddafi stated flatly, to the open disapproval of his listeners, that increased freedom for women was contrary to the principles of Islam. Gordon (1968, pp. 61ff.) found in Algeria a considerable gap between the promises and statements of the leaders of the independence movement and the reality of the status of women after independence.

to continue in the near future throughout the Arab East. Those patterns already emerging in the urban upper and middle classes, particularly in Beirut, will spread throughout the Levant, and Islamic culture will, we believe, play an increasingly important, but distinctive, role in the world-wide evolution of patterns of family life.

BIBLIOGRAPHY

Abu Khadra, Rihab. Recent changes in Lebanese Moslem marriage shown by changes in marriage contracts. Unpublished M.A. Thesis, Department of Sociology and Anthropology, American University of Beirut, 1959.

Abu-Lughod, Janet, "The emergence of differential fertility in urban Egypt," *Millbank Memorial Fund Quarterly*, Vol. 43, 1965, pp. 235-253.

Abu-Lughod, Janet, "Cairo: Perspective and prospectus," in *From Medina to Metropolis*, L. Carl Brown (ed.), Princeton: Darwin Press, 1973, pp. 95-113.

Adams, Bert N., *Kinship in an Urban Setting*. Chicago: Markham, 1968.

Anon., "Arab women today: the old ways are changing," *Daily Star* (Beirut), August 30, 1970, p. 8.

Anon., "Syria 1969: divorce one-third of marriages, "*An-Nahar, Economic and Financial Supplement* (Beirut), March 1, 1970, p. 14.

Anon., "Penetration de la television au Liban," *L'Orient-Le Jour Nouvelle Serie* (Beirut), No. 18, October 16-22, 1971, p. v.

Antoun, Richard T., "On the modesty of women in Arab Muslim villages," *American Anthropologist*, Vol. 70, 1968, pp. 671-697.

Antoun, Richard T., "The social significance of Ramadan in an Arab village," *The Muslim World*, Vol. 58, No. 2, 1968, pp. 95-104.

Antoun, Richard T., *Arab Village*. Bloomington: Indiana University Press, 1972.

Aswad, Barbara C., "Key and peripheral roles of noble women in a Middle Eastern plains village,"*Anthropological Quarterly*, Vol. 40, 1967, pp. 139-152.

Ayoub, Millicent R. Endogamous marriage in a Middle Eastern village. Unpublished Ph.D. dissertation. Cambridge, Mass.: Radcliffe College, 1957.

Baer, Gabriel, *Population and Society in the Arab East*. London: Routledge and Kegan Paul, 1964 (translated by Hanna Szoke).

211

Beck, Dorothy F., "The changing Moslem family of the Middle East," *Marriage and Family Living*, Vol. 19, 1957, pp. 340-347.

Bell, Norman W. & Vogel, Ezra F. (eds.) *A Modern Introduction to the Family*. New York: Free Press, 1968.

Bendix, Richard, "Tradition and modernity reconsidered," *Comparative Studies in Sociology and History*, Vol. 9, 1967, pp. 292-346.

Benedict, Burton, "Family firms and economic development," *Southwestern Journal of Anthropology*, Vol. 24, 1968, pp. 1-19.

Berelson, Bernard & Steiner, Gary A., *Human Behavior: An Inventory of Scientific Findings*. New York: Harcourt, Brace & World, 1964.

Berger, Morroe, *The Arab World Today*. Garden City, N.Y.: Doubleday & Co., 1964.

Berque, Jacques, "Selections from the social history of an Egyptian village in the twentieth century," in *Peoples and Cultures of the Middle East*, Louise E. Sweet (ed.), Garden City, N.Y.: The Natural History Press, 1970, Vol. 2, pp. 193-221.

Bliss, Frederick J., *The Religions of Modern Syria and Palestine*. New York: Charles Scribner's Sons, 1917.

Castillo, Gelia T., Weisblat, Abraham M., & Villareal, Felicidad R., "Concepts of nuclear and extended family: an exploration of empirical referents," *International Journal of Comparative Sociology*, Vol. 9, 1968, pp. 1-40.

Chatila, Khaled, *Le Mariage chez les Musulmans en Syrie*. Paris: Librairie Orientaliste Paul Geuthner, 1934.

Churchill, Charles W., *The City of Beirut: A Socio-Economic Survey*. Beirut: Dar el Kitab, 1954.

Churchill, Charles W., "An American sociologist's view of seven Arab cities," *Middle East Economic Papers*, Economics Research Institute, American University of Beirut, 1967, pp. 13-39.

Churchill, Charles W. & Sabbagh, Tony, "Beirut, two time levels," *Middle East Economic Papers*, Economics Research Institute, American University of Beirut, 1968, pp. 35-66.

Cohen, Abner, *Arab Border-Villages in Israel*. Manchester: University Press, 1965.

Daghestani, Kazem, *La Famille Musulmane Contemporaine de Syrie*. Paris: Leroux, 1932.

Davis, Kingsley, *Human Society*. New York: Macmillan, 1948.

Demographic Yearbook 1970. Statistical Office of the United Nations. Department of Economic and Social Affairs. New York, 1971.

212

Department of Statistics, The Hashemite Kingdom of Jordan, *First Census of Population and Housing: 18 November 1961. Vol. 1; Final Tables: General Characteristics of the Population. Vol. 2; Final Tables: Economic Characteristics of the Population.* Amman, Jordan: Department of Statistics Press, 1964.

Directorate of Statistics, Ministry of Planning, Syrian Arab Republic. *Census of Population 1960 in the Syrian Arab Republic.* Damascus, 1969.

Dodd, Peter C., "Youth and women's emancipation in the United Arab Republic," *Middle East Journal,* Vol. 22, 1968, pp. 159-172.

Dodd, Peter C., "Women's honor in contemporary Arab society." Paper presented to the section on Family Research, Seventh World Congress, International Sociological Association, Varna, Bulgaria, September 1970. Abstracted in *Sociological Abstracts,* Vol. 18, pp. 785-786, August 1970.

Dodd, Peter C., "Family honor and the forces of change in Arab society," *International Journal of Middle East Studies,* Vol. 4, 1973, pp. 40-54.

Farber, Bernard, *Family: Organization and Behavior.* San Francisco: Chandler, 1964.

Farsoun, Samih K., "Family structure and society in modern Lebanon," in *Peoples and Cultures of the Middle East,* Louise E. Sweet (ed.), Garden City, N.Y.: The Natural History Press, 1970, Vol. 2, pp. 257-307.

Friedl, Ernestine, "The position of women: Appearance and reality," *Anthropological Quarterly,* Vol. 40, 1967, pp. 97-108.

Fuller, Anne H., *Buarij: Portrait of a Lebanese Muslim Village.* Harvard Middle East Monographs, No. 6. Cambridge, Mass.: Harvard University Press, 1961.

Furstenberg, Frank F., "Industrialization and the American family: A look backward," *American Sociological Review,* Vol. 31, 1966, pp. 326-337.

Gardet, Louis, *La Cité Musulmane: Vie Sociale et Politique.* Paris: Librairie Philosophique J. Vrin, 1954.

Goode, William J., *World Revolution and Family Patterns.* New York: Free Press, 1963. (Paperback edition, 1970).

Gordon, David C., *Women of Algeria: An Essay on Change.* Harvard Middle East Monograph Series, No. 19. Cambridge, Mass.: Harvard University Press, 1968.

Government of Palestine, *Census of Palestine 1931.* Alexandria, Egypt: Whitehead Morris, 1933.

213

Granqvist, Hilma, *Marriage Conditions in a Palestinian Village*. Helsingfors: Societas Scientiarum Fennica, Part I, 1931; Part II, 1935.

Granqvist, Hilma, *Birth and Childhood among the Arabs*. Helsingfors: Soderstrom and Co., 1947.

Granqvist, Hilma, *Child Problems among the Arabs*. Helsingfors: Soderstrom and Co., 1950.

Greenfield, Sidney M., "Industrialization and the family in sociological theory," *American Journal of Sociology*, Vol. 67, 1961, pp. 312-322.

Gulick, John, *Social Structure and Culture Change in a Lebanese Village*. New York: Wenner-Gren Foundation for Anthropological Research, 1955.

Gulick, John, *Tripoli: A Modern Arab City*. Cambridge, Mass.: Harvard University Press, 1967.

Gulick, John, "The Arab Levant," in *The Central Middle East*, Louise E. Sweet (ed.), New Haven, Conn.: Human Relations Area Files, Vol. 1, 1968, pp. 111-193.

Gulick, John, "Village and city: cultural continuities in twentieth century Middle Eastern culture," in *Middle Eastern Cities*, Ira M. Lapidus (ed.), Berkeley, California: University of California Press, 1969, pp. 122-158.

Hacker, Jane M., *Modern Amman: A Social Study*. Durham: Durham Colleges in the University of Durham, 1960.

Hagen, Everette E., *On the Theory of Social Change*. Homewood, Illinois: Dorsey Press, 1962.

Hajjaj, Abdul-Wadud, "Divorce in Lebanon," *Daily Star Supplement* (Beirut), August 22, 1971, p. 9.

el-Hamamsy, Leila Shukry, "The changing role of the Egyptian woman," in Abdullah M. Lutfiyya & Charles W. Churchill (eds.), *Readings in Arab Middle Eastern Societies and Cultures*, The Hague: Mouton & Co., 1970, pp. 592-601.

Harris, George L., *Jordan*. New Haven: HRAF Press, 1958.

Hirabayashi, Gordon & Ishaq, May, "Social change in Jordan: A quantitative approach in a non-census area," *American Journal of Sociology*, Vol. 64, 1958, pp. 36-40.

Hollingshead, August B., "Cultural factors in the selection of marriage mates," *American Sociological Review*, Vol. 15, 1950, pp. 619-627.

Hourani, Albert, *Arabic Thought in the Liberal Age: 1798-1939*. London: Oxford University Press, 1962.

Hudson, Michael C., *The Precarious Republic*. New York: Random House, 1968.

Hussein, Aziza, "The role of women in Egypt," *Middle East Journal*, Vol. 7, 1953, pp. 440-450.

Issawi, Charles, "Economic change and urbanization in the Middle East," in *Middle Eastern Cities*, Ira M. Lapidus (ed.), Berkeley: University of California Press, 1969, pp. 102-121.

Issawi, Charles, "Growth and structural change in the Middle East," *Middle East Journal*, Vol. 25, 1971, pp. 309-324.

Kassees, Assad S., "Cross-cultural comparative familism of a Christian Arab people," *Journal of Marriage and the Family*, Vol. 34, 1972, pp. 538-544.

Kahl, Joseph A., *The Measurement of Modernism*. Austin: University of Texas Press, 1968.

Khalaf, Nadim, *Economic Implications of the Size of Nations with Special Reference to Lebanon*. Leiden: Brill, 1971.

Khalaf, Samir & Shwayri, Emilie, "Family firms and industrial development: The Lebanese case," *Economic Development and Cultural Change*, Vol. 15, 1966, pp. 59-69.

Khalaf, Samir, "Family associations in Lebanon," mimeographed, 1968.

Khalaf, Samir & Kongstad, Per, *Hamra of Beirut: A Case of Rapid Urbanization*. Leiden: Brill, 1973.

Khalaf, Samir & Kongstad, Per, "Urbanization and Urbanism in Beirut: Some Preliminary Results" in *From Medina to Metropolis*, L. Carl Brown (ed.), Princeton: Darwin Press, 1973, pp. 116-149.

Khuri, Fuad I., "Parallel cousin marriage reconsidered: a Middle Eastern practice that nullifies the effects of marriage on the intensity of family relationships," *Man*, Vol. 5, 1970, pp. 597-618.

Korson, J. Henry, "Age and social status at marriage: Karachi, 1961-1964," *Pakistan Development Review*, Vol. 4, 1965, pp. 586-600.

Korson, J. Henry, "Dower and social class in an urban Muslim community," *Journal of Marriage and the Family*, Vol. 29, 1967, pp. 527-533.

Korson, J. Henry, "Residential propinquity as a factor in mate selection in an urban Muslim society," *Journal of Marriage and the Family*, Vol. 30, 1968, pp. 518-527.

Korson, J. Henry, "The roles of dower and dowry as indicators of social change in Pakistan, *Journal of Marriage and the Family*, Vol. 30, 1968, pp. 696-707.

Korson, J. Henry, "Student attitudes toward mate selection in a Muslim society: Pakistan," *Journal of Marriage and the Family*, Vol. 31, 1969, pp. 153-165.

Korson, J. Henry, "Endogamous marriage in a traditional Muslim society: West Pakistan," *Journal of Comparative Family Studies*, Vol. 2, 1971, pp. 145-155.

Lane, Edward W., *The Manners and Customs of the Modern Egyptians*. London: Dent & Sons, Everyman's Library, 1963 (first published in 1835).

Lapidus, Ira M. (ed.), *Middle Eastern Cities*. Berkeley: University of California Press, 1969.

Lauer, Robert H., "The scientific legitimation of fallacy: Neutralizing social change theory," *American Sociological Review*, Vol. 36, 1971, pp. 881-889.

Lerner, Daniel, *The Passing of Traditional Society*. Glencoe, Illinois: Free Press, 1958.

Levy, Reuben, *The Social Structure of Islam*. Cambridge: Cambridge University Press, 1962.

Licthenstadter, Ilse, "The 'New Woman' in modern Egypt: observation and impressions," *Moslem World*, Vol. 38, 1948, pp. 163-171.

Lowe, Gordon R., *The Growth of Personality from Infancy to Old Age*. Harmondsworth, England: Penguin Books, 1972.

Lutfiyya, Abdulla M., *Baytin: A Jordanian Village*. The Hague: Mouton, 1966.

Mahmassani, Sobhi, *Legal Systems in the Arab States Past and Present*. Beirut: Dar al Ilm lil Malayiin, 1962 (in Arabic).

Mirande, Alfred M., "The isolated nuclear family hypothesis," in *The Family and Change*, J. N. Edwards (ed.), New York: Alfred Knopf, 1969, pp. 153-163.

Muhyi, Ibrahim A., "Women in the Arab Middle East," *Journal of Social Issues*, Vol. 15, No. 3, 1959, pp. 45-47.

Nahas, M. Kamel, "The family in the Arab world," *Marriage and Family Living*, Vol. 16, 1954, pp. 293-300.

Nahas, M. Kamel, "Married life in Iraq," in *Studies of the Family*, N. Anderson (ed.), Tubingen: J.C. Mohr, 1956, pp. 183-210 (from *Sociological Abstracts*, 1957, No. 3825).

Najarian, Pergrouhi, "Adjustment in the family and patterns of living," *Journal of Social Issues*, Vol. 15, 1959, pp. 28-44.

Ogburn, William F. & Nimkoff, Meyer F., *Sociology*. Boston: Houghton Mifflin, 1950.

Office of Statistics, Government of Palestine, *General Monthly Bulletin of*

Current Statistics of Palestine, Vol. 13, Nos. 1-2 (January-February), 1948.

Patai, Raphael, "Cousin right in Middle Eastern Marriage," *Southwestern Journal of Anthropology*, Vol. 11, 1955, pp. 371-390.

Patai, Raphael, *The Kingdom of Jordan*. Princeton: Princeton University Press, 1958.

Patai, Raphael, *Golden River to Golden Road*. Philadelphia: University of Pennsylvania Press, 1969.

Patai, Raphael, *The Arab Mind*. New York: Scribners, 1973.

Peristiany, Jean G. (ed.), *Honour and Shame: The Values of Mediterranean Society*. London: Weidenfeld and Nelson, 1965.

Peters, Emrys L., "Aspects of rank and status among Muslims in a Lebanese village," in *Mediterranean Countrymen*, J. Pitt-Rivers (ed.), Paris: Mouton and Co., 1963, pp. 159-200.

Petersen, Karen K., "Demographic conditions and extended family household: Egyptian data," *Social Forces*, Vol. 46, 1968, pp. 531-537.

Petersen, Karen K., "Kin network research: A plea for comparability," *Journal of Marriage and the Family*, Vol. 31, 1969, pp. 271-280.

Prothro, Edwin T., *Child Rearing in the Lebanon*. Harvard Middle East Monograph Series, No. 8. Cambridge, Mass.: Harvard University Press, 1961.

Quigley, Carroll, "Mexican National character and circum-Mediterranean personality structure," *American Anthropologist*, Vol. 75, 1973, pp. 319-322.

Rizk, Hanna, "National Fertility Sample Survey for Jordan, 1972: The Study and Some Findings," *Population Bulletin of the United Nations Economic and Social Office in Beirut*, No. 5, July 1973, pp. 14-31.

Rogers, Everett M., *Modernization among Peasants: The Impact of Communication*. New York: Holt, Rinehart and Winston, 1969.

Rosenfeld, Henry, "An analysis of marriage and marriage statistics for a Moslem and Christian Arab village," *International Archives of Ethnography* (Leiden), Vol. 48, 1957.

Rosenfeld, Henry, "From peasantry to wage labor and residual peasantry: The transformation of an Arab village," in *Peoples and Cultures of the Middle East*, Louise E.Sweet (ed.), Garden City, N.Y.: The Natural History Press, 1970, Vol. II, pp. 143-168.

Rosenfeld, Henry, "Social factors in the explanation of the increased rate of patrilineal endogamy in the Arab village in Israel." Paper presented at the Mediterranean Social Anthropological and Sociological Conference, Nicosia, Cyprus, September 7-12, 1970.

Rosenfeld, Henry, "An overview and critique of the literature on rural politics and social change," in *Rural Politics and Social Change in the Middle East,* Richard Antoun & Iliya Harik (eds.), Bloomington: Indiana University Press, 1972, pp. 45-74.

Safilios-Rothschild, Constantina, "Quelques aspects de la modernization sociale aux Etats-Unis et en Grèce," *Sociologie et Societés,* Vol. 1, 1969, pp. 23-37.

Safilios-Rothschild, Constantina, "The study of family power structure: A review 1960-1969," *Journal of Marriage and the Family,* Vol. 32, 1970, pp. 539-553.

Sayigh, Rosemary, "The changing life of Arab women," *Mid East,* Vol. 8, 1968, pp. 19-23.

Sayigh, Yusif A., *Entrepreneurs of Lebanon.* Cambridge, Mass.: Harvard University Press, 1962.

Schneider, Jane, "Of vigilance and virgins: Honor, shame and access to resources in Mediterranean societies," *Ethnology,* Vol. 10, 1971, pp. 1-24.

Smelser, Neil J., *Sociology of Economic Life.* Englewood Cliffs, N.J.: Prentice Hall, 1963.

Statistical Yearbook 1970. Statistical Office of the United Nations, Department of Economic and Social Affairs, New York, 1971.

Stephens, William N., *The Family in Cross-Cultural Perspective.* New York: Holt, Rinehart and Winston, 1963.

Stern, Gertrude H., *Marriage in Early Islam.* London: Royal Asiatic Society, James G. Forlung Fund, Vol. 18, 1939.

Sussman, Marvin B., "The isolated nuclear family: Fact or fiction," *Social Problems,* Vol. 6, 1959, pp. 333-340.

Sweet, Louise E., *Tell Toqaan: A Syrian Village.* Ann Arbor: University of Michigan, 1960.

Tannous, Afif I., "Social change in an Arab village," *American Sociological Review,* Vol. 6, 1941, pp. 651-662.

Tillion, Germaine, *Le Harem et les Cousins.* Paris: Editions du Seuil, 1966.

Tomeh, Aida K., "Reference-Group supports among Middle Eastern college students," *Journal of Marriage and the Family,* Vol. 32, 1970, pp. 156-165.

Toulmin, Stephen, *Human Understanding.* Volume I: General Introduction and Part I. Oxford: Clarendon Press, 1972.

des Villettes, Jacqueline, *La Vie des Femmes dans un Village Maronite Libanais: Ain al Kharoube*. Tunis: Publications de l'Institut des Belles Lettres Arabes, 1964. (Imprimerie: Bascone & Muscat, Tunis).

White, Leslie A., *The Evolution of Culture*. New York: McGraw Hill, 1959.

Williams, Herbert H., Some Aspects of Culture and Personality in a Lebanese Maronite Village. University of Pennsylvania Ph.D. Dissertation, 1958. Ann Arbor: University Microfilms, 1964.

Williams, Herbert H. & Williams, Judith R., "The extended family as a vehicle of cultural change," *Human Organization*, Vol. 24, 1965, pp. 59-64.

Williams, Judith R., *The Youth of Haouch el Harimi*. Harvard Middle Eastern Monographs, No. 20. Cambridge, Mass.: Harvard University Press, 1968.

Winch, Robert F., "Permanence and change in the history of the American family and some speculations as to its future," *Journal of Marriage and the Family*, Vol. 32, 1970, pp. 6-15.

Woodsmall, Ruth F., *Moslem Women Enter a New World*. London: George Allen and Unwin, 1936.

Yaukey, David, *Fertility Differences in a Modernizing Country*. Princeton: Princeton University Press, 1961.

Youssef, Nadia H., "Differential labor force participation of women in Latin American and Middle Eastern countries: The influence of family characteristics," *Social Forces*, Vol. 51, 1972, pp. 135-153.

APPENDIX

BASIC INTERVIEWING SCHEDULE

1. Duration of marriage in years:.................................

   Wife's feeling about time of marriage:

       1. Too early ....
       2. Just right ....
       3. Too late   ....

   b. Husband's feeling about time of marriage:

       1. Too early ....
       2. Just right ....
       3. Too late   ....

2. Age of Wife at marriage in years: ....

   a. Birth order of wife: ....

   b. Number of Siblings:

       1. Brothers   ....
       2. Sisters   ....

3. Age of Husband at marriage in years: ....

   a. Birth order of husband: ....

   b. Number of Siblings:

       1. Brothers   ....
       2. Sisters   ....

4. Husband's profession: ....

5. Education:

    a. No formal education

    b. Primary education—Certificat

    c. Secondary education—Brevet

    d. Secondary education—Bac. I

    e. Secondary education—Bac. II

    f. University education—(1) Sophomore (2) B.A. (3) M.A., Licence, (4) Ph.D., etc.

    Of the above alternatives, state which of them applies to each of the following:

    A. Wife: ....

    B. Wife's mother: ....

    C. Wife's father: ....

    D. Husband: ....

    E. Husband's mother: ....

    F. Husband's father: ....

6. How did wife meet her husband?

    a. Through a matchmaker

    b. Through in-laws

    c. Through her relatives

    d. Through friends

    e. In social gatherings

    f. In school or university

    g. Other (specify): ....

7. Degree of acquaintance with husband:

    A. a. Never saw him

        b. Never went out with him alone

        c. Went out with him once with family, but not alone

d. Went out with him several times with family, but not alone

e. Went out with him with a group of friends (without a relative chaperone)

f. Went out with him several times alone, without a chaperone

g. Other (specify): ....

B. Of the above alternatives, state which of them applies to each of the following:

a. Before engagement: ....

b. During engagement: ....

c. After marriage (but before living with husband): ....

8. Length of period of engagement:

a. No engagement

b. Less than one month

c. One month to six months

d. Six months to one year

e. More than one year (specify): ....

9. Length of period of marriage before actually living with husband:

a. During the same day

b. Less than one month

c. One month to six months

d. Six months to one year

e. More than one year (specify): ....

10. Husband's relation to Wife:

a. First cousin, father's side (ibn 'amm)

b. First cousin, mother's side (ibn khal)

c. Same family (father's family)

d. Mother's family

e. Not related, but of same religious sect (Sunni)

f. Not related, and of a different religious sect (specify) : ....

11. Number and ages of children in family :

 a. Boys : ....

 b. Girls : ....

12. Sexes of children born who died during infancy, childhood or adulthood :

 a. Sex................................Age ....Birth order ....

 b. Sex................................Age ....Birth order ....

 c. Sex................................Age ....Birth order ....

 d. Sex................................Age ....Birth order ....

13. What do you consider to be the ideal family size?

 a. Boys : ....

 b. Girls : ....

13 A. What do you think is your husband's estimate of an ideal family size?

 a. Boys : ....

 b. Girls : ....

14. If there is discrepancy between "actual" and "ideal" family size, ask for reasons :

 ....

15. Wife's relations with her in-laws (*husband's parents*) :

 A. *Residence* :

 a. Lived with in-laws since marriage

 b. Lived with in-laws for a period(s) of time : ....

 c. Lived only with husband since marriage.

 B. *Visiting* :

 a. I visit in-laws often : ....times per week

 b. My in-laws visit me often : ....times per week

 c. I visit in-laws only occasionally : ....times per ....

d. My in-laws visit me only occasionally: ....times per ......

e. Exchange visits only on formal occasions, e.g. feasts, weddings, sickness, funerals, etc...........

f. Do not visit.

C. *Proximity*:

My in-laws live in the:

a. Same building

b. Next building

c. Same neighborhood (quarter)

d. Same city

e. Another city (specify): ....

16. Wife's relations with *her own parents*:

A. *Residence*:

a. Lived with parents ever since marriage

b. Lived with parents for a period(s) of time: ....

c. Lived only with husband since marriage

d. Live occasionally with parents: ....

B. *Visiting*:

a. I visit my parents often: ....times per week

b. My parents visit me often: ....times per week

c. I visit my parents only occasionally: ....times per ....

d. My parents visit me only occasionally: ....times per ......

e. Exchange visits only on formal occasions, e.g. feasts, weddings, sickness, funerals, etc...........

f. Do not visit.

C. *Proximity*:

My parents live in the:

a. Same building

b. Next building

c. Same neighborhood

d. Same city

e. Another city (specify) : ....

17. Wife's relations with her in-laws (*husband's married brothers and sisters, if any*) :

A. *Residence*:

a. Lived with in-laws since marriage

b. Lived with in-laws for a period of time : ....

c. Lived only with husband since marriage

d. Live occasionally with in-laws : ....

B. *Visiting*:

a. I visit in-laws often : ....times per week

b. My in-laws visit me often : ....times per week

c. I visit in-laws only occasionally : ....times per ....

d. My in-laws visit me occasionally : ....times per ....

e. Exchange visits only on formal occasions, e.g. feasts, weddings, sickness, funerals, etc...........

f. At husband's parents' house : ....

g. Do not visit.

C. *Proximity*:

My in-laws live in the:

a. Same building

b. Next building

c. Same Neighborhood

d. Same city

e. Another city (specify) : ....

18. Wife's relations with her own family (*Wife's married brothers and sisters, if any*):

   A. *Residence*:

       a. Lived with family since marriage

       b. Lived with family for a period of time: ....

       c. Lived only with husband since marriage.

   B. *Visiting*:

       a. I visit my family often: ....times per week

       b. My family visits me often: ....times per week

       c. I visit my family only occasionally: ....times per ....

       d. My family visits me only occasionally: ....times per ....

       e. Exchange visits only on formal occasions, e.g. feasts, weddings, sickness, funerals, etc..........

       f. At her own parents' house ....

       g. Do not visit.

   C. *Proximity*:

       My family lives in the:

       a. Same building

       b. Next building

       c. Same neighborhood

       d. Same city

       e. Another city (specify): ....

19. Wife's work outside the home:

   A. Did you work outside the home, for pay, before marriage:

       a. Yes, full time: Nature of work ....

       b. Yes, part time: Nature of work ....

       c. No.

B. Did you work outside the home, with pay, after marriage:

    a. Yes, full time: Nature of work ....for how long? ....

    b. Yes, part time: Nature of work ....for how long? ....

    c. No.

C. If "Yes" to item B, how does your husband react to your working?:

    a. Very much in favor

    b. Does not object

    c. Would prefer that I stop working

    d. Very much opposed.

D. If "No" to items A or B, do you approve of women working outside home?:

    a. Yes, before and after marriage

        (1) only if there is need
        (2) only if children are taken care of

    b. Yes, but only before marriage

        (1) only if there is need

    c. No.

E. If "No" to items A or B, what do you believe your husband's opinion to be on the topic of women's work?:

    a. Approves of women working, before and after marriage

        (1) only if there is need
        (2) only if children are taken care of

    b. Approves of women working, but only before marriage

        (1) only if there is need

    c. Does not approve.

F. If "No" to items A or B, what kind of work do you think you would like to do, if any, if you wanted to work? (List in order of preference):

....

....

G. If "No" to items A or B, what kind of work do you think your husband would like you to do, if any, and if you wanted to work? (List in order of preference):

....

....

20. Wife—husband interaction:

For each of the following items, indicate who makes (or made) the final decision:

a. (1) Both of us (husband and wife) cooperate
   (2) Either of us, depending on circumstances

b. (1) I decide
   (2) I decide, in spite of my husband's interference

c. I decide (after consultation with my family)

d. My parents decide

e. (1) My husband decides
   (2) My husband decides, in spite of my objection

f. My husband decides (after consulting with his family)

g. My in-laws decide

h. Children decide (for 4 below).

The items are the following (Put a, b, c, d, e, f, or g along with any comments):

1. Place of residence: ....

2. Name of newborn (boy and girl): ....

3. Children's discipline: ....

4. Children's marriages (boy and girl): ....

5. "Who" to visit: ....

6. "How" you dress: ....

7. When to have children: ....

21A. Did you ever (check if positive): (a) smoke, (b) drink liquor, (c) swim, (d) dance, (e) go to the movies alone or with other women?

229

1. Before marriage: ....

2. After marriage: ....

3. In presence of parents: ....

4. In absence of parents: ....

5. In public: ....

21B. Wife's attitudes towards a variety of social issues:

For each of the following items, check either:

a. Strongly agree

b. Agree

c. Undecided

d. Disagree

e. Strongly disagree

The items are the following:

A. *Mixed Dancing*: (Specify *Place* and *Age* when "Agree"):

    1. Girls going to dancing parties:

        a. Unchaperoned ....

        b. Accompanied by a trustworthy person (Who?) ....

    2. My daughter going to dancing parties:

        a. Unchaperoned ....

        b. Accompanied by a trustworthy person (Who?) ....

    3. My son going to dancing parties: ....

B. *Swimming*: (Specify *Place* and *Age* when "Agree"):

    1. Girls swimming at a public beach:

        a. Unchaperoned ....

        b. Accompanied by a trustworthy person (Who?) ....

    2. My daughter swimming at a public beach:

    a. Unchaperoned ....

    b. Accompanied by a trustworthy person (Who?) ....

  3. My son going swimming: ....

C. *Going to movies*: (Specify *Place* and *Age* when "Agree"):

  1. Girls going to movies:

    a. Unchaperoned ....

    b. Accompanied by a trustworthy person (Who?) ....

  My daughter going to movies:

    a. Unchaperoned ....

    b. Accompanied by a trustworthy person (Who?) ....

  3. My son going to movies: ....

D. *Education and Coeducation*:

  1. Girls going to a woman's college ....

  2. Girls going to a coeducational college ....

  3. My daughter going to a woman's college ....

  4. My daughter going to a coeducational college ....

  5. My son going to a coeducational college...

E. *Smoking*: (Specify *Place* and *Age* when "Agree"):

  1. Girls smoking ....

  2. My son smoking ....

  3. My daughter smoking ....

F. Would you like your daughter to get married in the same way you did?

....

....

G. *Religious practices and rituals*:

  1. Do you pray, fast, and/or wear a veil:

    a. Before marriage: ....

    b. After marriage: ....

  2. Do your children pray, fast, etc.? ....

22. *Payment of Dowry*:

    a. Only symbolic "Advance" and "Late" payments

    b. Symbolic "advance" but actual "late" payment

        (Amount: ....)

    c. Actual "advance" but symbolic "late" payment

        (Amount: ....)

    d. Actual "advance" and "late" payments

        (Amounts: ....; ....).

23. Have you ever felt, at one time or another, that you would have been happier if you were a "man" rather than a "woman"?

    Yes.. No ....

    If "Yes", do you still feel the same way?

    Yes.. No ....

24. Do you use any methods of birth control? Yes ....

    No ....Never heard of it ....

    If "No", state why not ....

    ....

25. (Fill out as soon as possible after leaving).

    a. Number of rooms and size:...

    b. Bathroom? ....

    c. Radio? Other appliances?...

    d. General appearance of home (paint, repair) :...

    e. Servants? ....

    f. Over-all impression of socio-economic status: ....

    ....

INDEX

Bethuel the Syrian, 25
birth control, 114; in Lebanon, 95, 99-100; reasons for lack of practice in 115
Bliss, [Frederick], 6, 119, 127
Brazil, 63
bride price. See *mahr*
Britain, 178
Buarij, 11, 12, 13, 26, 36, 93; development of, 17-18; response of persons interviewed in, 20; primary schooling in, 21, 22; arranged marriages in, 28; age at marriage in, 30, 31; duration of wedding celebrations, in, 37; pre-marital attitudes of wives interviewed in, 43, 44, 48, 49, 50, 51; mean age of wives and husbands at time of marriage in, 45, 46; writting of the contract *(Katb al-Kitab)* and wedding ceremony in, 52; *mahr* payments in, 54, 55, 56, 59; cousin 74, 75, 76; marriage in, 63, 65 residential pattern in, 66, 67, 68-69, 77-89; family size in, 98, 99, 105-113; birth control in, 100, 114-115; infant mortality in, 116; veiling of women in, 119, 136, 137; religious observances of villagers in, 128, 129, 138, 139, 140, 141; movie attendance of women in, 128, 129; use of tobacco by women in, 129; decision-making in, 131; educational level of the parents of the sample interviewed in, 142, 143, 144, 145; attitudes of mothers to daughters attending college, 146, to employment outside the home, 147, 148, 149, to cinema attendance, 150, 151, 152, 153, to smoking, 154, 155, 156, to mixed dancing, 157, 158, 159, 160, to swimming, 161, 162, 163, to drinking alcohol, 164; wives cooperation in various aspects of decision-making in, 165, 166, 167, 168; role and status of women in, 169; divorce rate in, 172; polygyny in, 184

C

Cairo, 8, 67, 91, 171, 209 *n*
Castillo, [Gilia], 62
Chatila, [Khaled], 7, 30, 37, 39, 64, 182
Chicago, 67
Chtoura, 17
Churchill, [Charles], 14, 15, 16, 27, 30, 31, 39, 94, 119, 128
Cohen, [Abner], 67
conjugal family: as seen by Goode, 3-4; ideals of, 5
cousin marriage, 26, 27, 62-66; statisties on; 74-76; trend away from, 204

D

Daghestani, [Kazem], 7, 27
Damascus, 11, 12, 14, 15, 16, 17, 209; response of persons interviewed in, 20; primary schooling in, 21, 22; mean age of wives and husbands interviewed in, at time of marriage, 30, 45, 46; writing of the contract *(Katb al-Kitab)* and marriage ceremony in, 52, 56, *mahr* payment in, 39, 54, 55, 56, 59; pre-marital attitudes of wives interviewed in, 43, 44, 48, 49, 50, 51; residential patterns in, 69, 77-89; cousin marriage in, 74, 75, 76; birth control in, 100, 114-115; family size in, 105-113; infant mortality in, 116; veiling of women in, 119, 136, 137; religious observances of Muslim women in, 123, 138, 139, 140, 141; employment of women in, 125, 126; use of tobacco by women in, 129; decision-making in, 131; educational level of the parents of wives in the sample interviewed in, to daughters attending college, 146, to employment outside the home, 147, 148, 149, to cinema attendance, 150, 151, 152, 153, to smoking, 154, 155,

235

156, to mixed dancing, 157, 158, 159, 160, to drinking alcohol, 164; wives co-operation in various aspects of decision-making in, 165, 166, 167, 168; divorce in, 173, 179, 188
Davis, [Kingsley], 2
"demonstration effect", 7, 208
Detroit, 67
divorce, 6, 203; in pre-Islamic times, 171; rate of, 172-173, 206, in Lebanon, Jordan and Syria, 173-175; kinds of, 175-177, 186; duration of marriage before, 177-178; instigator of, 178-179, 187; causes for, 179-180; statistics on, in Lebanon, Jordan and Syria, 188-197
Dodd, [Peter], 18n, 118, 126n
dowry/bride price. *See mahr*

E

Egypt, 6; cousin marriage in, 63; family size in, 91; birth control in, 95; religious observances of Muslim women in, 121, 122; divorce in, 171-172; employment of women in, 125-127; engagement, 33-35; encounters of couple before and during, 42, 49, 50, 51, 204
Engels, 1
Evolutionary family theory, 1,2
Extended family, 2, 61-62; and industrialization, 4, 6, 8

F

Family size, 91-102; statistics on, 103-113
Farber, [Bernard], 1
Farsoun, [Samih], 8
Fertile Crescent, 11
France, 6, 174, 186; divorce in, 190
Friedl, [Ernestine], 131
Fuller, [Anne], 18, 19, 26, 30, 63, 66, 93, 119, 121, 123, 125, 127, 172, 184
functionalist theory, 2
Furstenberg, [Frank], 3

G

Gardet, [Louis], 175n
Genesis, 25
Ghaddafi, Colonel, 209n
Goode, [William], 3, 5, 6, 9, 26, 30, 31, 62, 67, 68, 72, 95, 101, 172, 173, 174, 175, 178, 180, 181, 182, 183, 186, 190n
Gordon, [David], 117, 209n
Granqvist, [Hilma], 11n, 19, 26, 30, 35n, 38, 63, 64, 119, 121, 122, 125, 128, 172, 173, 183; survey of family size in Artas by, 91-93
Greenfield, [Sidney], 3
Greensboro, 72
Gulick, [John], 7, 11, 16, 31, 62, 67, 94, 117, 121, 123, 125, 128, 184, 185

H

Hacker, [Jane], 15
Hagen, [Everette], 208
Hajjaj, [Abdul-Wadud], 174
Hamamsy, [Leila], 175n
Haouch el-Harimi, 66, 121, 124
Harris, [George], 121, 125, 183
Hirabayashi, [Gordon], 27, 33, 98, 119, 125
Hourani, [Albert], 7
Hudson, [Michael], 14, 15, 16, 17

I

industrialization, 9; relationship of to family, 2, 3, 4-5, 8, 202; development of, in Middle East, 14, 15
infant/child mortality, 91, 95, 96, 116; in: Artas, 93, Buarij, 94, 100-101, Iraq, 179
Isaac, 25, 34
Ishaq, [May], 27, 33, 98, 119, 125
Islamic family: changes in, 6-9
Israel, 15, 63, 67, 174, 183, 209; divorce in, 190

236

Issawi, [Charles], 11, 14
Italy, 174

J

Japan: family ties in, 3
Jedda, 8
Jerusalem, 16
Jordan, 11, 64; industrialization in,
  15; tourism in, 16; primary school
  population in, 23; (Katb al-Kitab)
  in, 35n; health conditions in, 101;
  family size in, 94, 95, 102n; religious
  observances of Muslim women in,
  120-121; employment of women in,
  125; divorce in, 173, 174, 175, 178,
  181, 188, 190; childless divorces in,
  180; polygyny in, 183-184, 185, 199,
  206; remarriage in, 187; marital status
  of brides and grooms in, 1958-1965,
  197
Jordan River, 190n
June War of 1967, 11-12

K

Kahl, [Joseph], 5
Karachi, 31, 39, 65n, 67
Kassees, [Assad], 63
Katb al-Kitab (marriage contract), 35,
  37; and marriage ceremony, 36, 52, 53
Khalaf, [Nadim], 15, 16
Khalaf, [Samir], 8, 14, 71
Khuri, [Fuad], 64, 65
Korson, [J. Henry], 28, 31, 38, 39, 65n,
  67
Krongstad, [Per], 14
Kuwait, 8, 29

L

Lahore, 65n
Lane, [Edward], 6, 27, 30, 63, 91, 121,
  122, 127, 171, 172, 182
Lapidus, [Ira], 14
Lauer [Robert], 207
Lebanon, 6, 7, 12, 32; industrialization

in, 15; religious composition of population of, 11; tourism in, 16; primary
school population in, 23; arranged
marriages in, 27; cousin marriages
in, 64; extended family in, 70-71;
family size in, 94; birth control in,
95; employment of women in, 125;
recreation of women in, 127; divorce
in, 172, 173, 174, 175, 179, 186,
188, 190; polygyny in, 184, 185,
187, 206
Lerner, [Daniel], 5
Levant, changes in the Islamic family
in, 6-9; geographical location of, 11;
characteristics of, 14-19; selection of
mate in, 26-27; marriage ties in,
62-66; women's age at marriage, 31;
concept of romantic love in, 33;
residential patterns in, 66-70; family
associations in, 71, 72-73; studies
of Muslim families in, 94; trends
in family size in, 101-102; religious
observances of Muslim women in,
120, 121, 122; employment of women
in, 125-127; recreation of women in,
127-128; attitudes to the consumption
of alcohol by women in, 130-131;
changing role of women in, 134;
divorce rate in, 172-174, 180; remarriage in, 180; polygyny in, 182, 183n;
description of the Arab family in the
early twentieth century in, 202-204,
after mid-century, 204-210. See also
Arab Levant and Middle East
Levy, [Reuben], 63, 117, 118
Liberation of Women (Amin), 6
Lichtenstadter, [Ilse], 38n
Lowe, [Gordon], 69n, 178
Lutfiyya, [Abdulla], 26, 38, 121, 172

M

Mahmassani, [Subhi], 175
mahr (dowry/bride price), 34, 35, 206;
  types and amount of 37-41, 42;
  statistics on payment of, 54-59; in
  cases of: divorce, 172, 175, polygyny,
  182

237

in, 23; age of male at marriage in, 30; cousin marriage in, 64; family size in, 94; employment of women in, 125; recreation of women in, 127; divorce in, 173, 174, 175, 178, 180, 188, 190; remarriage in, 181, 187; polygyny in, 182-183, 184, 185, 198, 200, 201, 206

Syrian Arab Republic. *See* Syria

T

Tannous, [Afif], 8

Tillion, [Germaine], 119n

Tohmeh, [Aida], 71

Toulmin, [Stephen], 2n

Transjordan, 15, 207. *See also* Jordan

Treaty of San Remo, 207

Tripoli, 12, 14, 15, 16, 209; response of persons interviewed in, 20; primary schooling in, 21, 22; arranged marriages in, 27; mean age of wives and husbands at time of marriage in, 32, 45, 46, 47; writing of the contract (*Katb al-Kitab*) and marriage ceremony in, 36, 52; *mahr* payment in, 39, 40, 54, 55, 56, 57, 58, 59; premarital attitudes of wives interviewed in 43, 44, 48, 49, 50, 51; cousin marriage in, 65, 74, 75, 76; residential patterns in, 68, 69, 77-89; family size in, 98, 105-113; birth control in, 100, 114-115; infant mortality in, 116; veiling of women in, 119, 134, 136, 137 religious observances of Muslim women in, 121, 138, 139, 140, 141; employment of women in, 125, 126; recreation of women in, 128; use of tobacco by women in, 129; educational levels of the parents of the sample interviewed in, 142, 143, 144, 145; wives attitudes in, to daughters attending college, 146, to employment outside the home, 147, 148, 149, to cinema attendance, 150, 151, 152, 153, to smoking, 154, 155-156, to mixed dancing, 157, 158, 159, 160, to swimming, 161, 162, 163, to drinking alcohol, 164; wives

co-operation in various aspects of decision-making in, 165, 166, 167, 168; divorce in, 173, 175, 176-177, 178, 179, 180, 187, 188, 189, 192, 194, 195, 196, polygyny in, 184

Tur'an, 183

Turkey, 63

U

United Nations *Demographic Yearbook*, 1970, 190n

United Nations *Statistical Yearbook*, 23n, 16

Union of Soviet Socialist Republics (USSR); divorce in, 174, 206

United States, 16, 64; nuclear family in, 3, 174, 181n, 186, 206; family ties in, 71-72; divorce in, 190

urbanization, 9, 11, 15; relationship of to family, 2, 3, 4-5

V

Vatican, 174

veiling of women, 6, 7, 26, 205; changing patterns in, 118-120, 134; statistics on, 136-137

des Villettes, [Jacqueline], 36

Vogel, [Ezra], 1

W

Wedding ceremony: and *Katb al-Kitab*, 36, 52, 53; duration of celebrations for, 37, 42

White, [Leslie], 2n

Williams, [Herbert], 8, 36, 38, 63, 66, 71

Williams, [Judith], 8, 36, 38, 63, 66, 70, 71, 94, 121, 124, 125, 128, 172, 184

Winch, [Robert], 3

Woodsmall, [Ruth], 7, 118, 119, 125

World Revolution and Family Patterns (Goode), 3

World War I, 6, 11n, 12n, 203, 207

World War II, 17, 134

239